IMAGES
of America

MARYVILLE

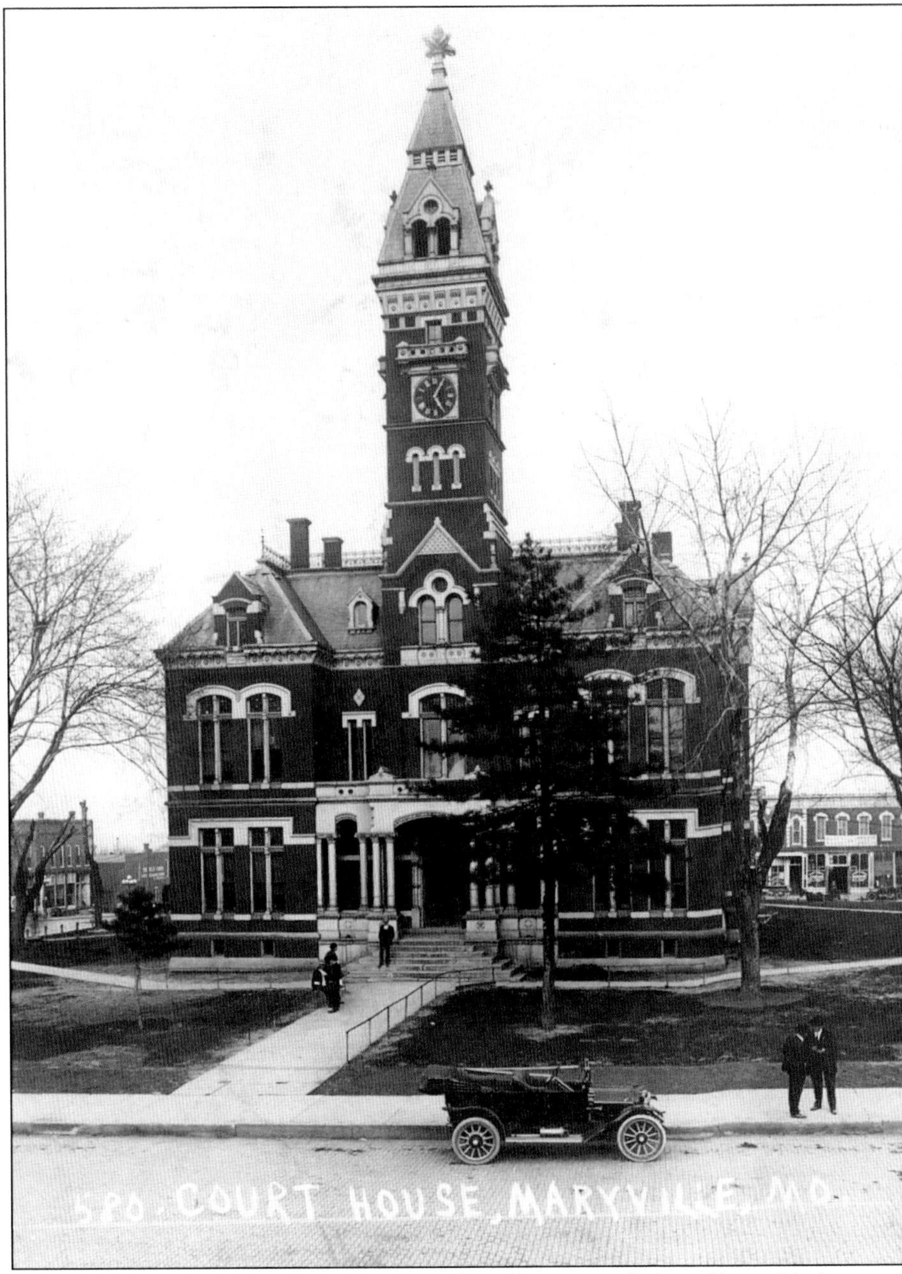

The iconic clock tower of the courthouse stands high at the center of Maryville, visible from most parts of the town. Edmund Eckel's design, constructed of red brick from St. Joseph and trimmed with sandstone from Parkville, is capped by a pinecone that symbolizes the ever-renewing life of the community. The structure is now listed in the National Register of Historic Places. (Courtesy of Coby Lamb.)

On the Cover: Serving satisfied customers at King's Cafe, from left to right behind the counter in 1952 are owner Jennie King, Helen Parker, Carol Jean Osborn, Christie West, and Elsie Mueller. Patrons could enjoy the 3-4-1 special, including an American Dairies Taste-A-Shake, hamburger, and French fries for 59¢. Passing truckers, residents, and farmers in town for business were all greeted by friendly faces and good food at King's. (Courtesy of Suzi Schneider-Anderson.)

IMAGES
of America

MARYVILLE

Michael J. Steiner and Brent Trout

ARCADIA
PUBLISHING

ISBN 978-1-4671-1079-2

Published by Arcadia Publishing
Charleston, South Carolina

Printed in the United States of America

Library of Congress Control Number: 2013936146

For all general information, please contact Arcadia Publishing:
Telephone 843-853-2070
Fax 843-853-0044
E-mail sales@arcadiapublishing.com
For customer service and orders:
Toll-Free 1-888-313-2665

Visit us on the Internet at www.arcadiapublishing.com

To our neighbors, friends, and family in Maryville,
who make it a wonderful place to live.

CONTENTS

ACKNOWLEDGMENTS

We owe gratitude to many people and organizations for their assistance in the production of this book. The Nodaway County Historical Society furnished most of the images for this book and we offer our thanks to the many volunteers and staff at the museum who have helped in innumerable small ways. Particular thanks go to Margaret Kelley and Melissa Middleswart for their wonderful assistance in procuring images from generous folks who help to preserve our local heritage through their contributions. Our appreciation also extends to the board of the Historical Society for its support for the organization. All images, unless otherwise indicated, are from the collection of the Nodaway County Historical Society.

The staff of the Northwest Missouri State University Archives has also provided considerable support. In particular, Beth Juhl, Northwest archivist, has provided enthusiastic support and assistance in identifying excellent images of the alma mater we share. Many thanks also to Leslie Galbreath, director of academic and library services, for opening doors for us, both figuratively and literally. Many of the images in this volume appear courtesy of the Northwest Missouri State University Archives (Northwest).

Many residents of Maryville have provided images over the years, either directly to this project or through their generous contributions to the Nodaway County Historical Society's print and digital archives. Thanks again to Coby Lamb, and also to Suzi Schneider-Anderson, Jim Bagby, Cheryl M. Cockrell, Ron and Janet Moss, Virgina Spoor, Joyce Miller Holt, Chuck Zeiler, Harold Hall, Mary Graham, and JoAnn Outs.

Janice Brandon-Falcone's superb *Transitions: A Hundred Years of Northwest* provided information for this book and her work as an educator and enthusiasm for Northwest Missouri State University has also inspired the Town and Gown chapter of this book. Virgil and Delores Albertini's excellent *Towers in the Northwest* also provided insights for segments on the university since the late 1950s, and we thank them as well for their role in preserving the history of that part of our community.

Thanks go again to Tom Carneal for the wonderful photographs he has taken and contributed to the Nodaway County Historical Society, for his steadfast support for local history, and for his ample knowledge and sound advice.

Michael J. Steiner

INTRODUCTION

Adventurous settlers who had migrated up the valley of the Nodaway and One Hundred and Two Rivers to settle the Platte Purchase region platted the town of Maryville in September 1845 in the Nodaway County court. Amos Graham bought the first lot for $5.25, and it was for his wife, Mary, that the town was named. Over the next decade, a string of settlers moved in, primarily from Kentucky and Tennessee, bringing with them ambition in business and their love for breeding horses. Situated on a knoll amid fertile prairie between two rivers, the town experienced vibrant growth, even before the railroads arrived. Merchants, blacksmiths, lawyers, brewers, wagon-wrights, and people of a wide array of other trades followed. The first structures were made of lumber hewn from local trees. Pine lumber imported up the river from St. Joseph followed, and in 1852, John Saunders erected the first brick building. The first rail line, operated by the Kansas City, St. Joseph, and Council Bluffs (Burlington) Railroad, established a depot on the low eastern side of town in 1869. The Council Bluffs and St. Louis (Wabash) line arrived in 1879, and between the two intersecting rail lines optimistic residents had raised nearly a quarter of a million dollars in cash and bonds to secure their presence.

Optimism paid off as the railroads ushered in rapid growth in the 1880s, marked by the construction of dozens of brick buildings, numerous local industries, impressive hotels, four banks, and over four hundred homes. By 1893, the town boasted four miles of brick paving on its streets and it approached the 20th century roiling with the excitement of a highly prosperous town. For the next half century, it added businesses, social organizations, educational institutions, an impressive array of structures, and a diverse cast of characters that made life both comforting and interesting. The arrival of automobiles changed the shape, sights, and sounds of the square around the courthouse as machines and animals positioned for space in the transition era. The automobiles won, and local dealers, mechanics, and motorists replaced their keen interest in fine horses with a love for machines. Festivals and parades trumpeted confidence in local businesses and organizations, and while they brought an interesting variety of outside entertainment to town, they mostly gave town folk an opportunity to show off for one another. Tremendous energy went into enticing the state of Missouri to establish a normal school for the education of teachers for the region, leading to a college being built in the northwest corner of town that would evolve into one of the most dynamic features of the community. Over the next seven decades, the Fifth District Normal School turned into Northwest Missouri State Teachers College, Northwest Missouri State College, and finally, Northwest Missouri State University. The school not only provided education for local youths, but brought to the town a steady flow of outsiders who continue to this day to exert significant influence on the economy and the culture of the community. The first half of the 20th century saw some old industries disappear and new ones arrive to replace them. Elements of local culture persisted and others changed with time and technology. Disasters, often in the form of fire, but also the weather and instances of both global and local inhumanity, tested the people of the community but always demonstrated their resolve to move forward with pride in their town.

Maryville, Missouri, rather than being separate from the life of the nation, or merely a bland homogenization of its center, like thousands of other small towns around the country, embodies the life of the nation. At each stage of its historical development, the major movements that formed American culture found expression in this small community. While towns like Maryville hasten to run local claims to importance up the flag pole on the public square—and they do have many legitimate such claims—local histories often fail to attach the essential life of the community to those transcendent forces that ebb and flow through the whole of the nation. In so doing they often diminish themselves with simply peculiar claims to fame. Maryville and its people, while they do indeed have their own interesting exceptionalities, merit celebration because they are like hundreds of other communities and an expression of America's development and its place in the world.

This photographic history will illustrate the ways in which a town planted in the middle of a tall-grass prairie frontier evolved into a community of people woven together by their economic interdependence and cultural identity, and, sometimes, how they were connected to the larger developments and movements that shaped America through the first half of the 20th century. These developments include the economic vitality of Midwestern towns, the cultural associations that shaped emerging communities, the unique dynamics of a small town hosting a state college, and the interesting community of people, both ordinary and outstanding, that make up a Midwestern community.

One

An Enterprising Town

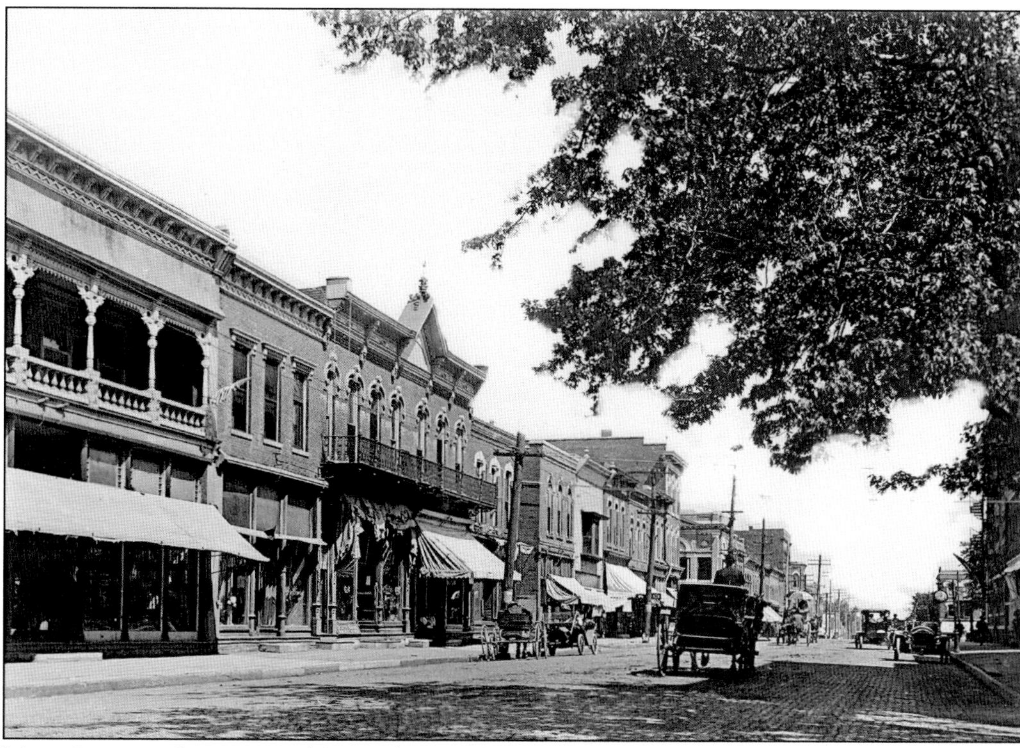

Main Street at the corner of Second Street bustles with traffic at the turn of the 20th century as wagons and horses blend with the earliest automobiles. On one side of this single block in 1900, shoppers could patronize three grocers, a meat shop, a bakery, two druggists, a millinery, a hardware store, a tin shop, and a notions and wallpaper store.

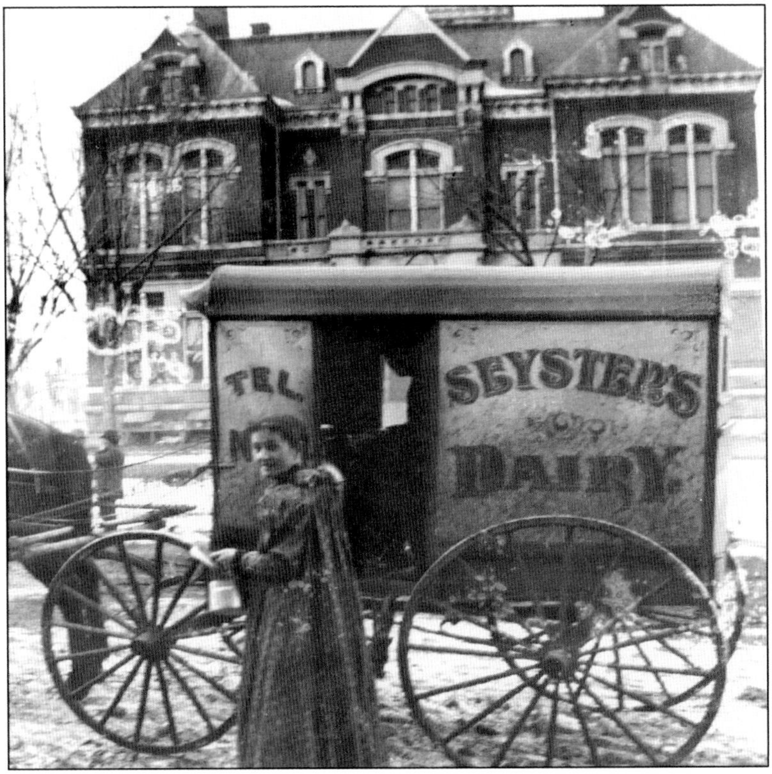

Hettie Anthony makes a purchase from Seyster's Dairy wagon on the east side of the square. For milk not yet pasteurized, customers brought their empty bottles to the wagon that kept the product moving to customers without spoiling. Soon, sterilized bottles and pasteurized milk would allow delivery wagons to drop milk off at homes on scheduled routes.

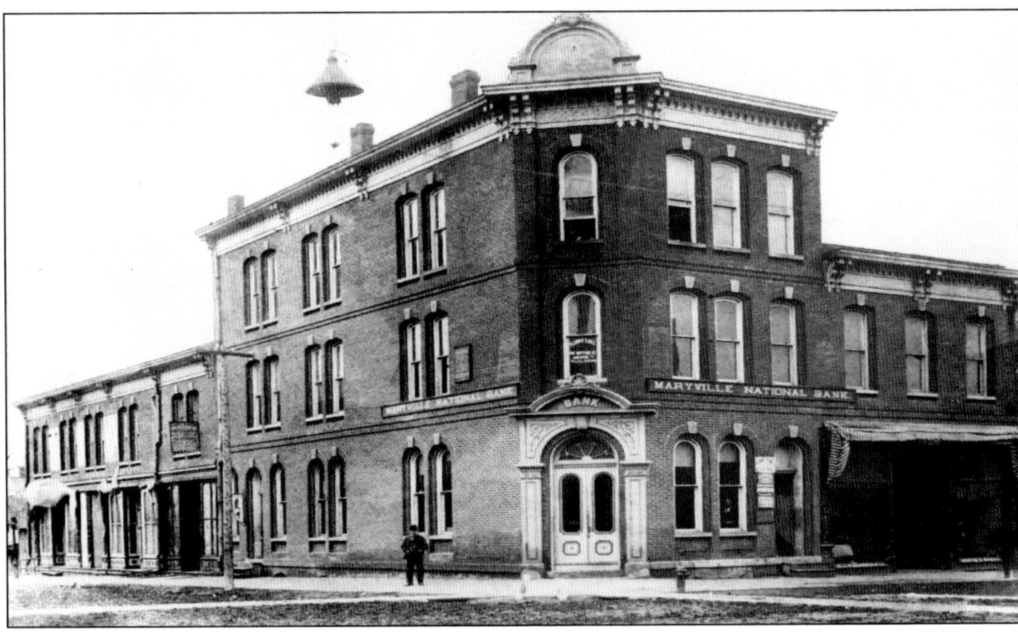

Founded in 1874 by George Baker, John Saunders, and Richard Saunders, Maryville National Bank erected this three-story structure at the corner of Fourth Street and Main Street. Seen in 1889, adjoining on Fourth Street to the left, are a shoe shop, gunsmith, and cabinetry shop. This brick block structure was replaced in 1917 with the impressive Greek revival structure that remains there today, owned by Bank Midwest.

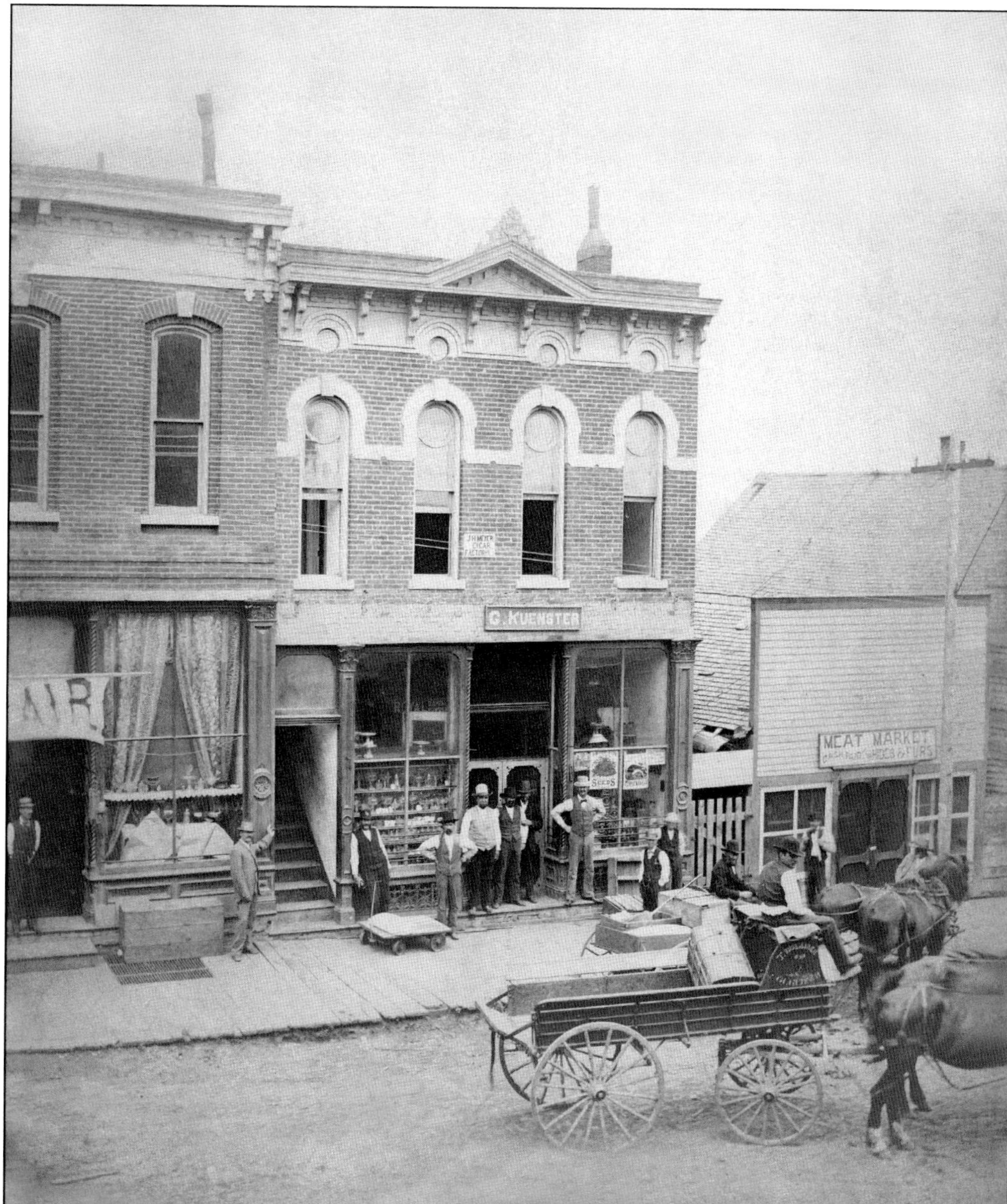

Gottlieb Kuenster operated this grocery and dry goods store, seen here in 1869 in perhaps the earliest surviving image of commerce in Maryville. Having started as Kuenster, Kessler, and Kraen, the business frequently used the unfortunate KKK advertising hook, including their pitch for Kutting, Klothing, and Kash. On the second floor, J.H. Meyer operated a cigar factory. A dray wagon operated by T. Shoemaker pauses for the photograph, perhaps already cognizant of the power of advertising opportunities.

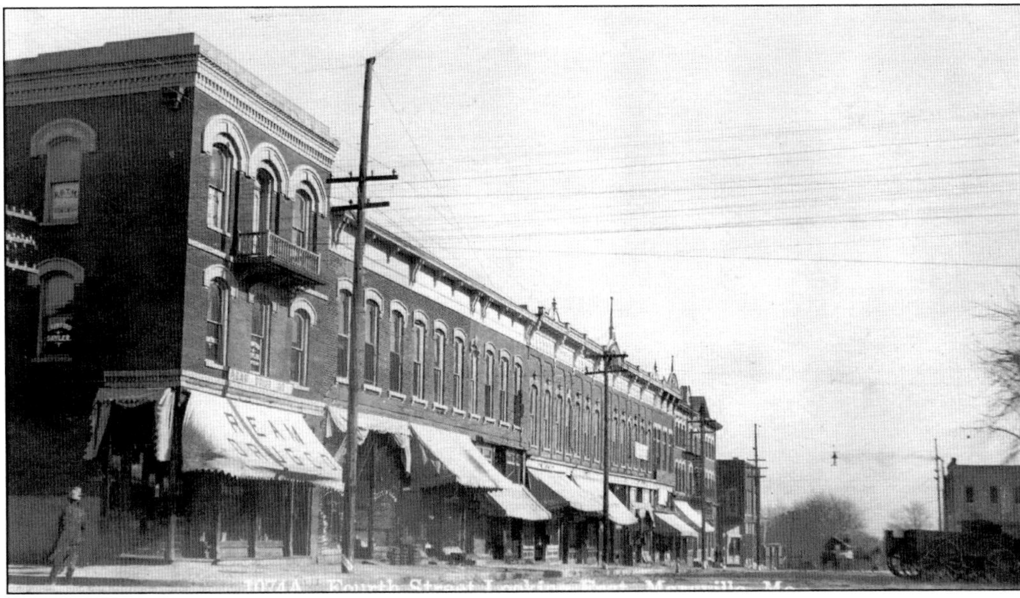

This image shows early Fourth Street looking east, sometime during the late 1880s or early 1890s. The dominant business on this end was Dr. Robert Ream's drug store. Ream gave up practicing medicine in 1897 and focused on his pharmacy from then after. An astute businessman, he also invested in a cigar shop in the space next door that was said to produce a fine quality cigar. The Knights of Maccabees lodge was on the third floor. Two other druggists shared the block, along with a hotel, bakery, restaurant, clothing shops, and the post office.

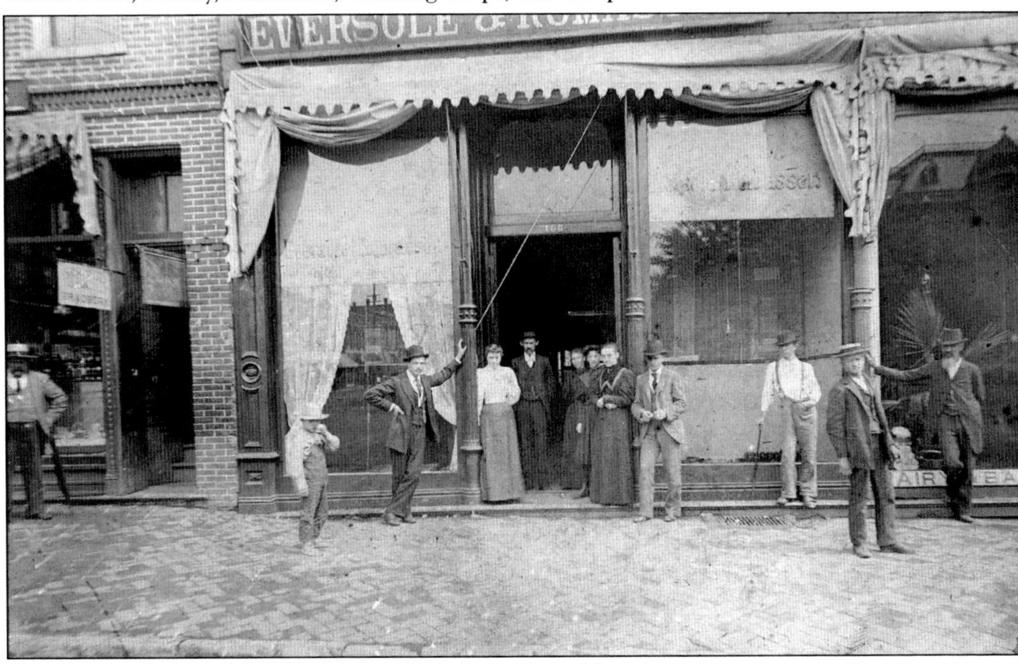

D.R. Eversole opened a shop in Maryville in 1874, and was joined in a partnership for a time as Eversole and Romassen, seen here in 1895 at 103 North Main Street. He later joined his son, Ralph, in operating a large dry goods store at 312 North Main Street. The shop offered carpets and rugs, ladies' ready-to-wear goods, notions, and assorted other dry goods.

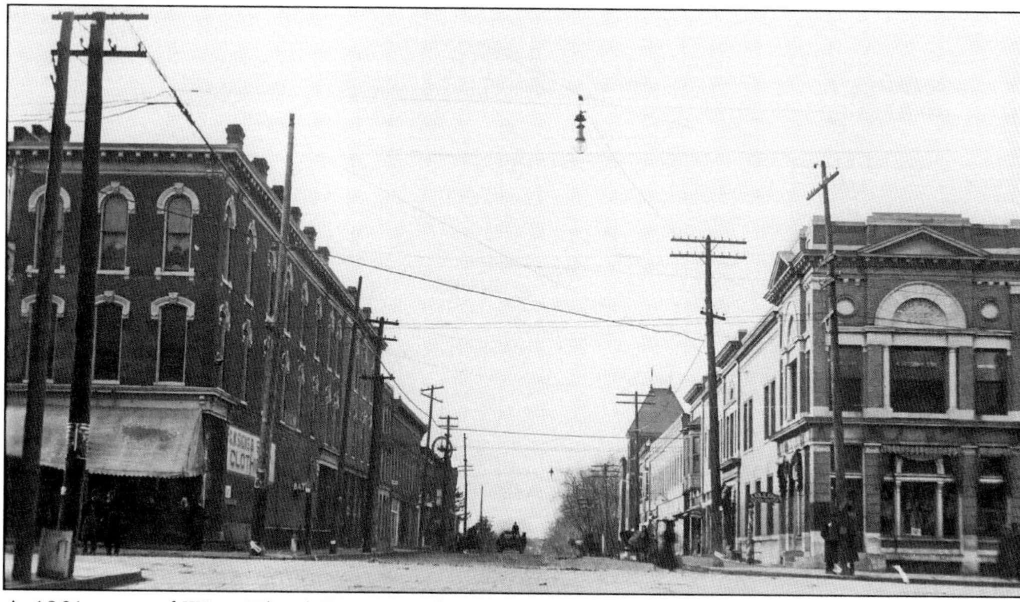

A 1901 view of West Third Street at the intersection with Main Street is bracketed by the impressive Smith Brothers building on the left and the new Nodaway Valley Bank building on the right. Signs and Sons Clothiers occupy the ground floor of the Smith Building

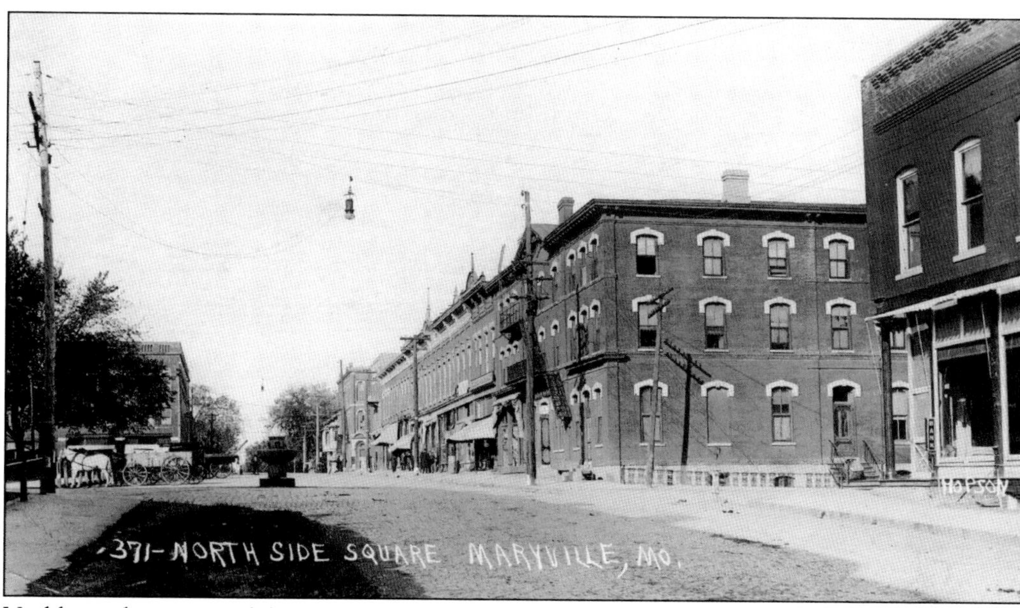

Visible in the center of the intersection of Fourth and Market Streets is a fountain provided to the city by Harmon Lee Ensign's National Humane Alliance. Mayor Garrett's beautification plan of 1925 moved the fountain to the corner of Dunn and Fourth Streets until 1969, when it was moved to the east side of the Administration Building on the college campus.

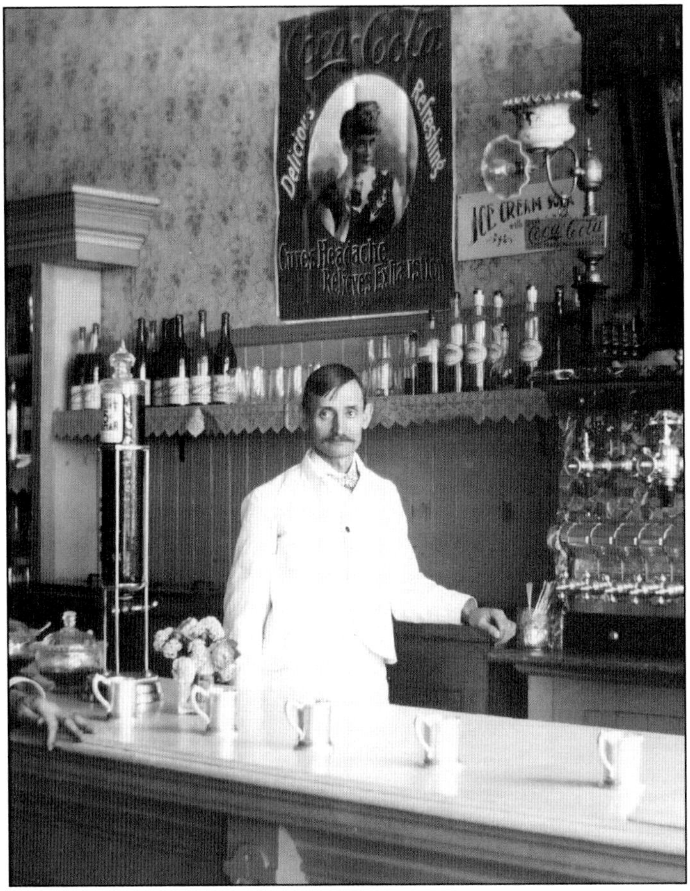

The Brenker Brothers Bakery Shop brought to Maryville the town's first soda fountain. The sign above the fountain advertising Coca Cola, indicative of the late 1890s, promised that it "cures headaches and relieves exhaustion." A variety of phosphate syrups behind the counter gave soda "jerks" liberty to mix a wide variety of their own flavors. A dispenser of "fruit nectar" on the counter, sold as an additive to either soda or simply water, allowed for even further enhancement of an afternoon beverage. The Brenker Brothers delivery wagon, shown below, pauses at the corner of Third and Buchanan, perhaps for a stop at Moffitt's hardware shop. Linneman Carriage and Wagon Repair, whose sign declares it home of "The Buggy Man," stands behind the wagon on the opposite corner.

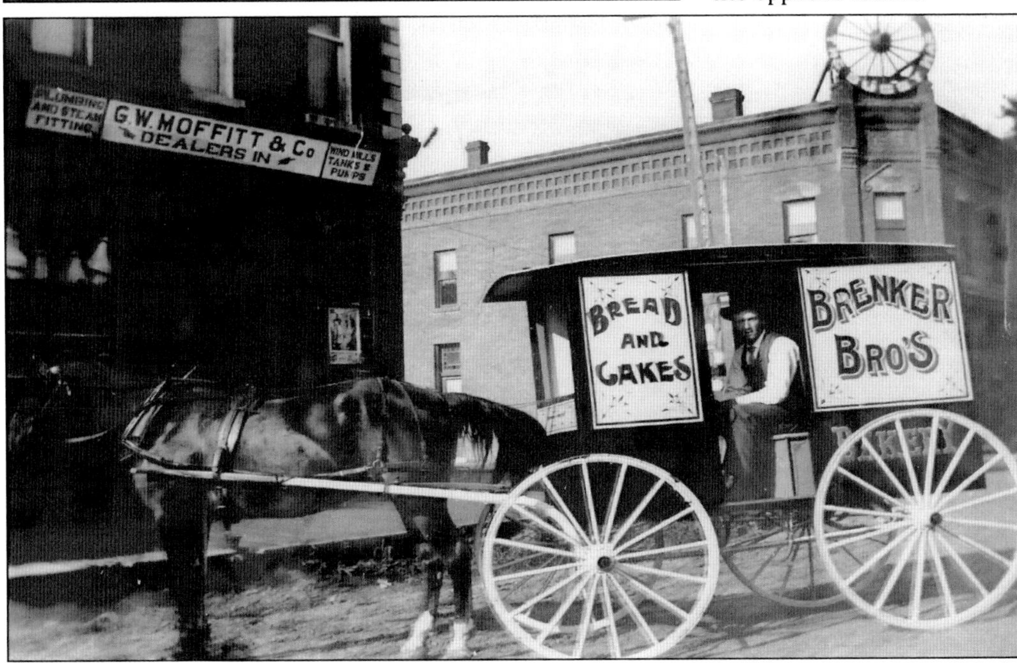

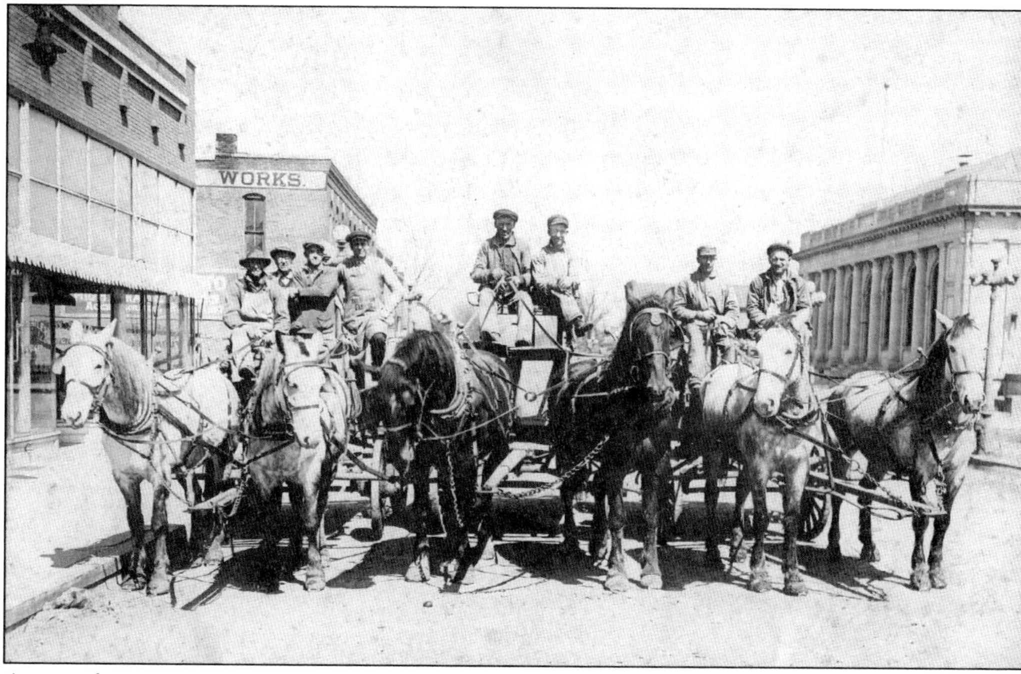

A trio of teamsters pause on North Main Street near the intersection with Fifth Street to show off their animals and rigs, sometime in the 1910s. While automobiles were quickly taking over the roads during this transition period, heavy loads of general stock for shops, groceries, and lumberyards around town still moved by dray wagon well into the 1920s.

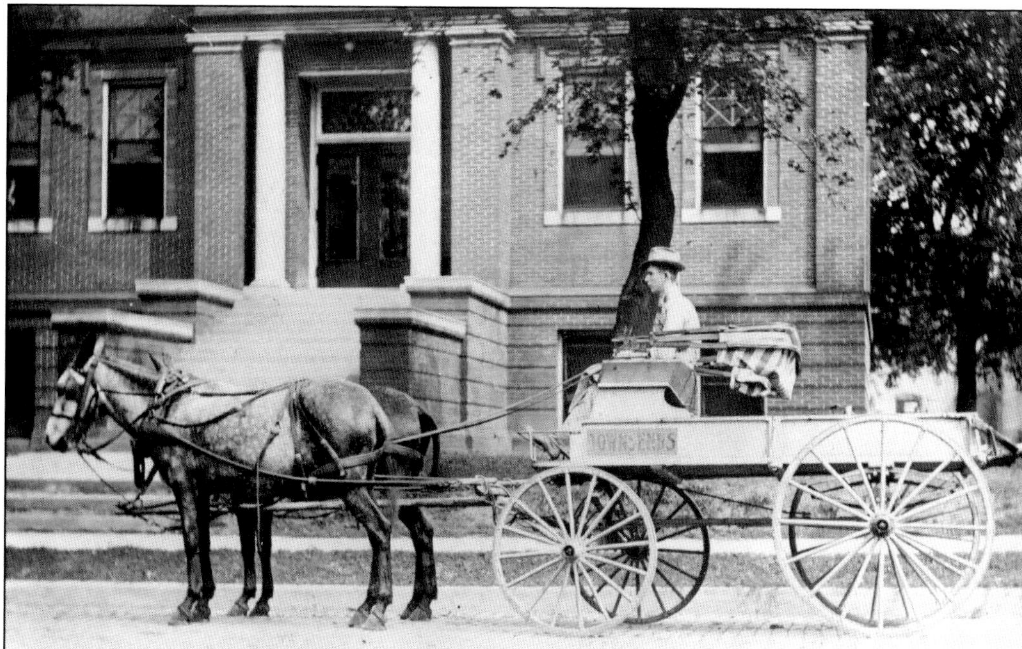

Dappled gray mules stand ready with Ray Kenny at the reins of a Townsend's delivery wagon. The team and driver sit on brick streets in front of the Carnegie library on Second Street between Main and Buchanan Streets, just after the turn of the century.

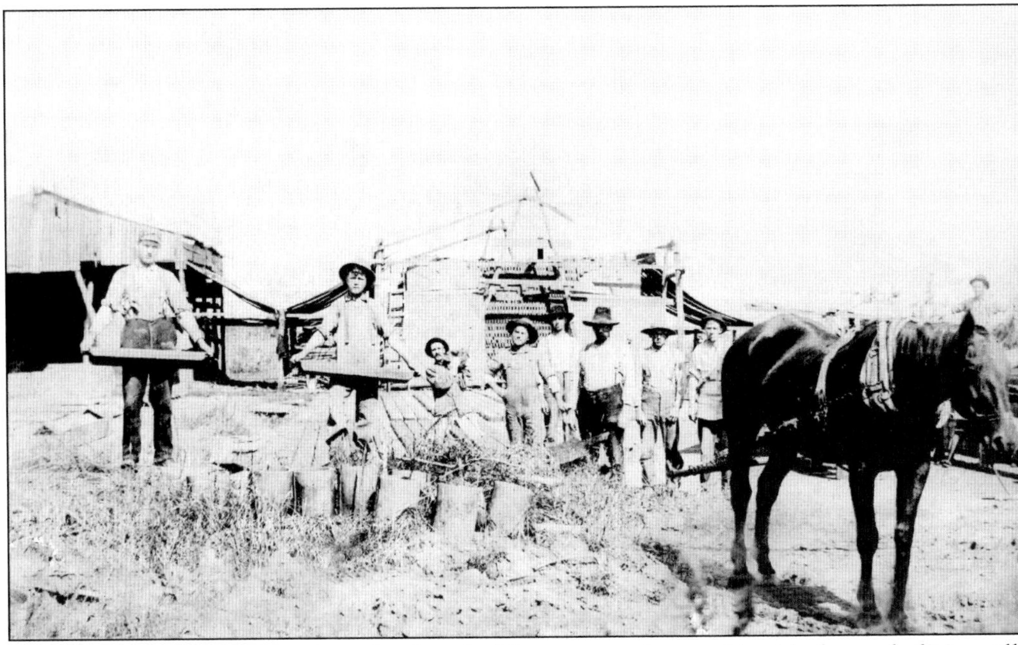

Workers at one of several local area brickworks labor to meet the considerable demand of Maryville builders at the turn of the century. The demand was caused by rapid construction expanding the commercial district of the town to several square blocks, as well as contractors demanding large quantities of brick to pave the streets of the business district and main thoroughfares.

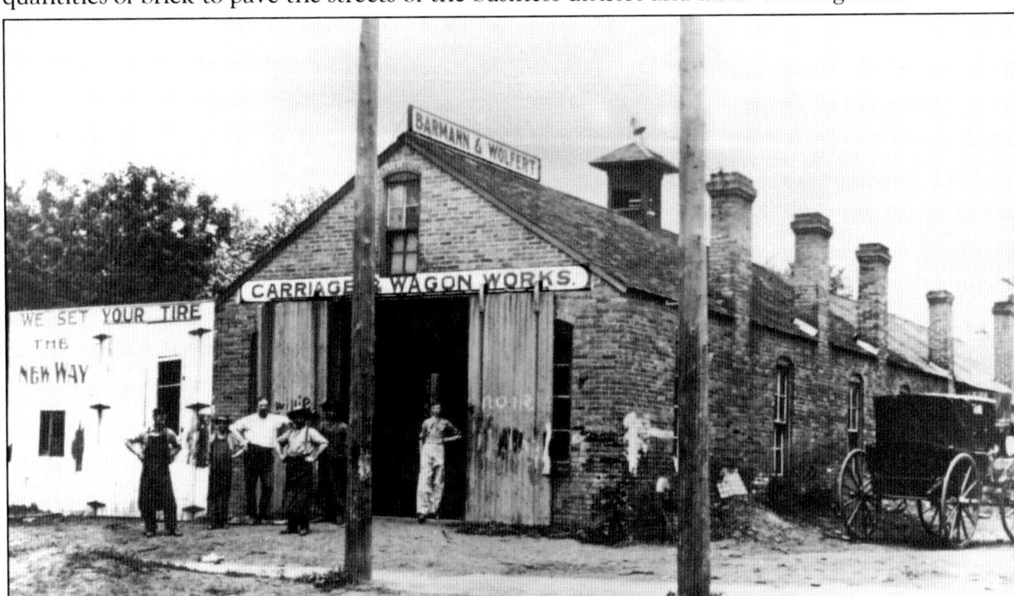

Organized in the late 1870s, the Barmann and Wolfert Carriage and Wagon Works at the corner of Fifth and Buchannan Streets was among the earliest, and by 1900, the busiest, carriage and wagon shops in the county. Frank Barmann originally owned a shoe store and sold it to get into the carriage business. He specialized in buggies, carriages, phaetons, and spring wagons. Starting with locally crafted buggies, they added factory-made models and later automobiles.

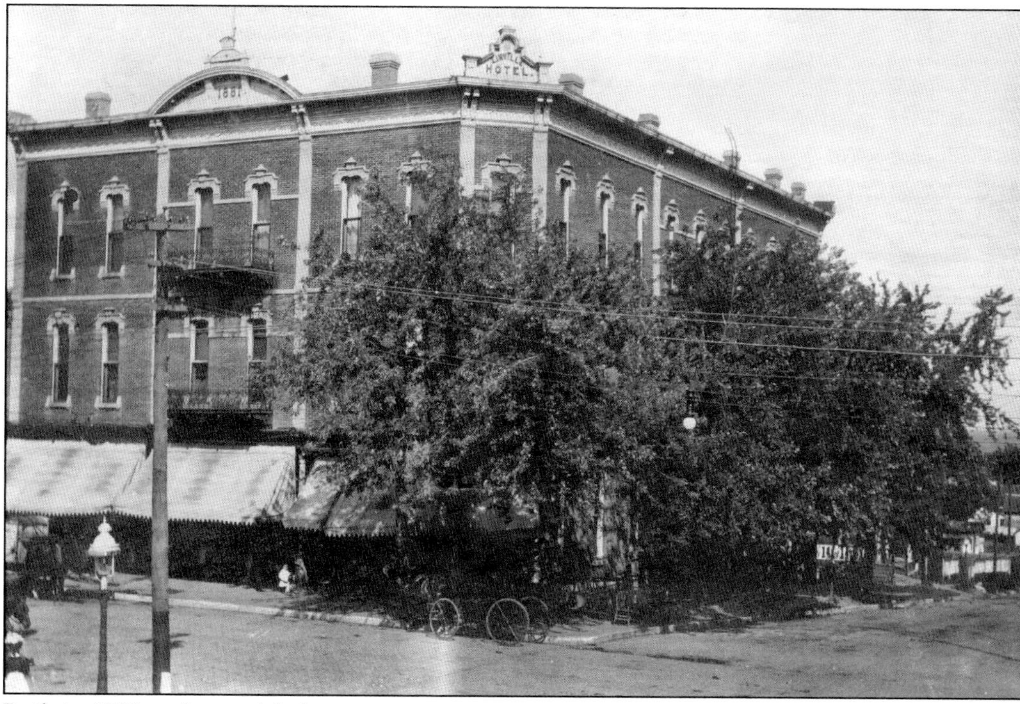

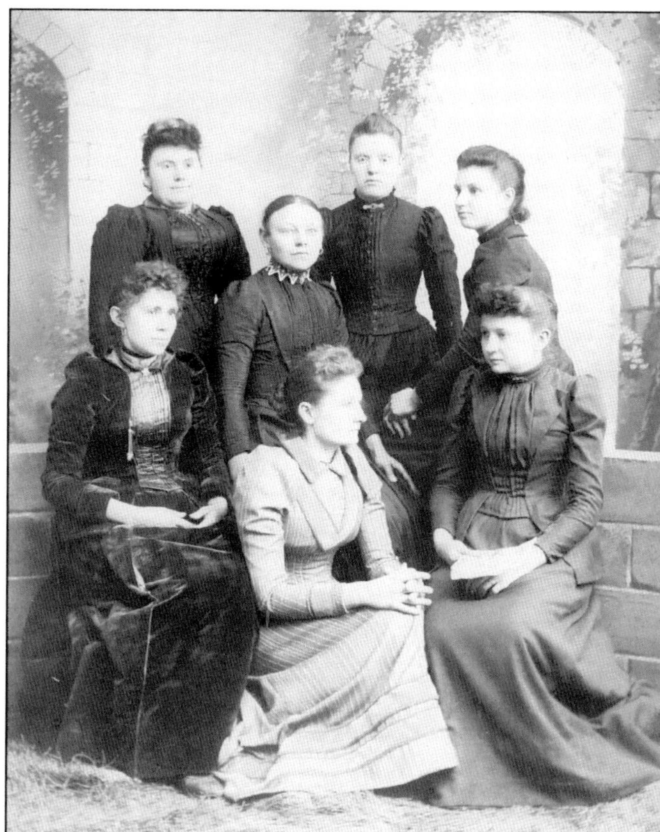

Built in 1881 and remodeled many times thereafter, the Linville hotel, after an initial period of mediocrity, became Maryville's finest hotel under the able management of George W. Fink. At the turn of the century, rates were $2 per day, or $2.50 with a bath. At the time of this photograph, around 1900, the "Traveling Man's Headquarters" hosted itinerant doctors who saw patients at the hotel. Buses to and from both railroad stations and its fine restaurant also made the hotel a destination for regional meetings. Newspapers attributed the success of the hotel to Fink's application of a strict code of conduct to himself and the Linville staff, shown to the right.

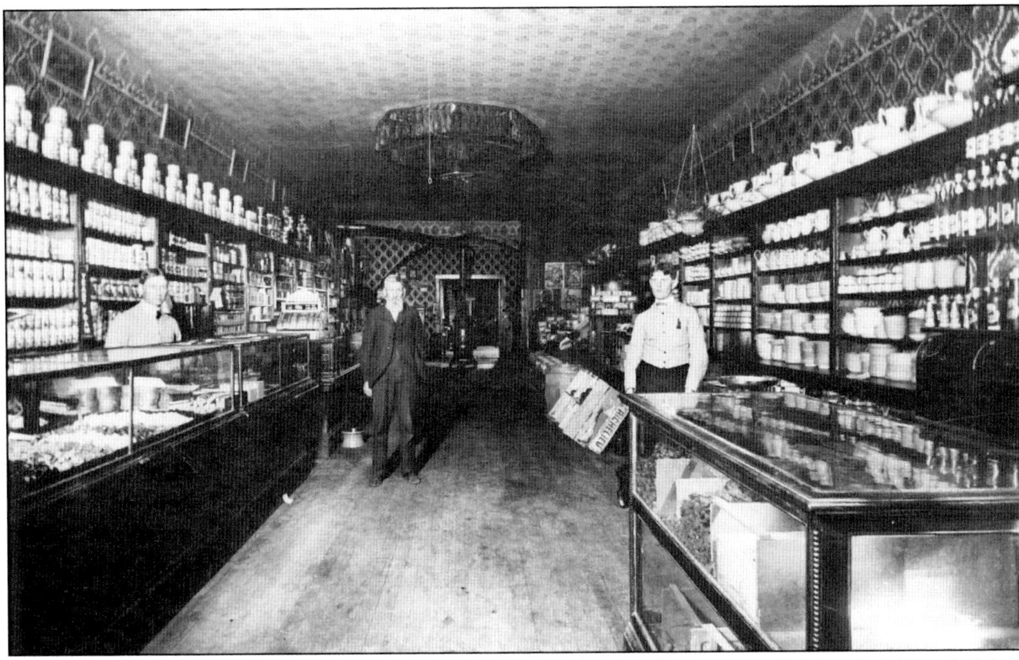

A wide assortment of goods fill the shelves of Airy and Sons Grocery in 1904 at 211 North Main Street. Carl Murry, on the left, joins the elder Mr. Airy and his son, Emery, at the store in 1904. A fixture among the numerous grocers of Maryville for many years, Airy and Roseberry advertised "goods delivered promptly to all parts of the city." Recognizing that customers spread their trade among more than a dozen grocers in town, Airy and Sons advertised modestly that "a portion of your patronage would be appreciated."

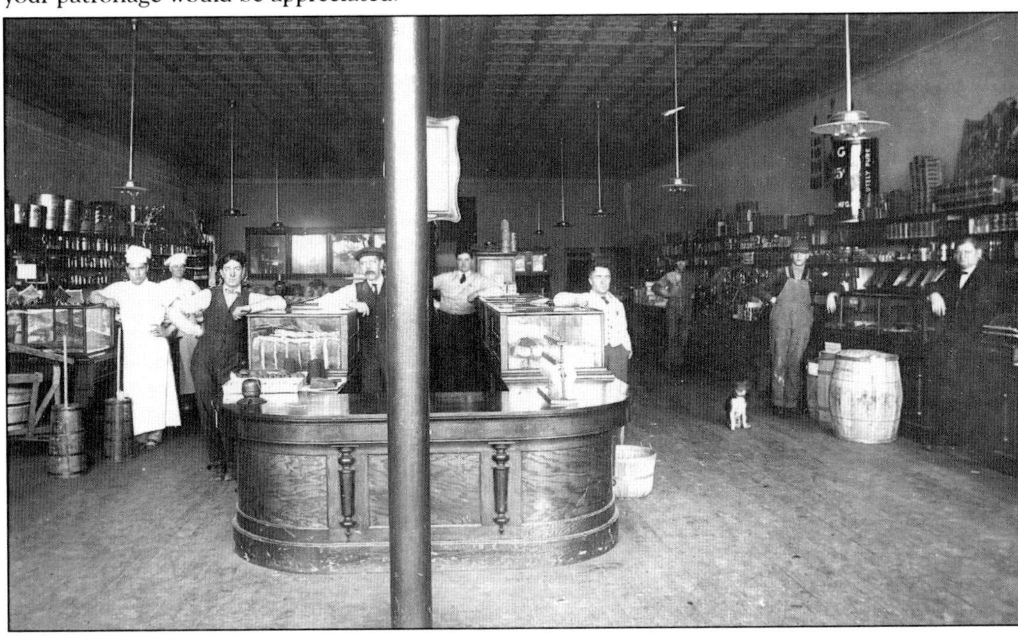

Located near the corner of East Fourth and Main Streets on the square, Andrews and Hempstead grocers, like several others in town, served diverse food and dry good needs. This particular enterprise joined two others in the local manufacturing of cigars for its patrons.

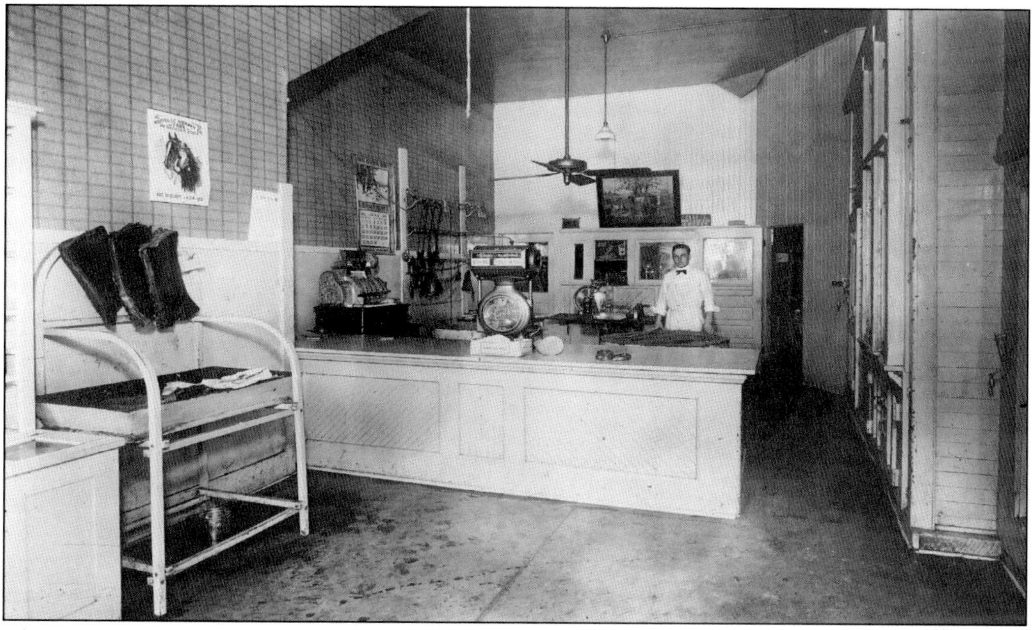

The summer of 1905 brought the problems of hot weather and raw meat for a Maryville butcher shop. A banner on this day advertises the Maryville Nodaway County Fair and Agricultural Association. On the counter sits a Toledo Electric Scale with its trademark slogan "No Springs, Honest Weight." This cash-on-the-barrelhead business also posts a sign that implores customers to "please don't ask for credit."

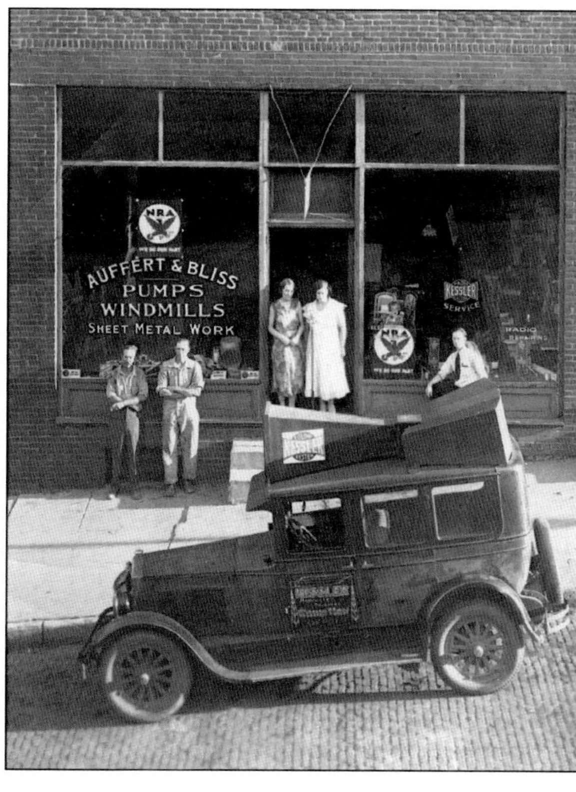

Making the most of commercial space, the Auffert and Bliss windmill shop shares a storefront with Kessler's Radio Electric, "Maryville's Original Radio Man." The classic "blue eagle" National Recovery Administration poster in the window suggests that Auffert and Bliss were supporters of the fair practice guidelines designed to reduce cut-throat competition and support minimum standards for workers nationwide from 1933 until 1935, when it was declared unconstitutional.

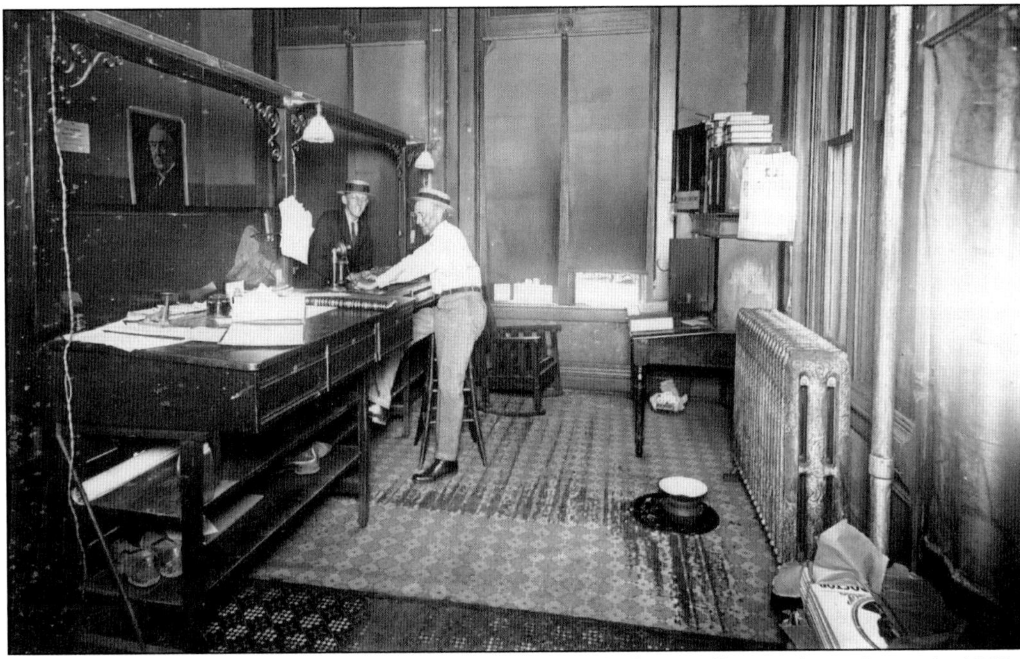

A couple of local businessmen share the trappings of white-collar work in the early 1920s. Telephone, ledgers, and notary stamps share a sparse décor with a print of President Warren G. Harding and a "wanted" poster adorning the walls. With leaky plumbing, leaky windows, and shades battered by summer breezes, such offices showed wear quickly.

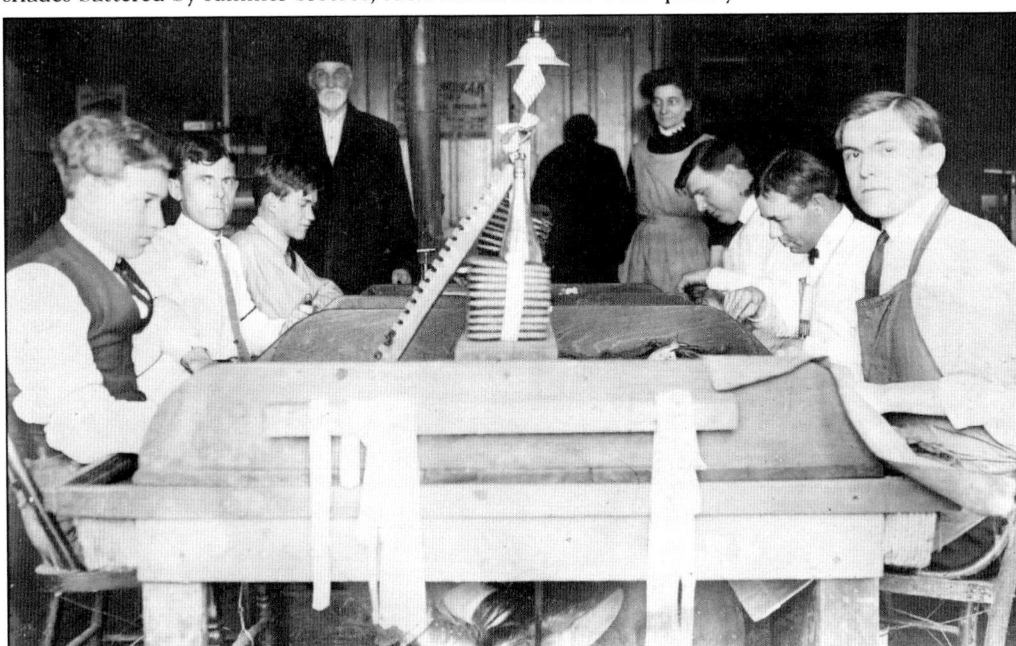

The craftsmen at Dietz and Keck on Main Street pause for a photograph in the 1910s. While the business district was lined with shops furnishing ready-made clothes, patrons who could afford to do so still relied on tailors for fine suits and alterations to better ready-wear garments that came in a limited variety of sizes.

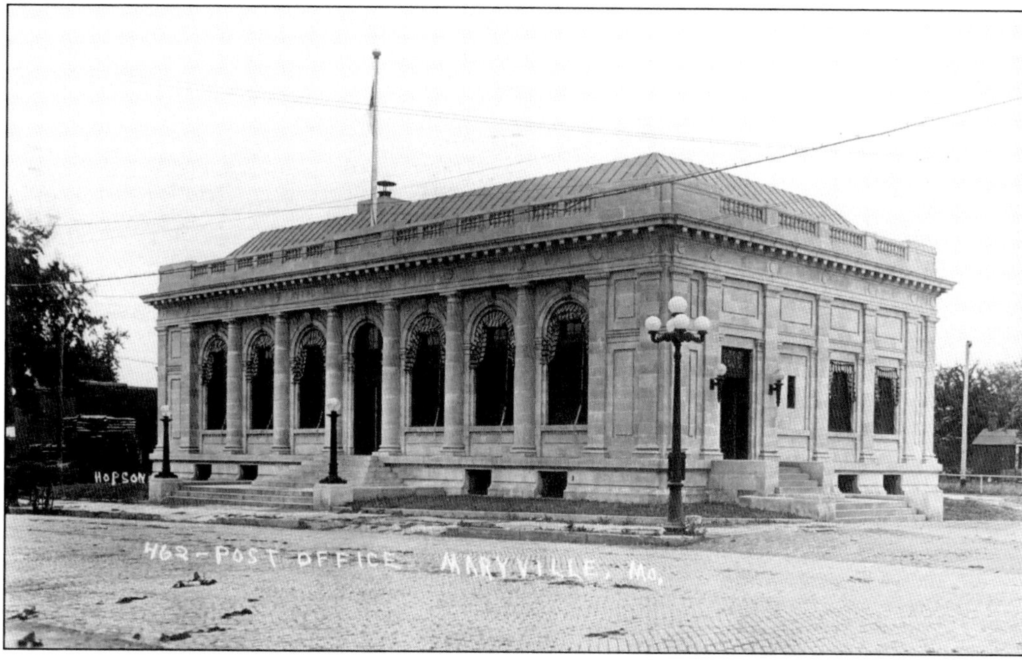

Serving today as the Maryville Public Library, this fine structure was built in 1912 as a United States Post Office. Architects James, Knox, and Taylor blended Beaux Arts Classical and Neoclassical styles in a durable and attractive public building. From the late 19th through the early 20th centuries, the Postal Service commissioned a wide variety of architecturally interesting structures for communities of all sizes. In the second half of the century, many of these fine structures were abandoned for smaller, nondescript, functional buildings. The US government gave this building to city of Maryville in 1962 to establish a library.

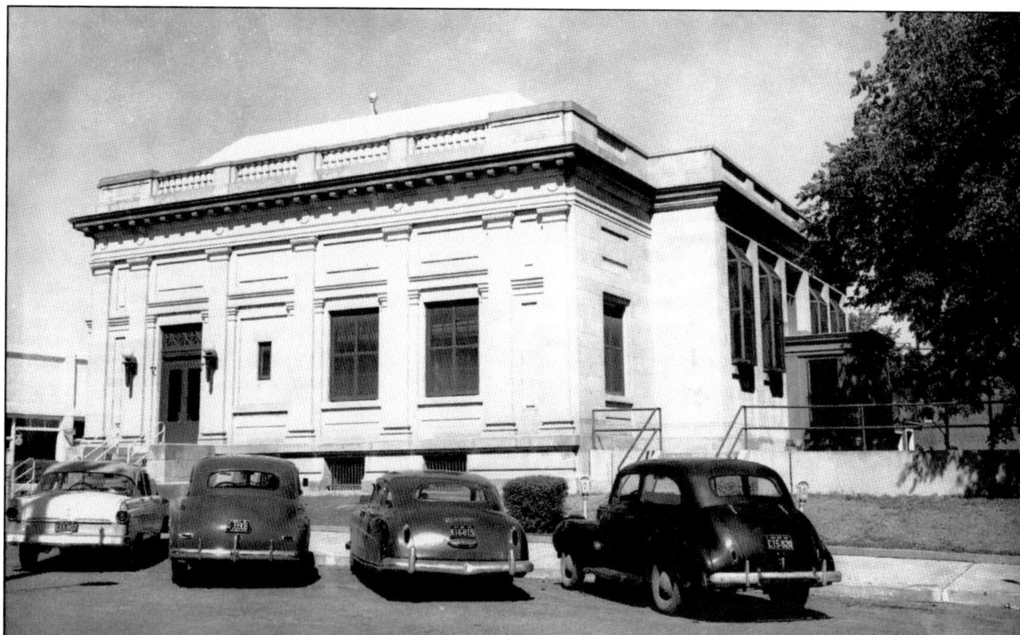

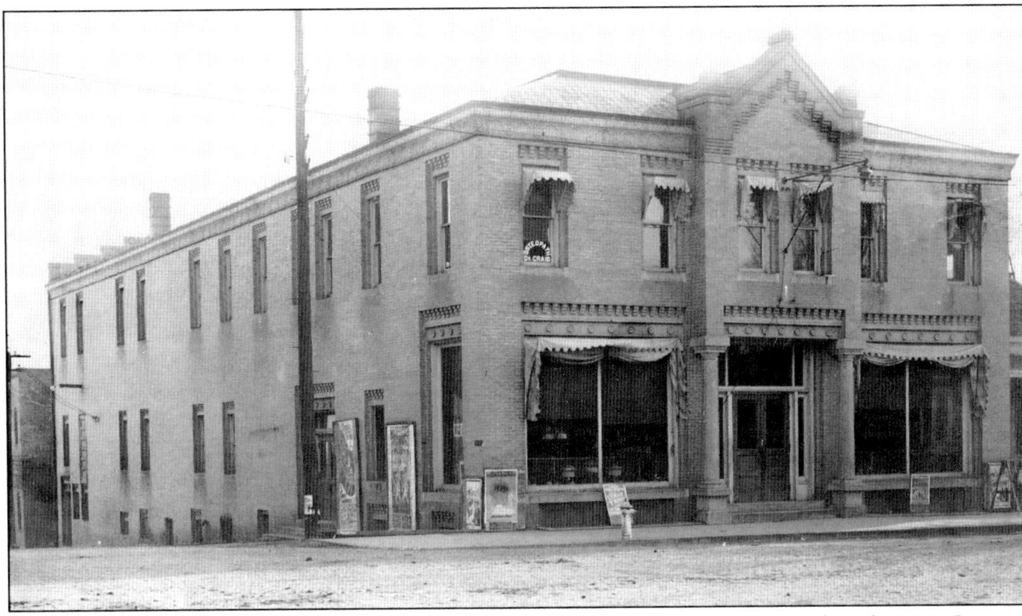

The Empire Theater was erected in 1903 at the southeast corner of Second and Main Streets. It contained a grand stage and supported 392 floor, 238 balcony, and 10 box seats. The theater hosted a wide variety of entertaining acts, such as movies, vaudeville, and minstrel shows, and even became a funeral viewing area for citizens requiring a larger space. Shown here around 1909, the Empire is preparing for the Lyman Twins, a nationally renowned stage act set to perform Yankee Drummers. Owners Cook and Sons also ran an electric light and power business out of the front offices of the theater.

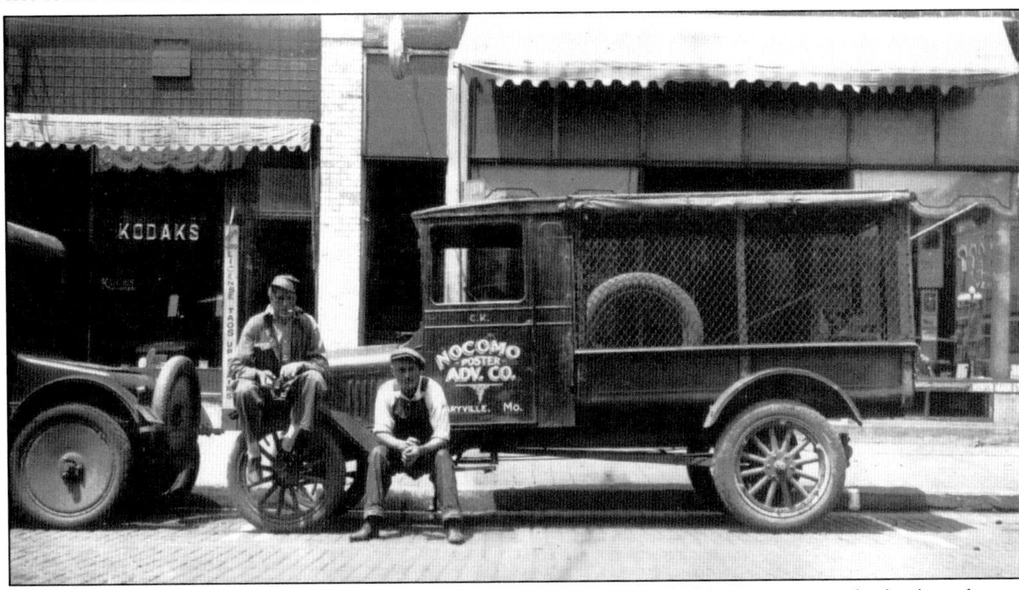

For a century and a half, Nodaway County, Missouri has provided businesses with the handy and euphonious acronym of NOCOMO. A pair of hard-working men with the NOCOMO Poster Advertising Company pause on North Main Street, apparently having delivered their signs for the day. The Ford Model TT with the express bed configuration was easily customized to fit the varied needs of commercial users.

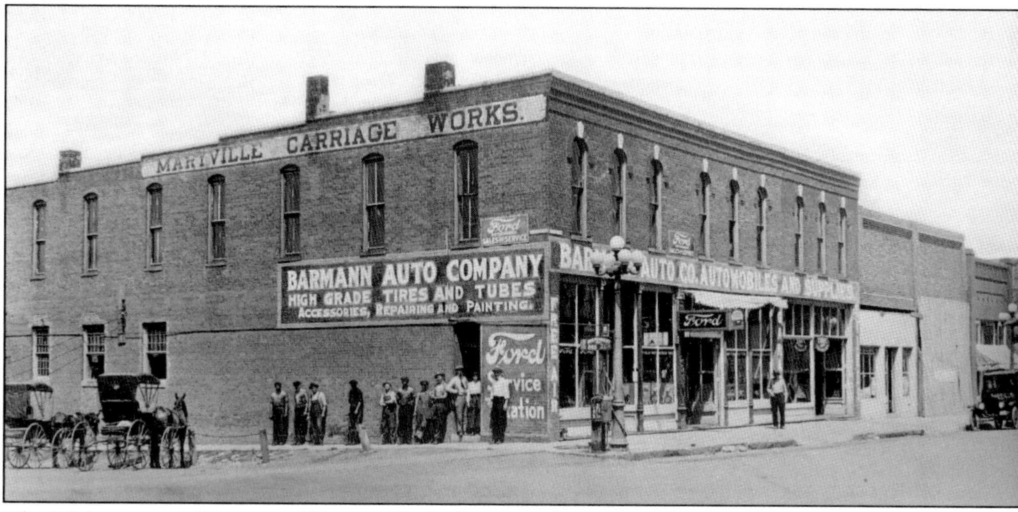

The 19th century Barmann Wagon Works became the Maryville Carriage works in its impressive new building at the corner of Fifth and Main Streets. Jumping in early on the advent of the automobile, the Barmanns gained a Ford service and sales dealership as the Barmann Auto Company. Gasoline could also be purchased at a curbside hand gas pump that appeared on the corner, probably in 1910. The family resided in apartments in the second floor of the building.

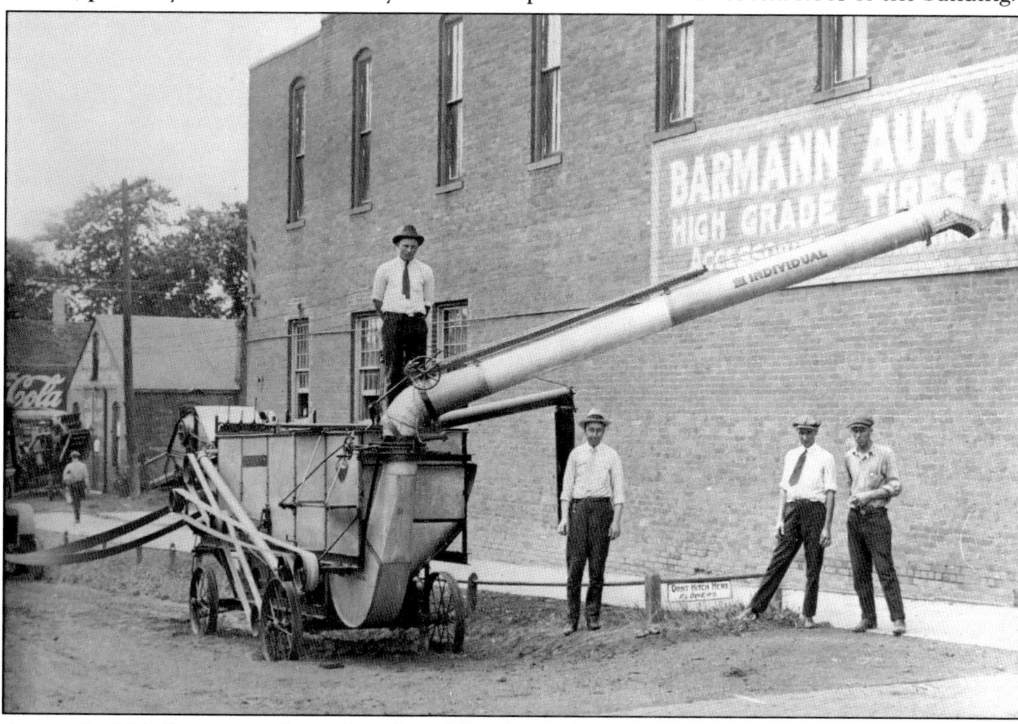

Around 1924, Barmann Auto Supply sold "The Individual," a compact version of the Wood Brothers successful Humming Bird Thresher. The Individual promised to save all your grain with 100 percent of its market value intact. Standing atop the machine is Austin Spoor, and on the ground are, from left to right, Earl Barmann, Leslie Roberts, and Homer Hanline. Barmann's original wagon works can be seen down the hill, with the transition from the age of horses to the automobile further marked by a sign on the old railing that reads "don't hitch here, flowers."

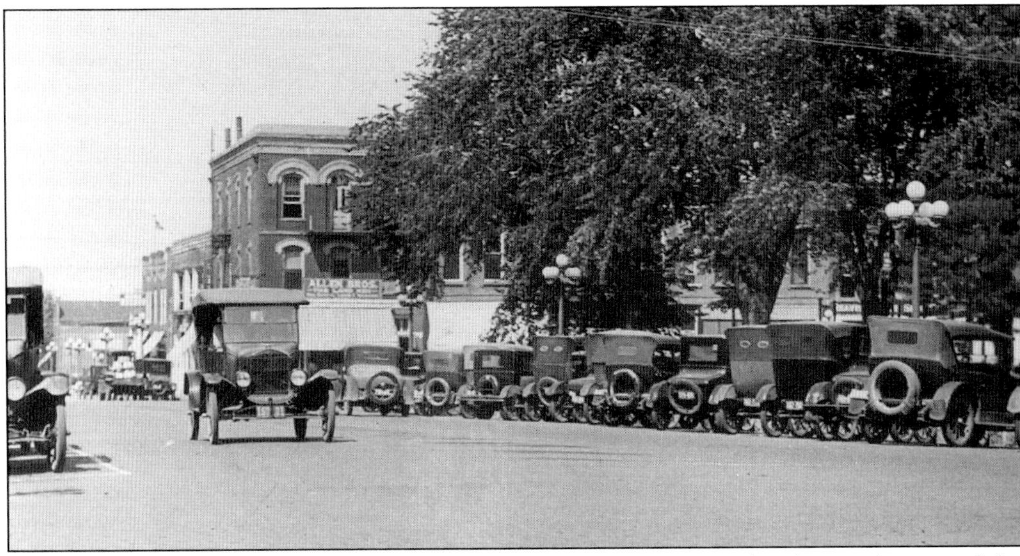

By the late 1920s, the downtown (or, locally, the "uptown") square was bustling with automobiles, and Maryville, like every other town across the country, had to address the problem of parking them. The pattern followed essentially the common-sense method used earlier with wagons and carriages, though with more orderly lines and spaces. Fortunately for these motorists, the parking meter would not be invented until 1935. (Courtesy of Coby Lamb.)

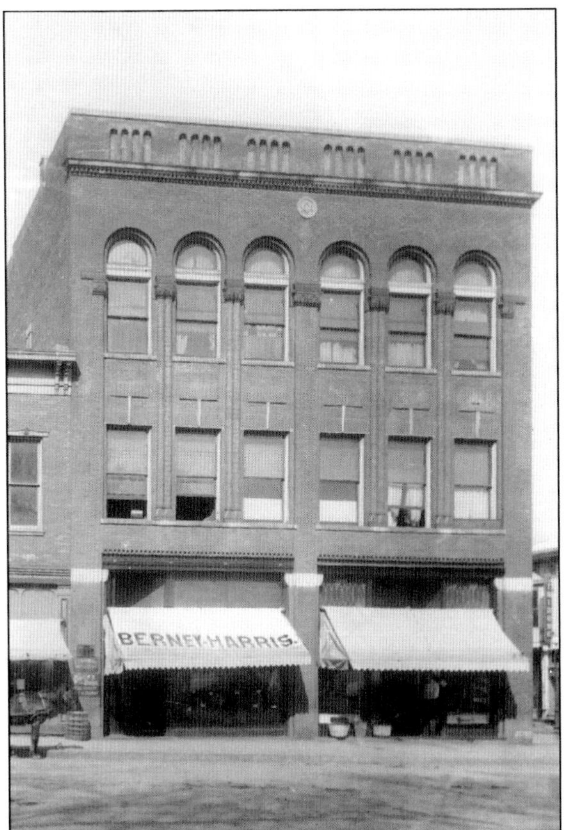

This landmark three-story brick block structure appeared in 1891 as a commercial venture of the highly successful Lavencour Michau. The ambitious businessman came to Maryville in 1856, and was joined in a dry-goods partnership with John Lieber in 1872. Michau's property housed numerous businesses, as well as the Masonic Lodge on the third floor. Michau died in 1901, and the "Michau Block" succumbed to fire in 1918, though he left to the community one of its most impressive residential homes.

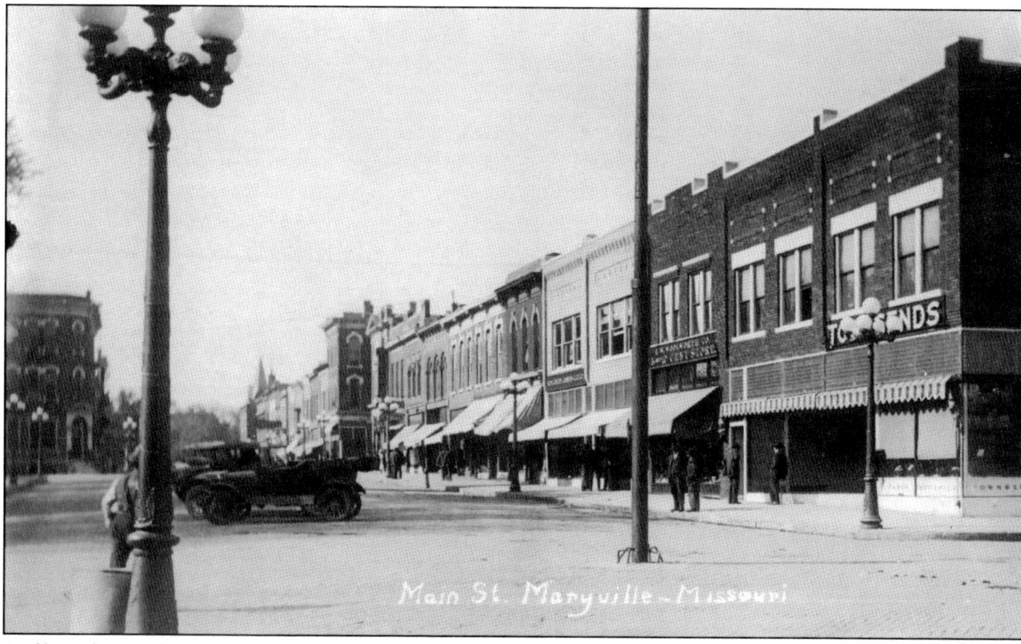

Still seeking the right solution to the problem of parking, Maryville, along with many other communities, experimented for a time in the mid-1920s with center-street parking. By that time, the west side of the square had already changed its face significantly as a result of fires and elective re-building. The great three-story Michau building that had stood on the near corner was replaced after its fire by the more modest brick block buildings common to the post–World War I era.

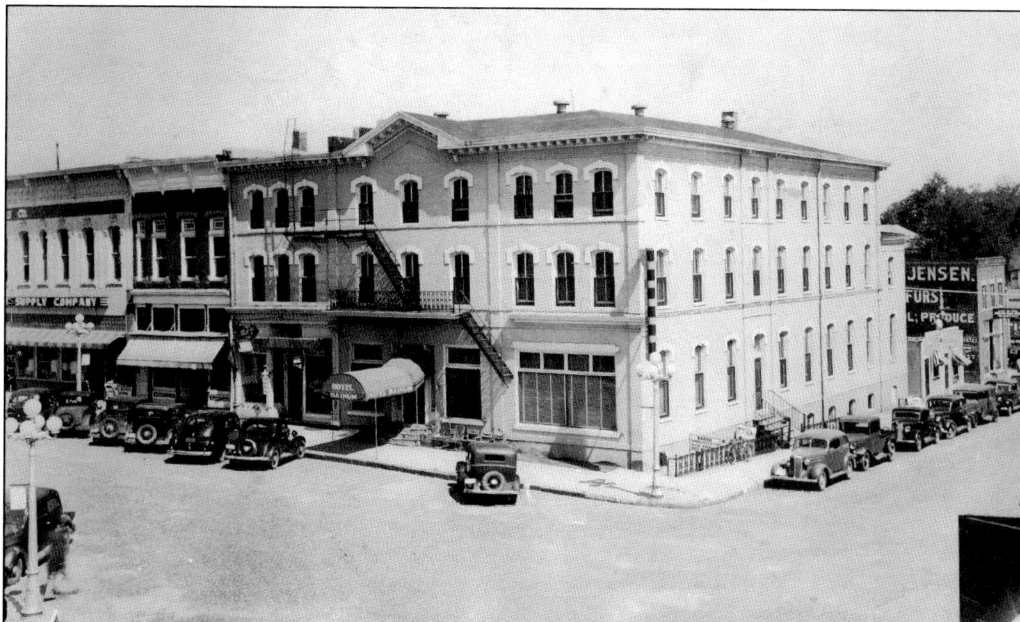

The grand Hotel Bainum, at the northwest corner of Fourth and Market Streets, challenged the Linville for status as Maryville's finest. By the 1930s, the 35-room hotel might well have laid claim to that status. A room in 1936 ranged from $1.25 to $1.75 per night under the ownership of Russel Day. A radio service shop and shoe repair rented space in the basement level.

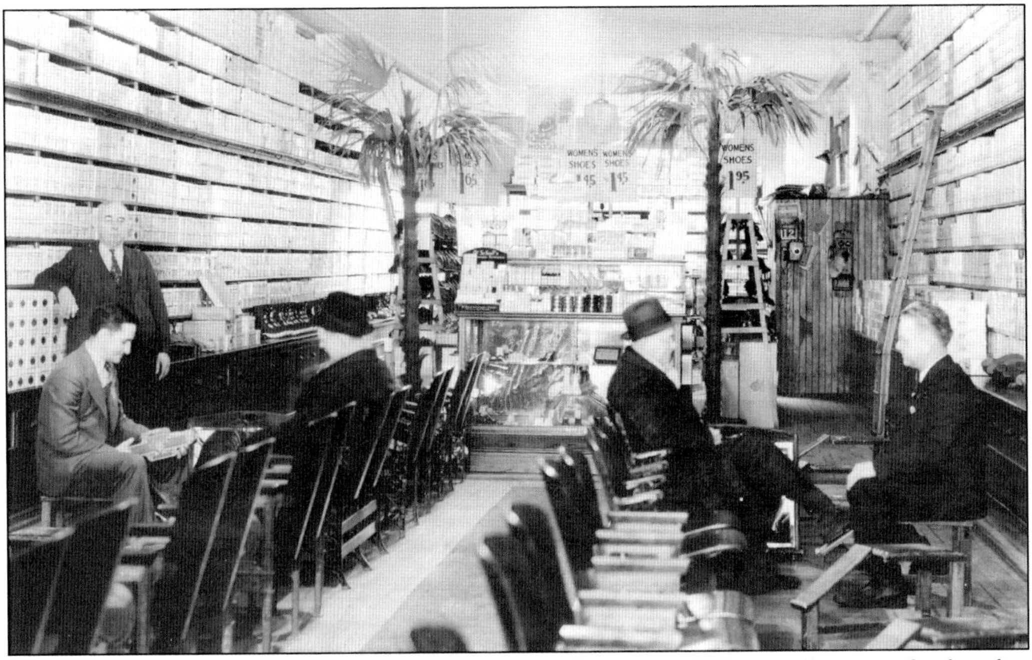

The Beehive Shoe Store, "home of good shoes," was a fixture on the Maryville square for decades, serving the town's footwear needs for men, women, and children. Palm trees put customers in a warm frame of mind during this February 1936 shopping day. Men's and women's shoes could be purchased for as little as $1.45 per pair.

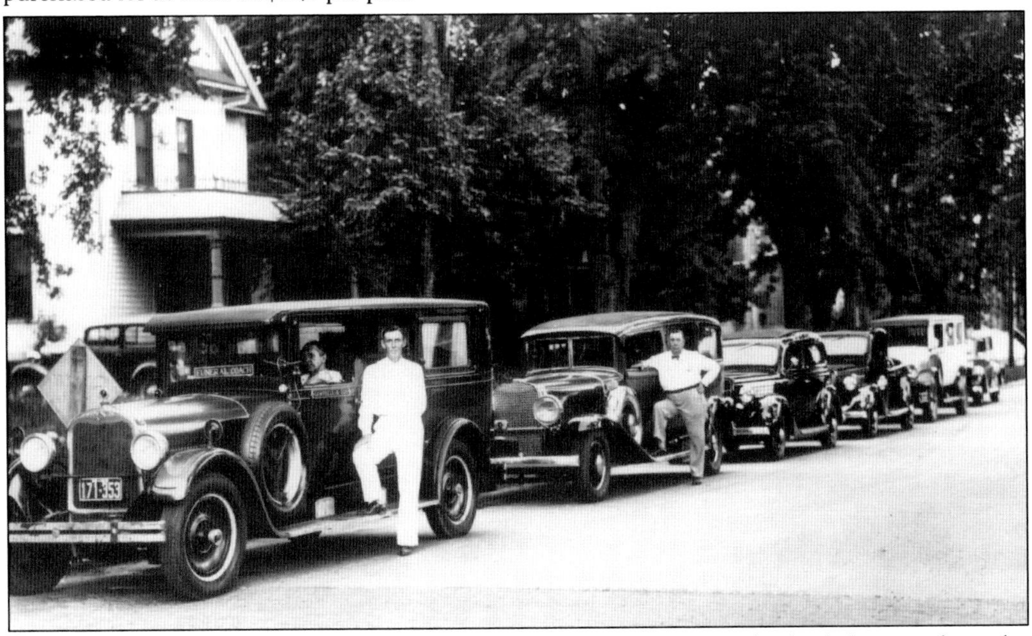

Campbell's funeral home at 951 South Main Street in the early 1930s bridged the span from the 19th century, when the business of preparing loved ones for burial was largely a family "undertaking" in the home, to the 20th-century business. For Lowell Campbell, the business, among other enterprises, also served as the foundation for a career in local politics. Mayor Campbell and his son show off their fleet of coaches in front of their home.

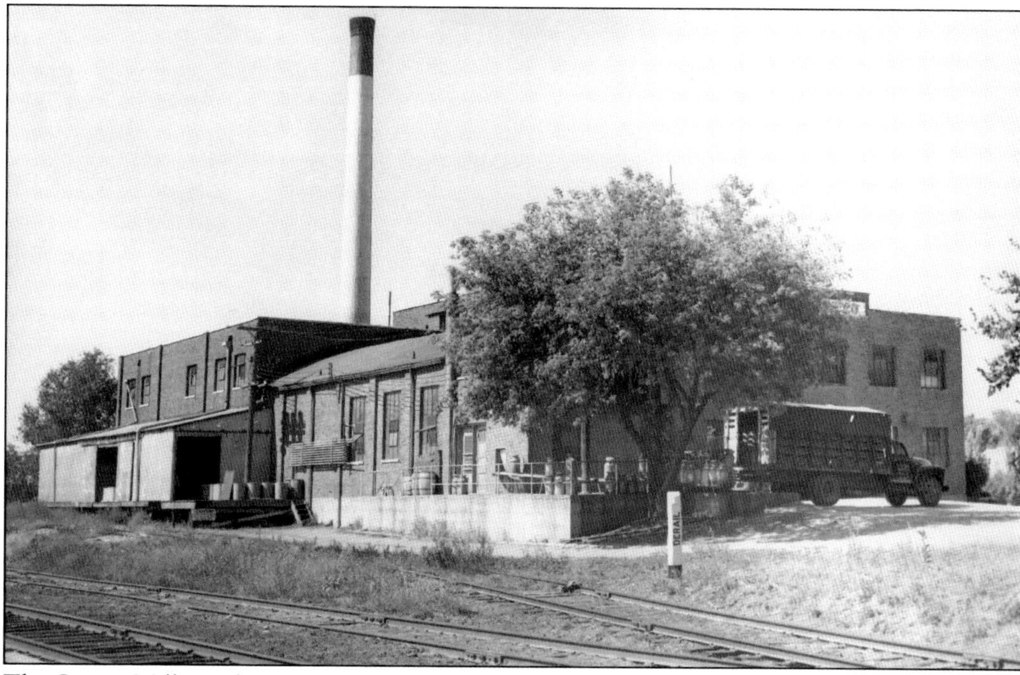

The Center Milk Products processing plant was located on a siding across the main line from the Wabash depot on the north side of town. The firm marketed powdered milk, bottled milk, and semi-solid buttermilk for animal feed. By the mid-1930s, the company paid more than $300,000 a year for milk from area dairy farmers.

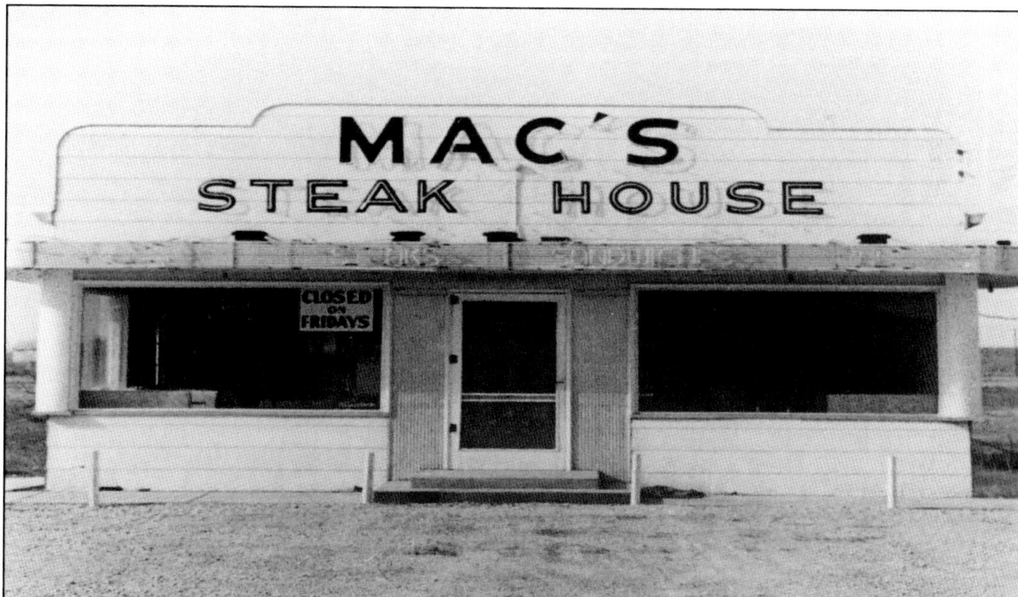

Mac's Steak House joined the cafes in the 1950s that dotted South Main along Highway 71 as part of the emerging movement of businesses away from the central district. Bucking the trend, however, Mac's moved into the downtown business district in the late 1960s. As is commonly the case, the building that once served diners on the south end of town has seen varied uses since, including as a Laundromat, and today the Hair It Is! salon.

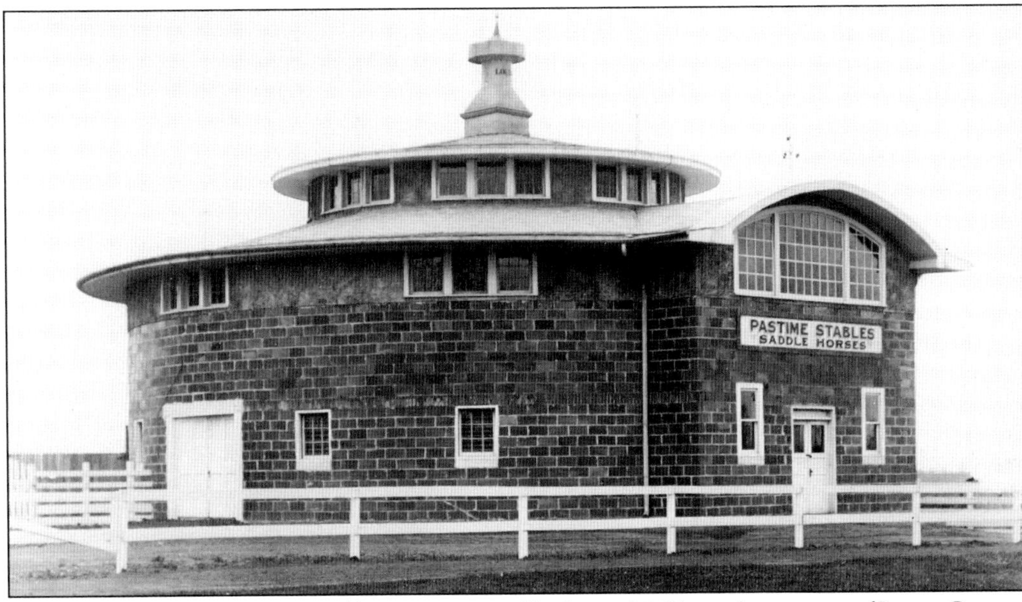

The unusual, round Pastime Stables was operated by James H. Tapp, the mentor of Lester Swaney of the famous Faustiana Farms. Pastimes was the last stable owned by Tapp, known to locals as "Colonel Tapp" and by those who knew him best as "Gentleman Jim." In addition to breeding fine Saddlebreds, Tapp also procured horses for the federal government during World War I, and once told of also filling a commission for the Mexican government of seven matched teams of Golden Saddlebreds. He retired in 1947.

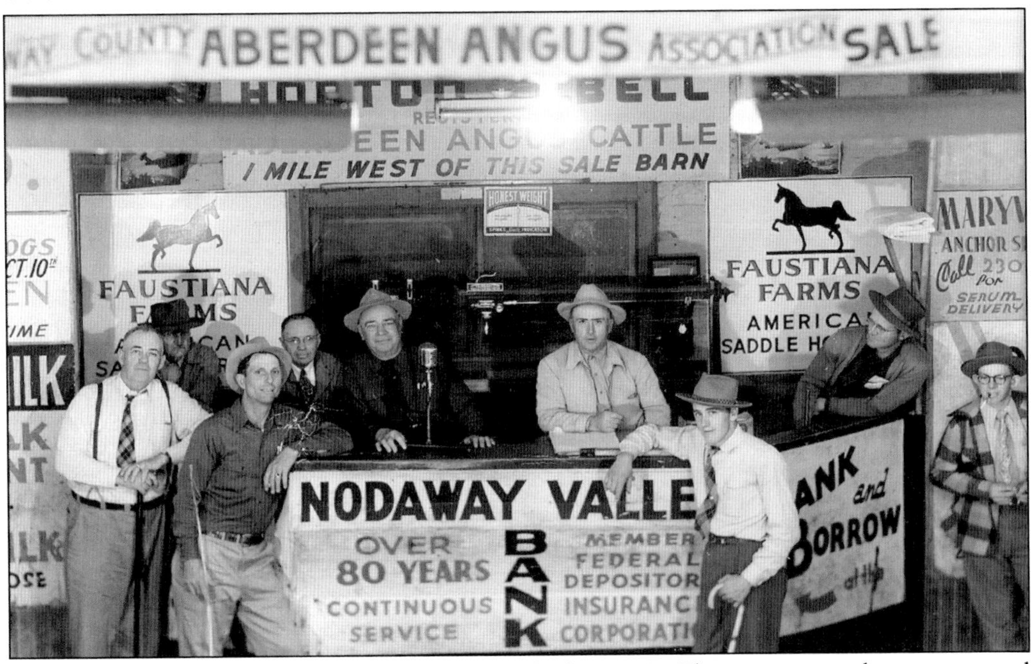

Auctioneers and handlers gather at the sale barn in the late 1940s. The association sale was an annual event starting in 1940, typically taking place during the fall around the first week of October. With numerous farmers and livestock men in attendance, auctions also proved an excellent opportunity to advertise breeding stock and the credit to buy them. (Courtesy of Mary Graham.)

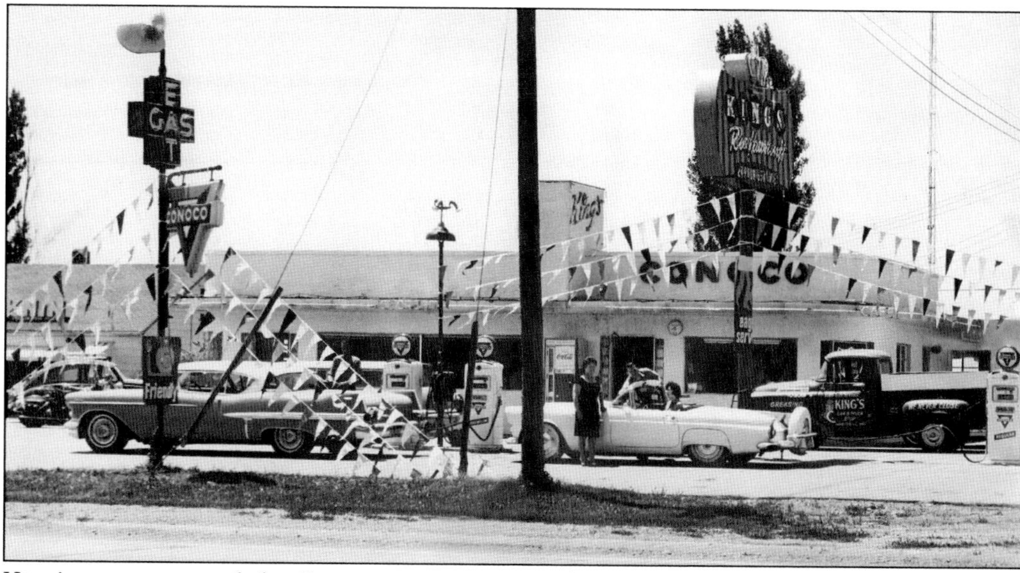

King's restaurant and the Conoco station on South Main Street helped to usher Maryville in the 1950s into the age of the 24-hour truck stop. These icons of American life in the 20th century generally appeared first in the 1940s with wider bays, diesel fueling pumps, and cafes not found at earlier filling stations. The Continental Oil Company's Conoco brand spread rapidly throughout the Midwest from its home base in Ponca City, Oklahoma, in the years after World War II. Proprietor Jennie King stands next to a fine new 1956 Ford Thunderbird passing through. (Courtesy of Suzi Schneider-Anderson.)

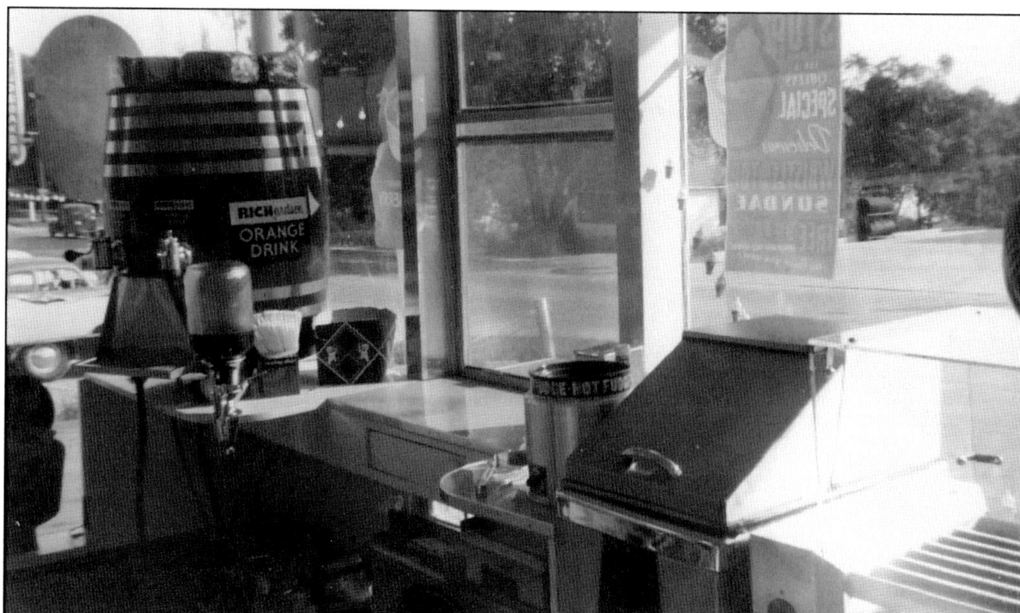

Another fixture on South Main Street for decades has been the Dairy Queen, seen here from the perspective of one of its first employees, JoAnn Outs, during its inaugural season in 1954. In addition to their trademark ice cream, patrons could enjoy Richardson orange drink and root beer. On this day, the DQ was also offering the "Queens Special," a whistle-top sundae that came with a free dairy queen whistle shaped like a cone. (Courtesy of JoAnn Outs.)

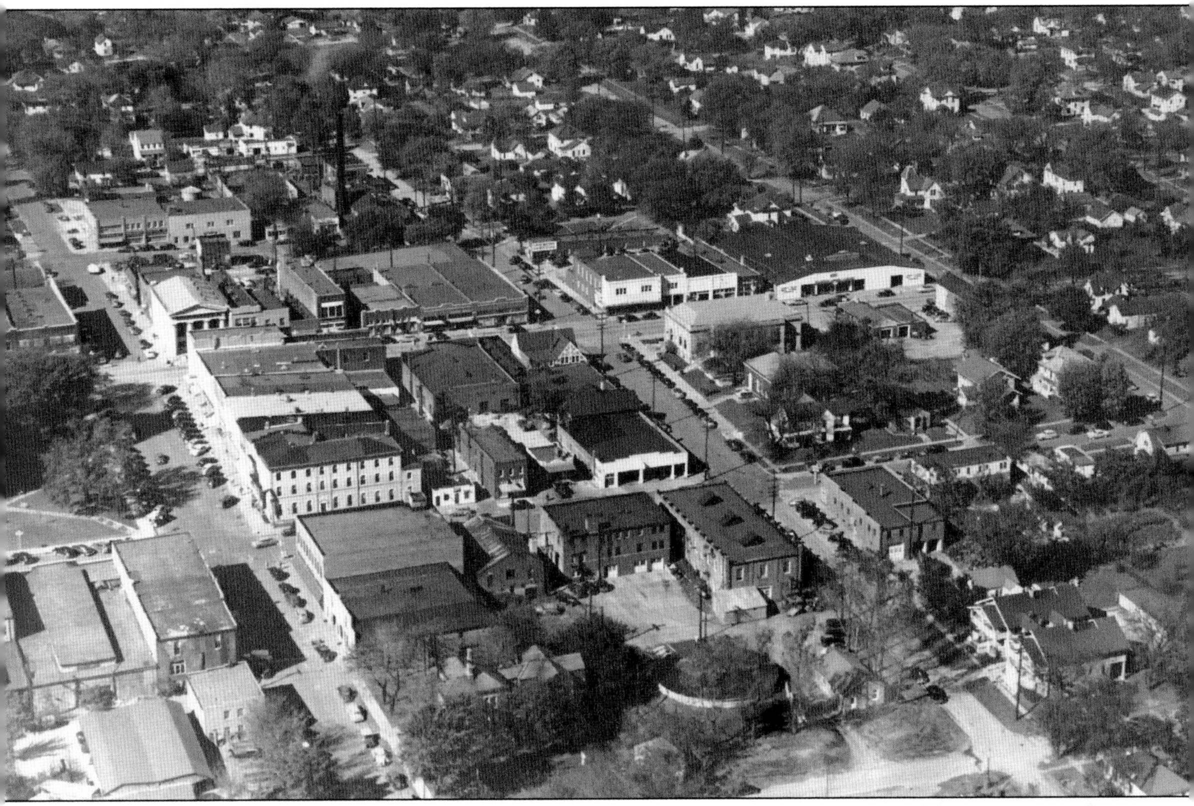

An aerial view looking west along Fourth and Fifth Streets just after World War II reveals a prosperous community looking ahead to the second half of an enterprising century. Most of the commercial structures visible here are no longer present, and have fallen victim to the vicissitudes of time and transformations in the marketplace. Some of them have been replaced by newer, and typically lower, structures, and others simply by parking lots. Bigger chain store franchises, fast-food, housing developments on the periphery of town, and a highway bypass all transformed the town considerably over the coming decades.

Two

Organizational Life

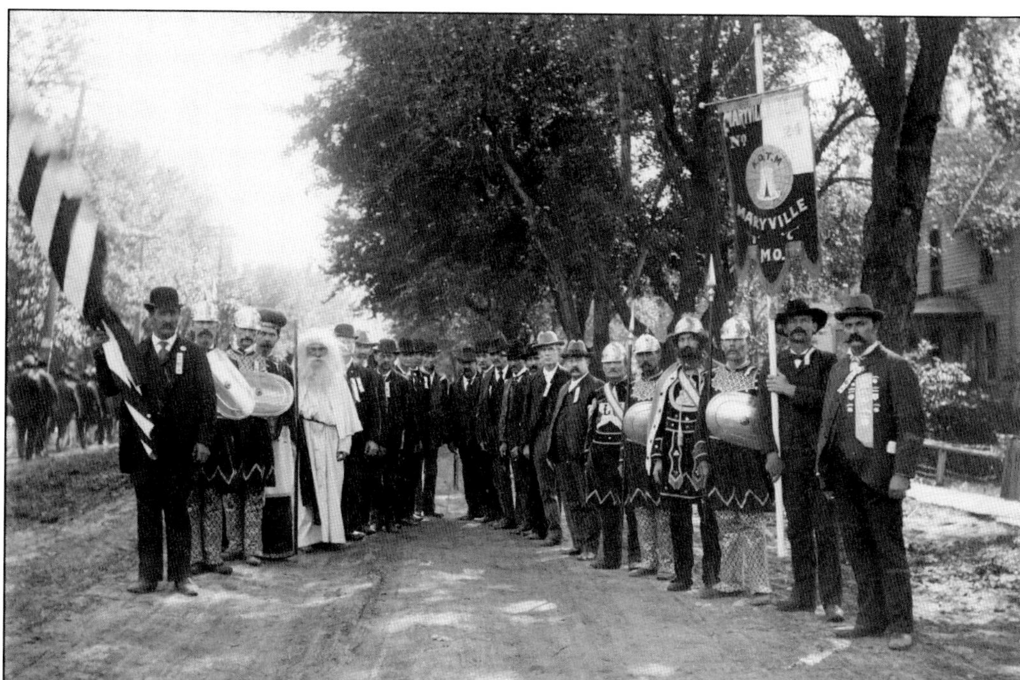

The Knights of the Maccabees, post Number 24, prepares to join a parade. Though the order had members in Maryville by the 1890s, it was not among the most popular, or well-known, of the region's numerous fraternal orders. While members clearly enjoyed social activities and dressing up for parades, the order's chief benefits were its insurance cooperative and burial expense benefits. By the 1920s, the order formed a parallel organization, the Ladies of the Maccabees.

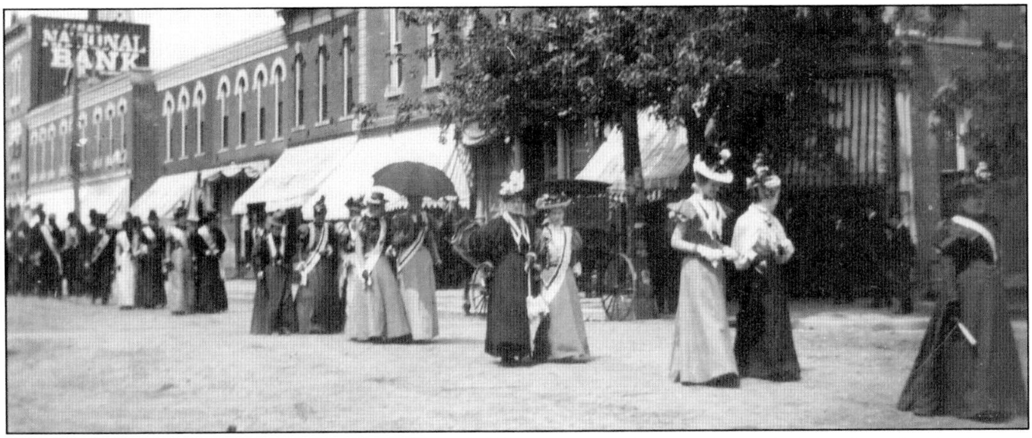

A parade of the Independent Order of Odd Fellows passes by the Linville Hotel on Main Street in 1897. The first IOOF lodge in Nodaway County was the White Cloud Lodge founded in Maryville in 1856. Fourteen other lodges followed in Nodaway County, with one in nearly every other community. By the end of the 19th century, there were over 1,200 members in the county who regularly joined in parades. As the image suggests, in 1851 it became among the first fraternal organizations to include women.

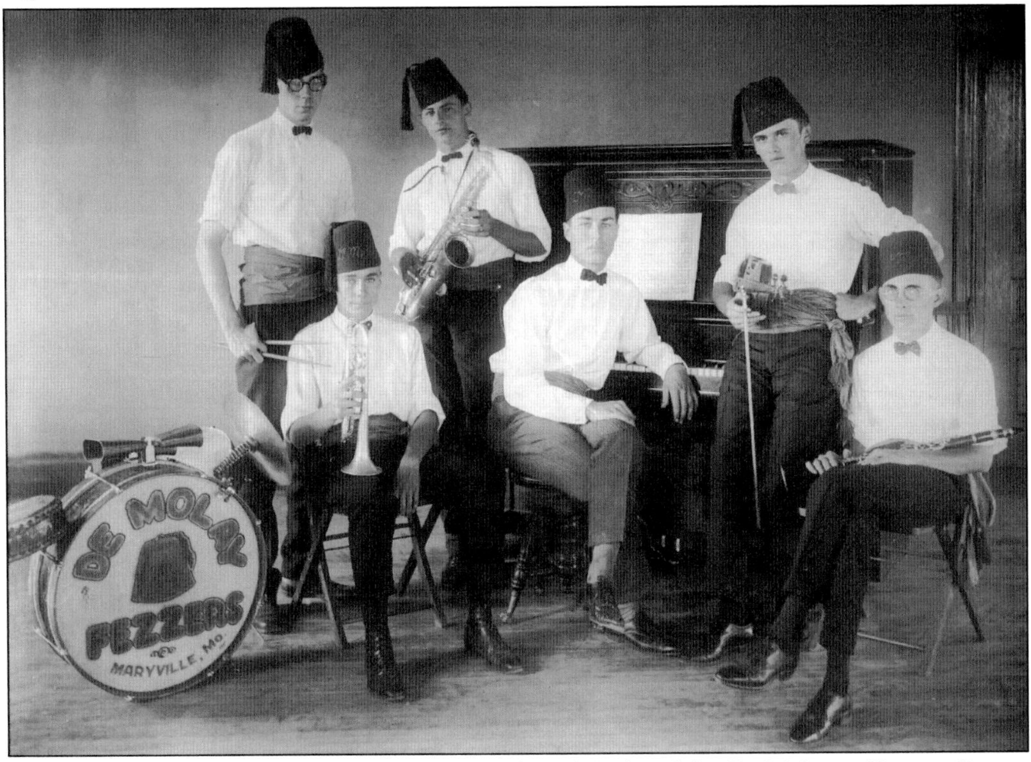

Businessman Frank Land founded the Masonic-based Order of the De Molay in Kansas City in 1919, not long before the time of this photograph. Named after the last grand master of the Knights Templar, Jaques De Molay, Land created the organization specifically for young men aged 12 to 21 to serve alongside a litany of other fraternal and social orders engaging young citizens in civic service. The De Molay Fezzers provided the local order with the band that was also requisite for such organizations.

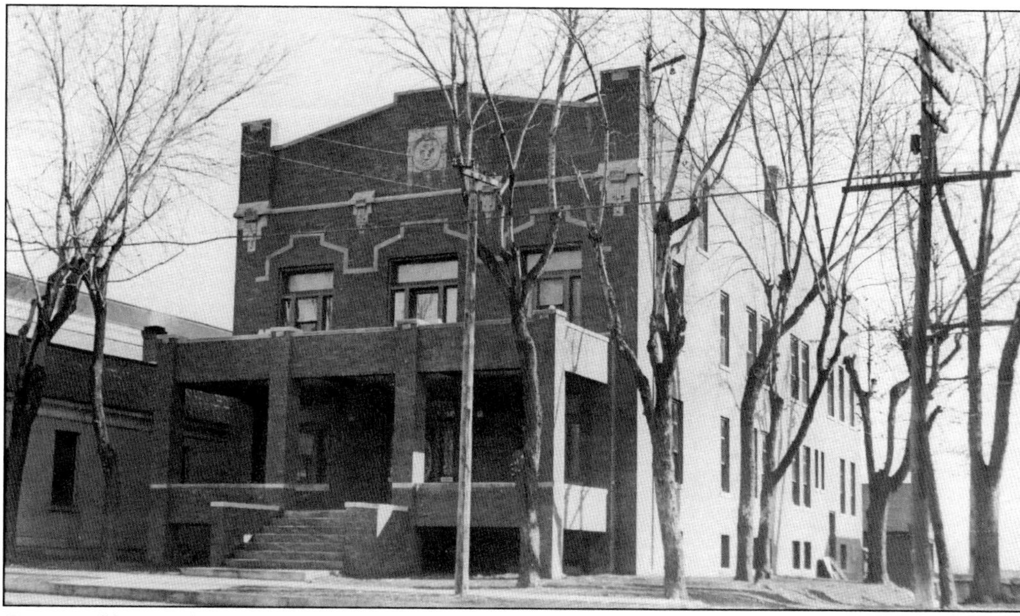

Civic and benevolent societies abounded at the turn of the century. In Maryville, the Elks joined in service the Masons, Eastern Star, Royal Arch Masons, Knights Templar, Independent Order of Odd Fellows, Daughters of Rebekah, Knights of Pythias, and others. District Deputy Exalted Ruler C.H. Fitzgerald instituted the Maryville Elks Lodge in March 1902, with 50 charter members paying the $15 initiation fee and $12 annual dues. After moving through several rental spaces the Elks built the permanent Club House, seen here in 1909, which still stands.

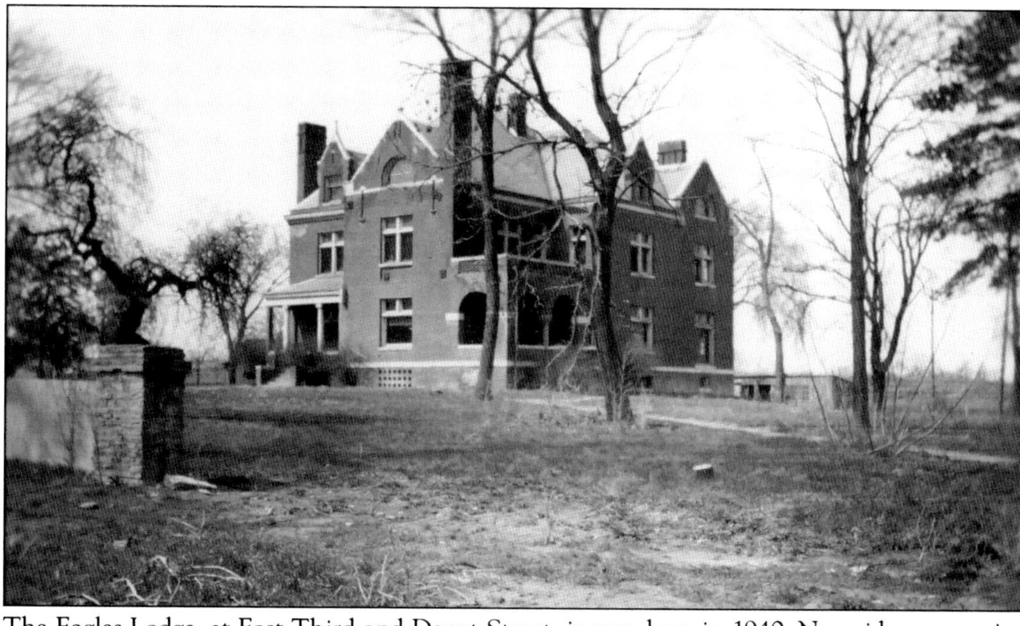

The Eagles Lodge, at East Third and Depot Street, is seen here in 1940. No evidence remains today of the impressive brick structure and little information about it remains. Miss Ida Nicholas snapped this photograph in 1940 for a project in a college class. Her student project preserved a collection of images of homes and structures in Maryville, most of which are gone and would have been lost to local history were it not for her work.

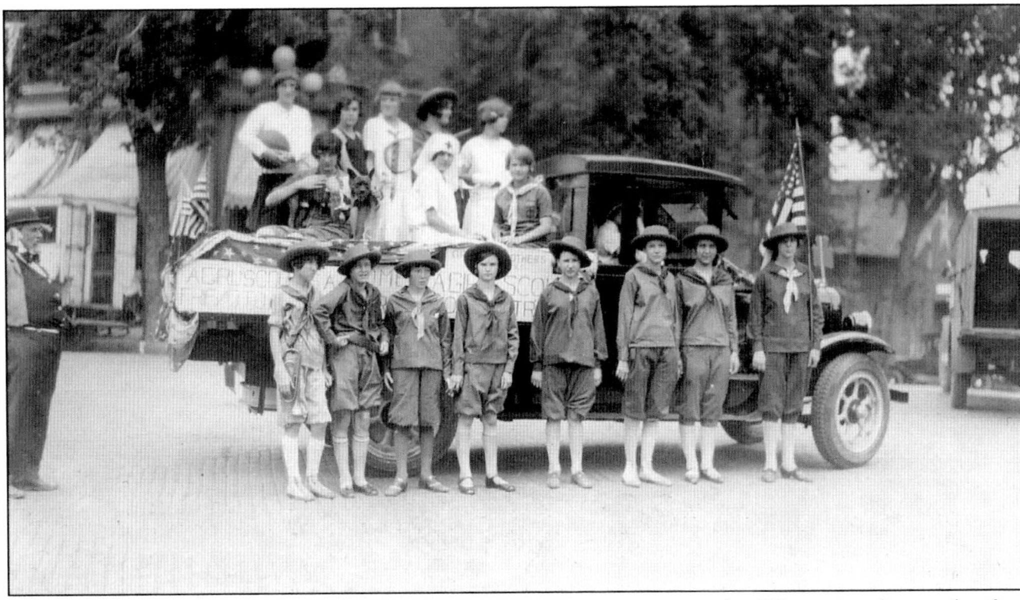

The intrepid Girl Scouts prepare for their turn in a summer parade. Their sign bears the first and fourth laws of the 1912 Girl Scout Law, instituted just a few years prior to this troop's day in the parade, which states, "a Girl Scout's honor is to be trusted; a Girl Scout is a friend to all." To the left stands ubiquitous local entertainer Albert Butherus, likely trying to tease the young ladies into a laugh.

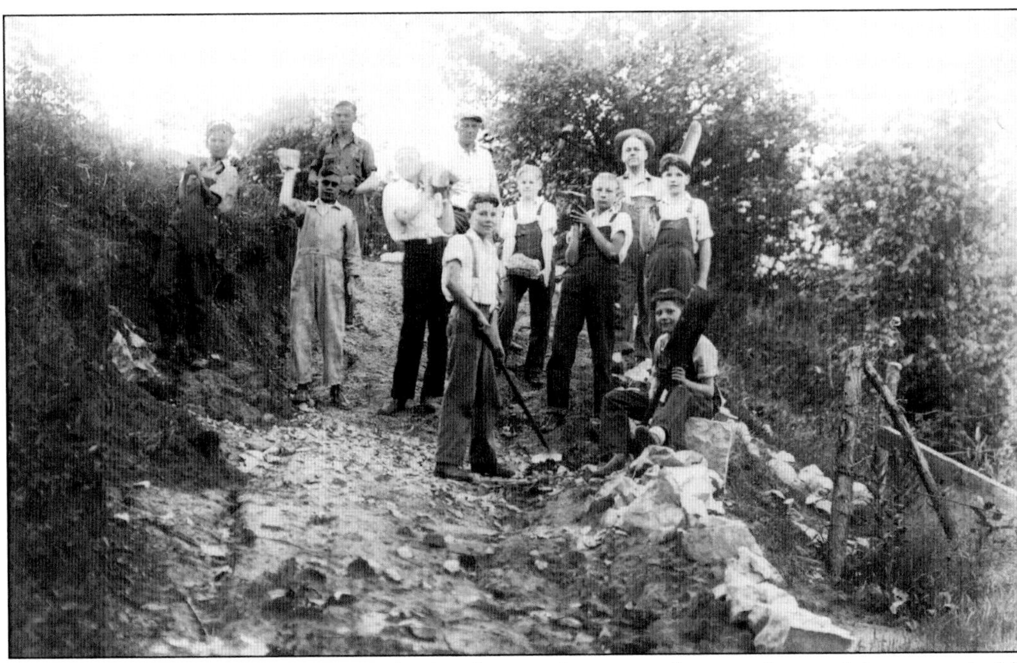

In June 1929, these eager Boy Scouts display their might in transforming the earth into a navigable road towards their camp on the northeast corner of town. One of the young men captioned the bottom of the original print proudly with "this is the way we do it."

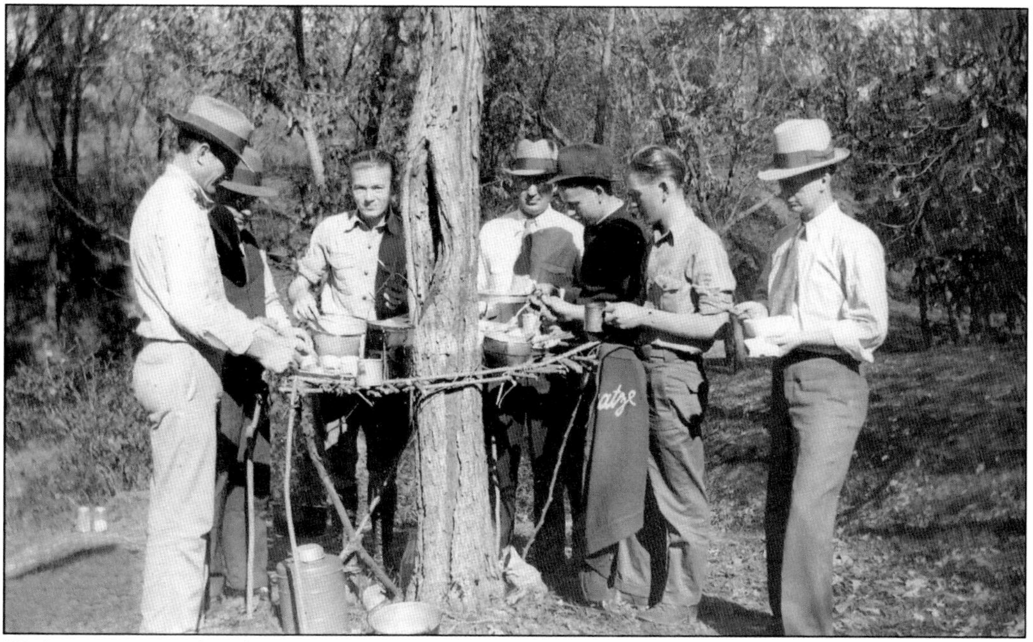

With a new manual and some organizational reforms in 1934, the process of becoming a scoutmaster in the Boy Scouts of America became more rigorous and required additional hours of field education. Shown here in October 1934, the Scout leaders prepare a hearty boiled egg breakfast with a makeshift tree trunk kitchen station.

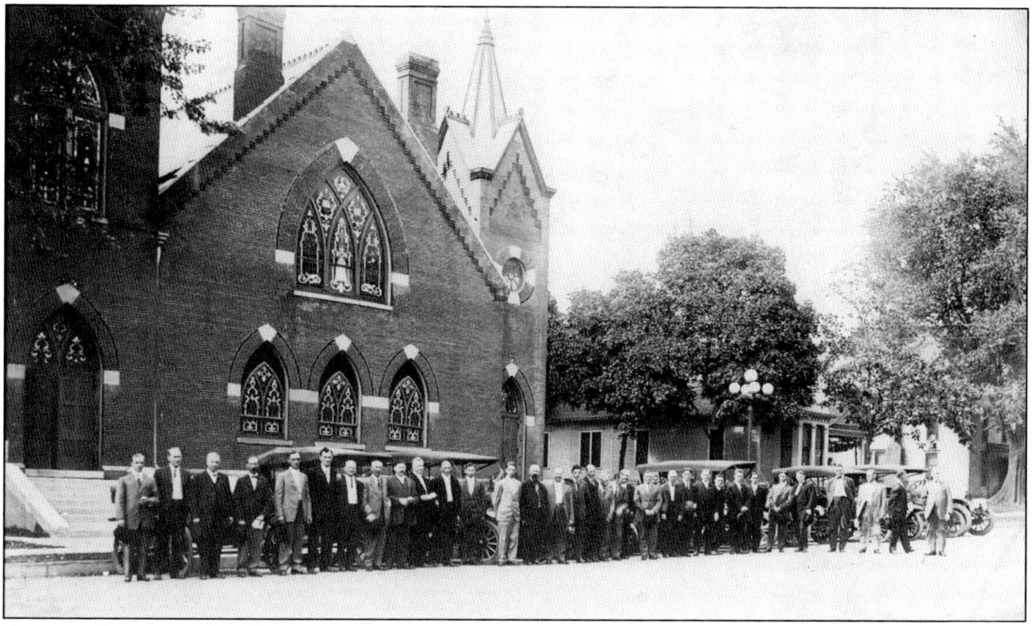

Among the more durable associations within communities are their churches. The men of the Methodist Episcopal Church gather on Main Street in the late 1910s in this photograph. Methodists in the 1850s met in various homes and schoolhouses until erecting a church building in the late 1860s. The structure behind these men, which still stands today with significant modifications to the towers, was completed in May 1894 at a cost of $30,000, which included the organ.

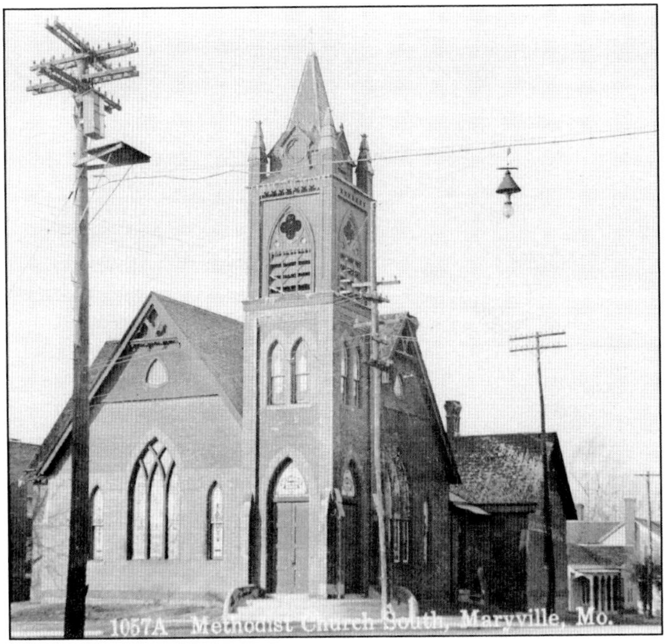

Well into the 20th century, Methodist congregations bore the imprint of the Civil War, with congregations divided into "North" and "South." Southern Methodists broke from the parent church in Maryville in 1844, before the town was even platted. The Methodist Church South met in the courthouse during its early years, suspended services for three years during the Civil War, and then erected a frame church in 1867. The congregation erected this brick structure in 1890 at the corner of Second and Buchanan Streets. In 1939, the congregations rejoined as First United Methodist Church.

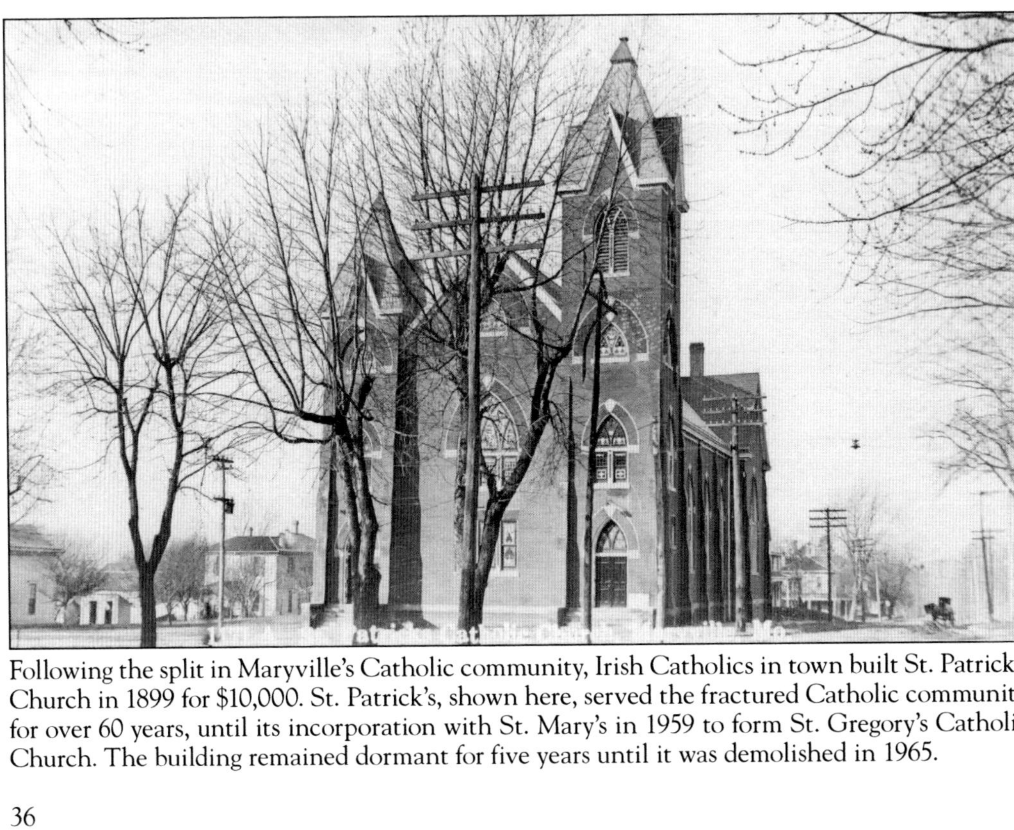

Following the split in Maryville's Catholic community, Irish Catholics in town built St. Patrick's Church in 1899 for $10,000. St. Patrick's, shown here, served the fractured Catholic community for over 60 years, until its incorporation with St. Mary's in 1959 to form St. Gregory's Catholic Church. The building remained dormant for five years until it was demolished in 1965.

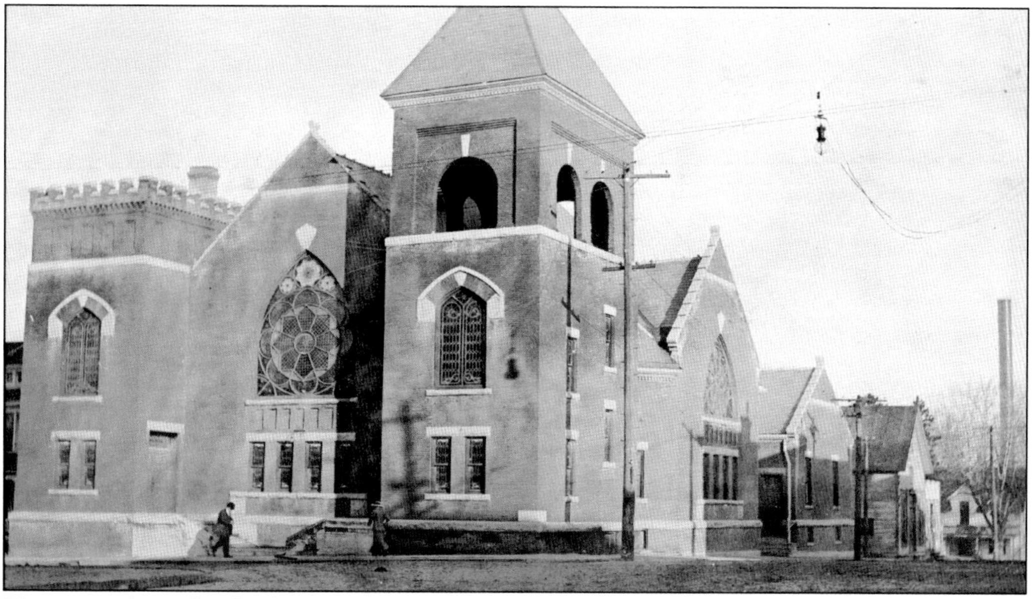

The magnificent brick Christian Church, dedicated in December 1893, provided an impressive sanctuary for a congregation that had previously met in private homes, other churches, the old courthouse, the old school house, and a modest frame structure of their own. The building had cost $27,000, and the region's best pipe organ, with 1,043 pipes, was added in 1910 at the cost of another $4,000—settling for good an earlier dispute within the congregation over the use of instrumental music. This structure was demolished and replaced with a modern design in 1982.

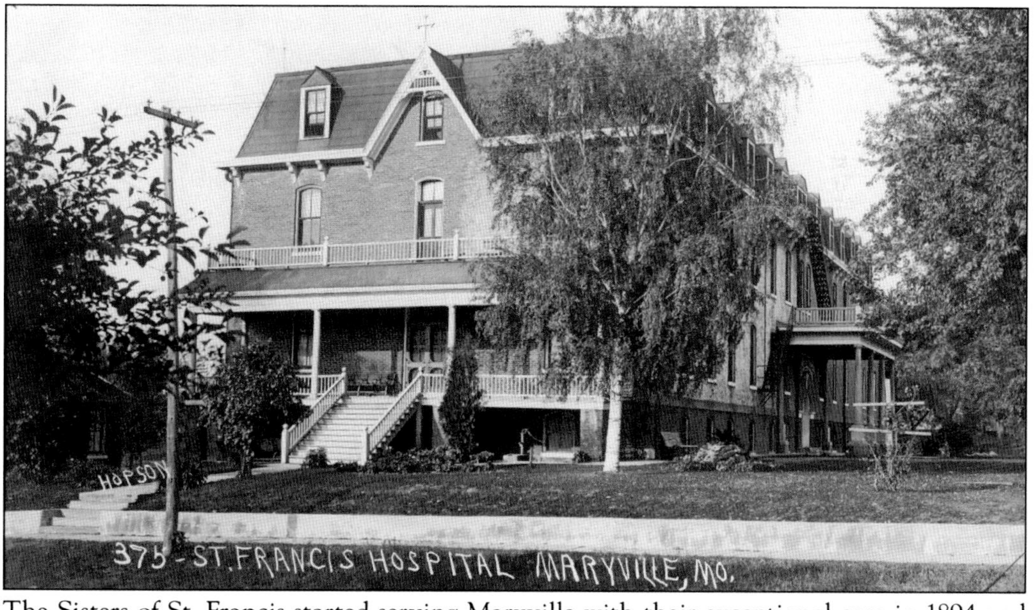

The Sisters of St. Francis started serving Maryville with their exceptional care in 1894 and purchased land on First Street and commissioned the construction of this hospital in 1895. The hospital served many residents of the area, some of whom could afford care and others who did not have the means to pay. Over the next 25 years, numerous additions and improvements were made to the building, seen here shortly after a major 1921 addition. The hospital moved to a new location on the south end of town in 1970.

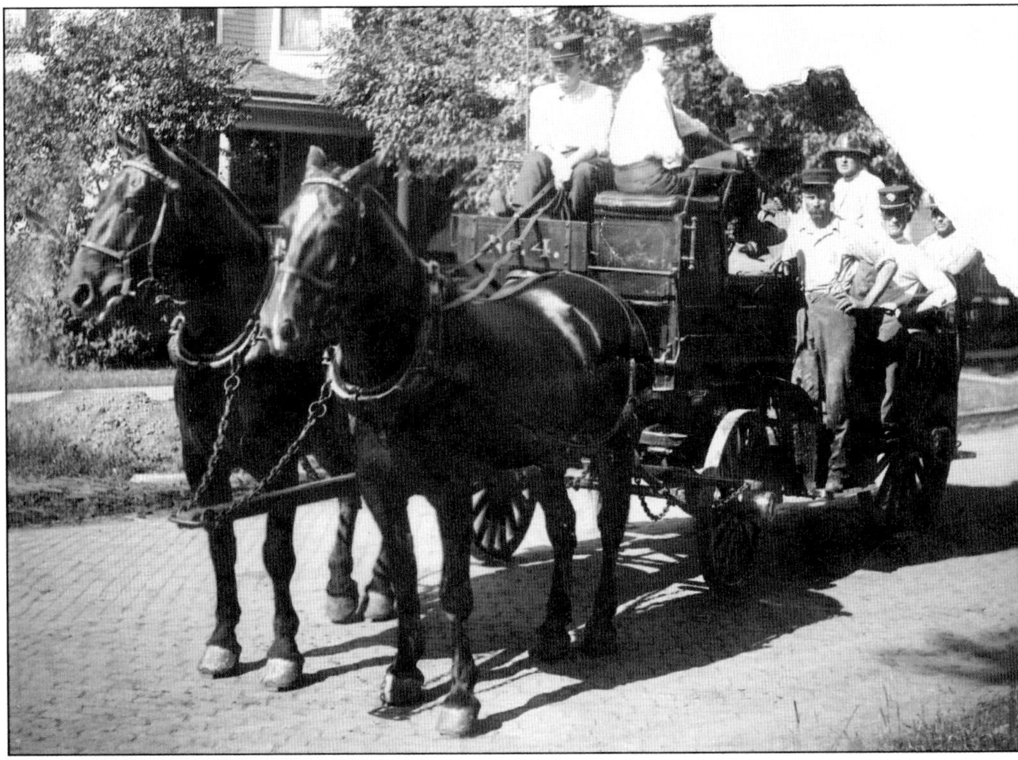

Maryville's fire brigade in 1886 had no steam or hand engines, no hose cart, poor water supply, and a handful of unpaid, irregular volunteers. By 1900, two hose carts, 80 pounds-per-square-inch of water pressure, and 64 double hydrants provided seven regular volunteers a better chance. The seven-man volunteer crew that made up the Maryville Volunteer Fire Brigade in the early 1900s included, from left to right, Steve Viles, John McCoy, Jim Kegin, Percy Jensen, Bill Porter, Byron Frost, and Emmet Scott. These men were paid $2.50 each per fire. Their express wagon held 1,800 feet of 2.5-inch hose. One paid man and a volunteer company of eight with rotating night patrols upped the odds a bit further against blazes in 1909. By the late 1910s, the sharply uniformed fire crew of 15 (below) appear even more prepared. Unfortunately, the occasional infernos that plagued the business district and homes typically proved unmanageable, and fire continued to reshape the community.

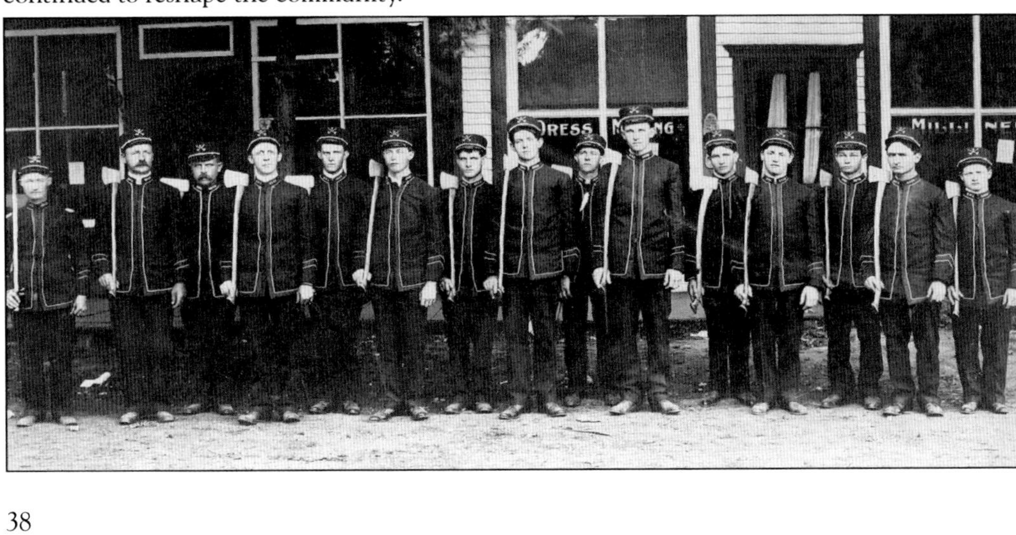

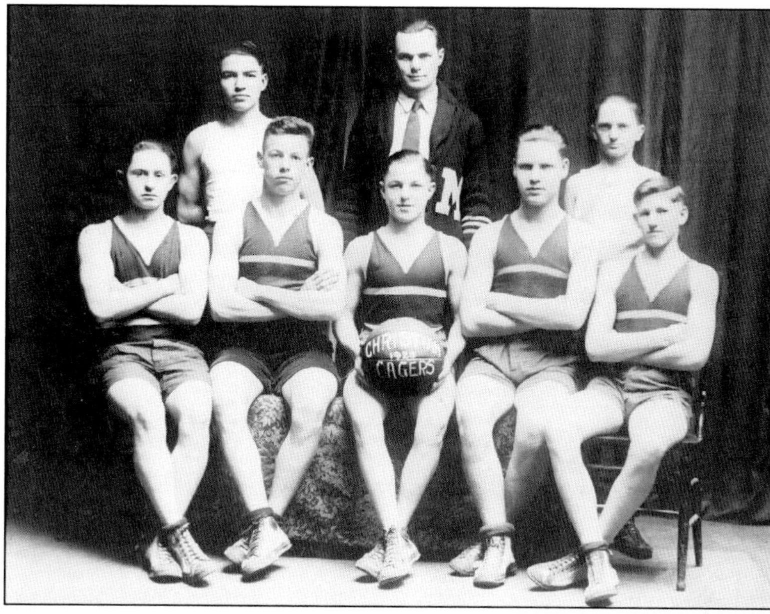

The origin and affiliation of the Christian Cagers basketball team, seen here in 1923, is unclear, but local sources make mention of them infrequently as late as 1963. The Cagers played other municipal teams, and occasionally college teams, with scores noted against the Northwest Bearcats in 1943 and 1944.

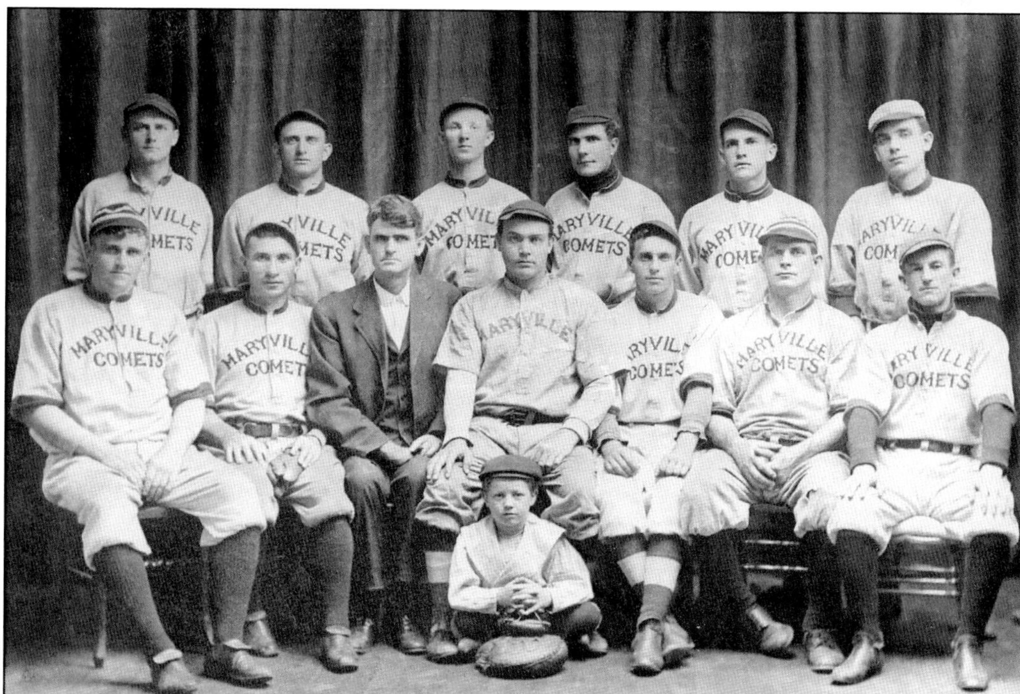

The Maryville Comets pose for their first team photograph in 1910. They started the season in May with two wins against the Oregon, Missouri, team. Under the leadership of Coach White, the star of the Comets was third baseman Joe Wintz, who won a bonus box of cigars for hitting the season's first triple. The team name was likely in honor of the pending brush with Halley's Comet on May 19, though town-folk joined others around the region in blaming the visitor for the season's erratic weather.

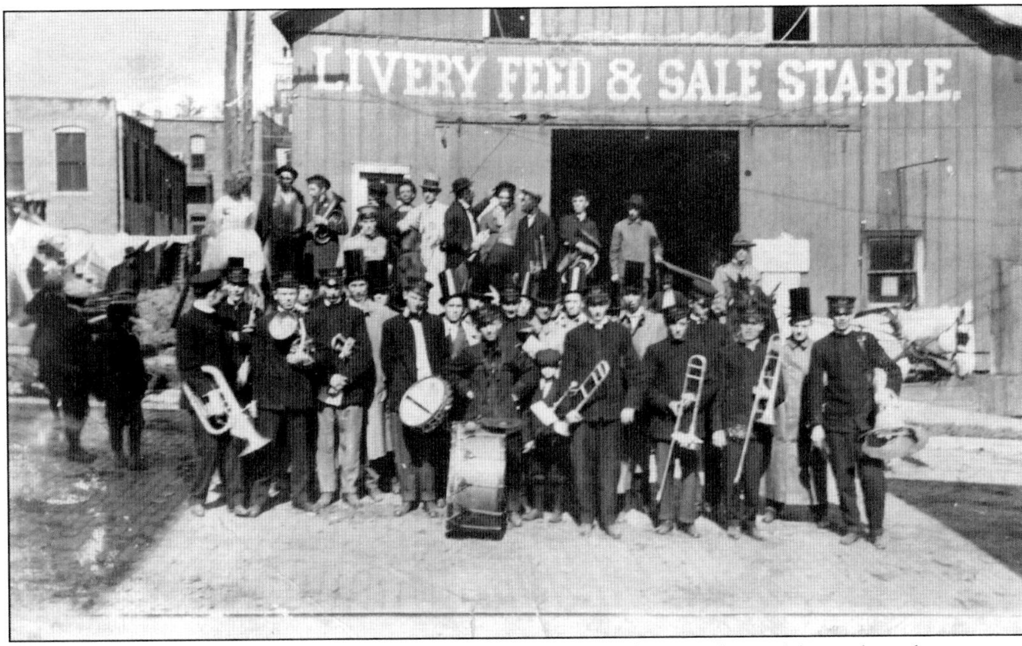

A gathering of Maryville musicians, many of whom performed at parades and festivals and sometimes on theater stages, like the Empire on Main Street, pose in the early 1900s on a makeshift open-air stage in front of the Starr Livery Stable. At least one of the town's more respectable association bands shares space with a wider cast of amateur vaudevillians. Those in the image below, seated and standing on the raised planks, performed as the Catfish Martin Band—an unusual troupe that defied conventions of all sorts, including their multi-racial composition and use of their African American trombonist's moniker and surname for the band. Bill Price, astride the horse, regularly performed in drag, while Albert "Slim" Butherus, seated at left, made numerous appearances in photographs of local events from the 1900s to 1930s.

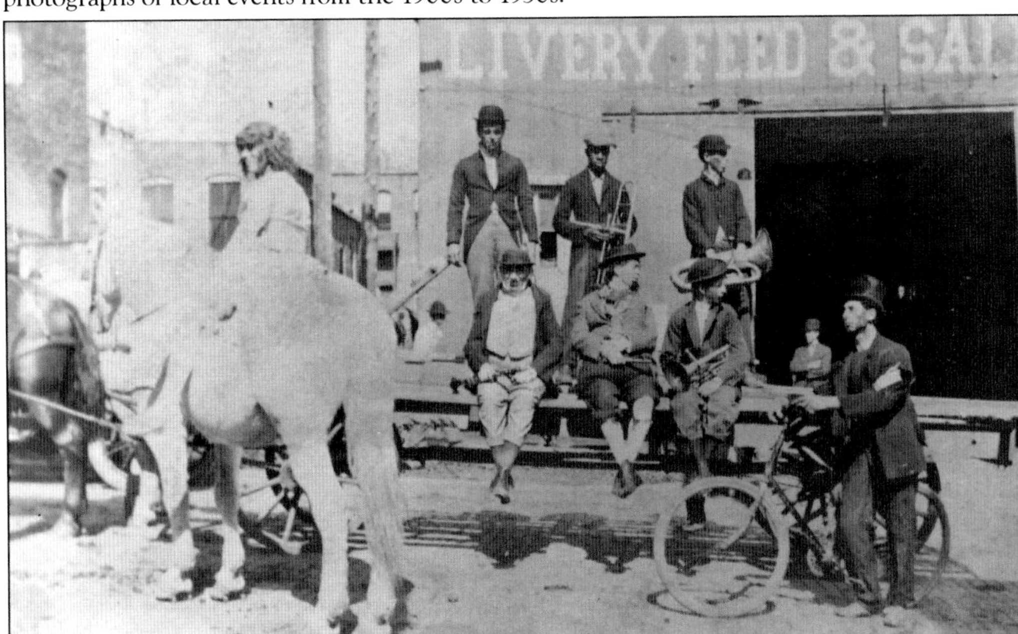

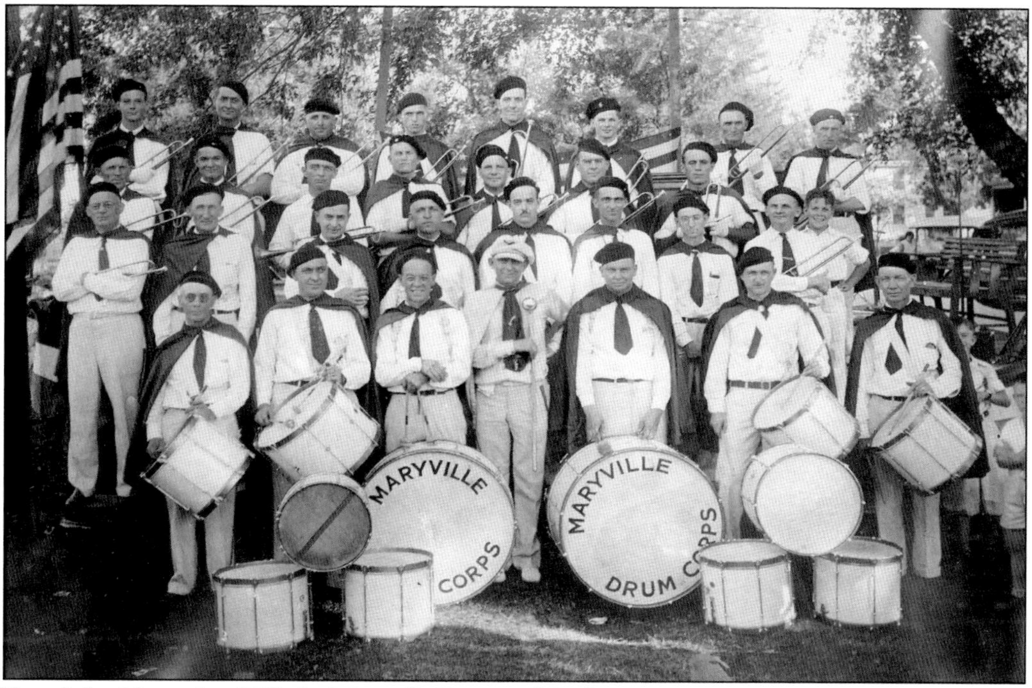

Founded in November 1932, the Maryville Drum and Bugle Corps entertained crowds throughout the region for several years. The organization elected officers on November 9, received their instruments by the 20th, and on December 5 marched for visiting legislators at the state college. During their first year, the amateur corps appeared in 45 community events around the county, including, according to the 1933 minutes by corps historian Ralph Marcell, a two-day blitz advertising the Maryville Fall Fair with stops in 20 towns in two days. For its first several years, the Maryville Drum Corps raised funds with an annual car raffle. Members of the corps purchased the car and worked on it for several weeks. They sold 2,906 tickets at 50¢ each, including one to former President Herbert Hoover on a visit to the county where he owned a farm. The winner, shown below, with his lucky horseshoe still in hand, was Charlie Shackelford of Burlington Junction.

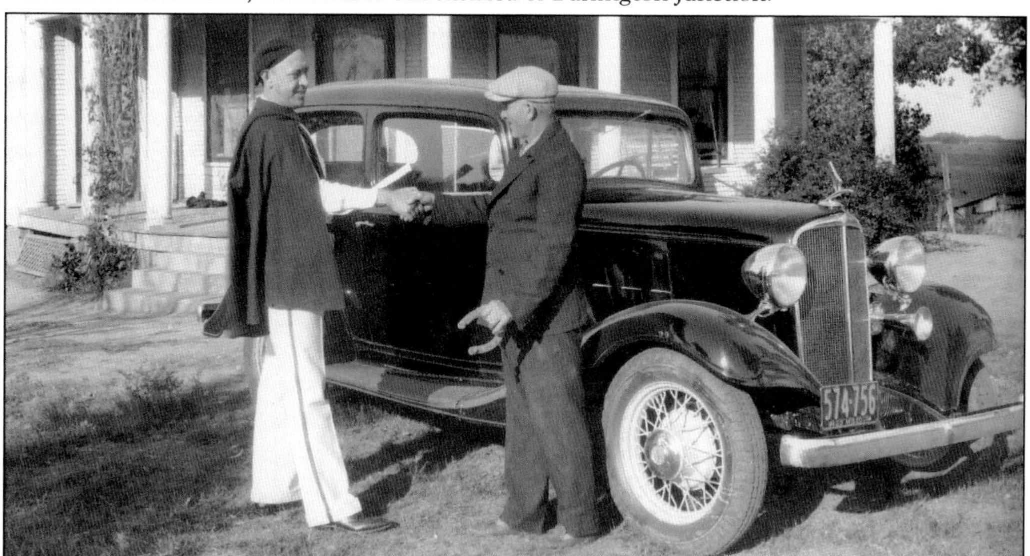

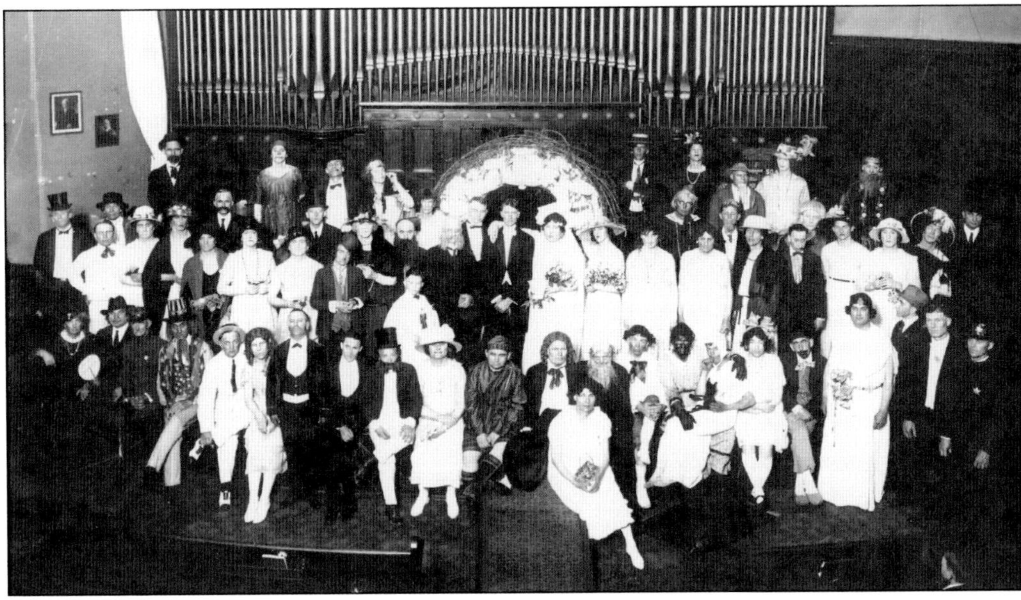

"The Womanless Wedding" was a local amateur production in towns across the country to raise money for charity causes, popular from the 1910s through the 1950s. The all-male production at the First Christian Church in Maryville in the early 1920s followed the typical version: a lone couple is tying the knot and upon discovering she is pregnant over 30 former lovers, including the King of England and Uncle Sam are exposed. Prominent businessmen participated in order to raise money for various causes.

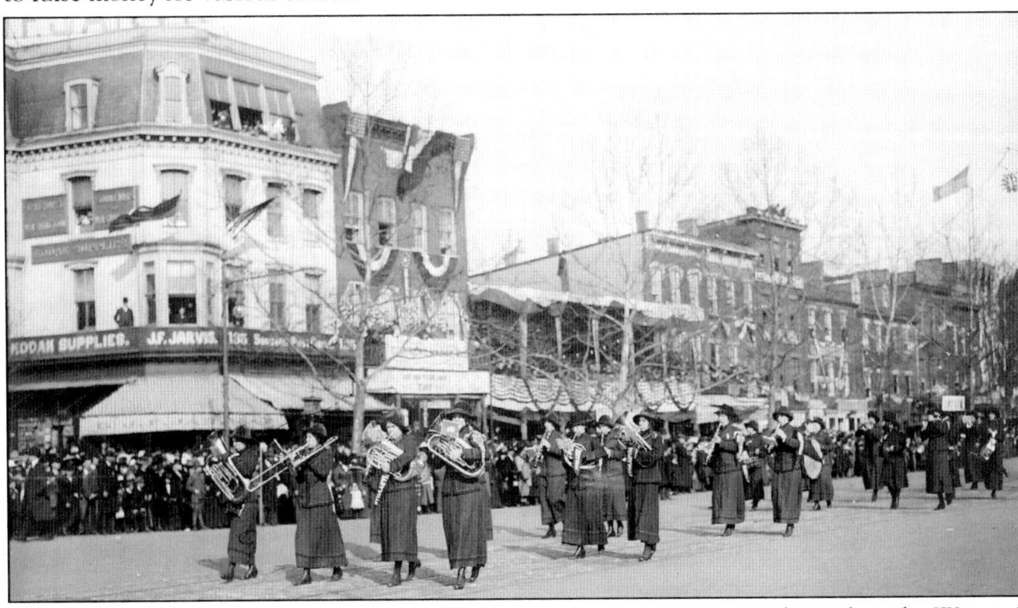

Alma Nash and the Maryville women of the Missouri Ladies Military Band march at the Women's Suffrage Parade in Washington, DC, on March 3, 1913. The daughter of a Maryville surgeon, Nash demonstrated a gift for music and the courage to stand out. Local benefactors J.S. Shinabarger and Dr. F.M. Ryan added $300 to the $500 already provided by the National Suffrage Association to send the only all-female band to the event. The Maryville ladies marched unmolested through a mostly-hostile crowd along the parade route and returned home as heroes.

Three

BECOMING MODERN

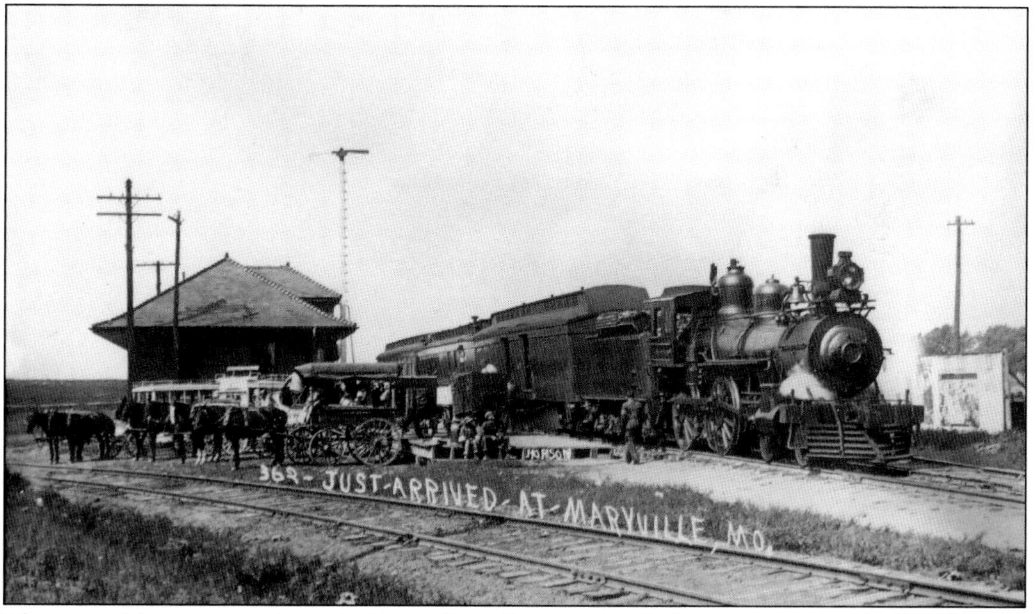

The second line to pass through Maryville, following the Burlington, was the Wabash Line in 1878. This line demanded $50,000 of Maryville citizens, along with another $75,000 from the surrounding countryside. Citizens raised the funds in cash and bonds, and the railroad laid the line within a year. The Wabash was famously known as the only line with direct connections to St. Louis, Kansas City, Omaha, St. Joseph, and Hannibal. A wooden depot, constructed in 1873, was replaced by this brick structure sometime after 1879. It was remodeled in 1945, and the last passenger train passed through in 1967.

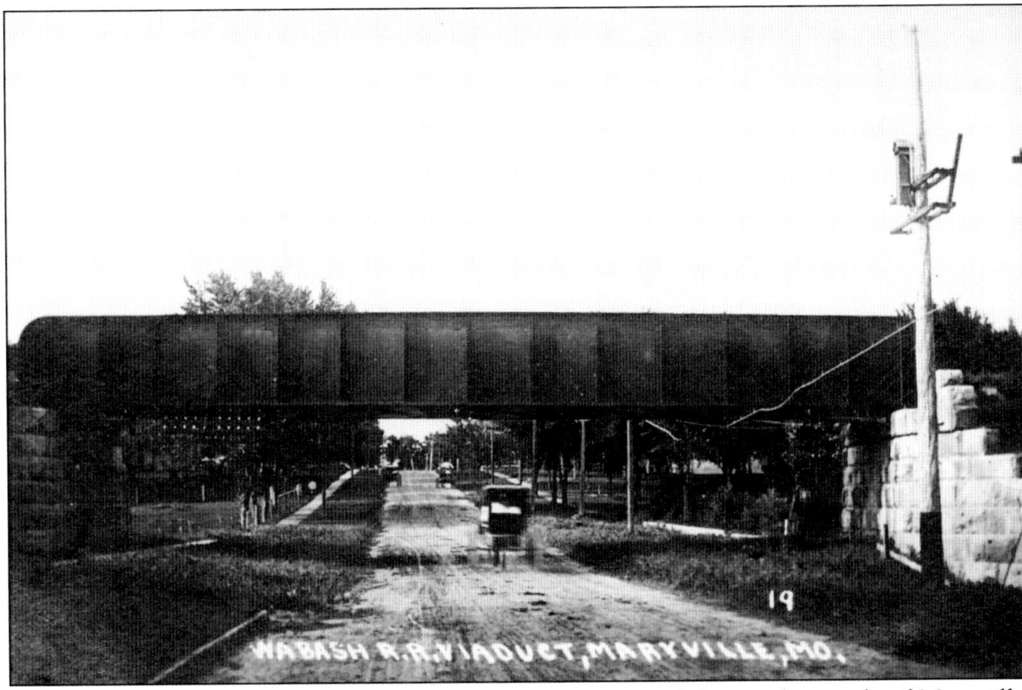

The Wabash line crossed North Main Street on its transit of the northern side of Maryville, making its way from the station on the northwest corner of town east to cross the Burlington line at Depot Street. Locomotives crossing this bridge rattled doors and pierced the quiet of homes along the stretch.

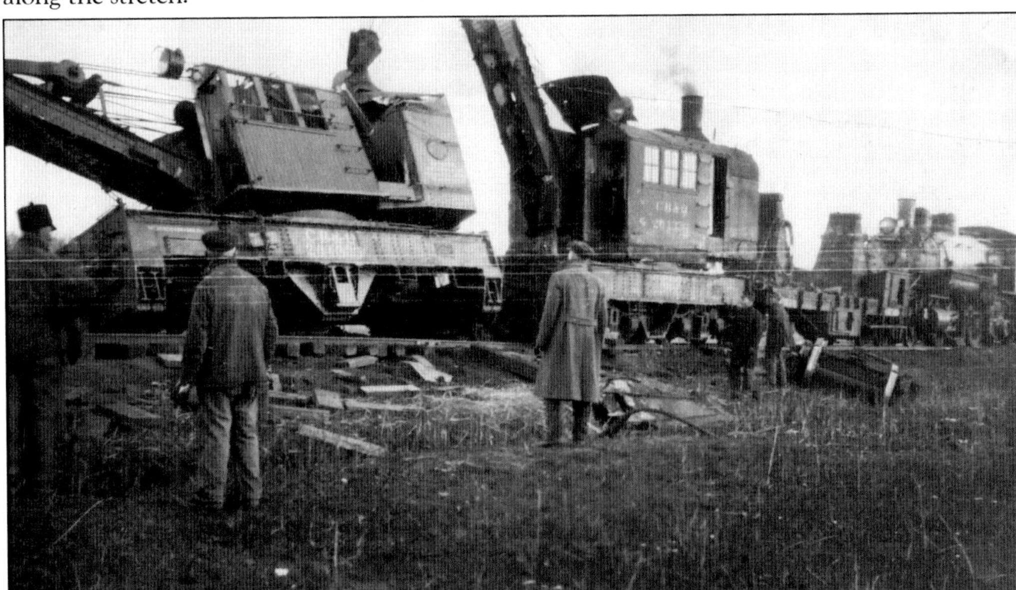

With over 12,000 miles of track in 14 states by 1920, the Chicago, Burlington & Quincy held a relatively safe record for transport. When a train did derail, it was protocol to send a wrecking crane to salvage the wreckage and clear the track. Around 1904, protocol was rewritten when a wrecking crane derailed near Maryville during a basic sweep, requiring another wrecking train to follow. (Courtesy of Coby Lamb.)

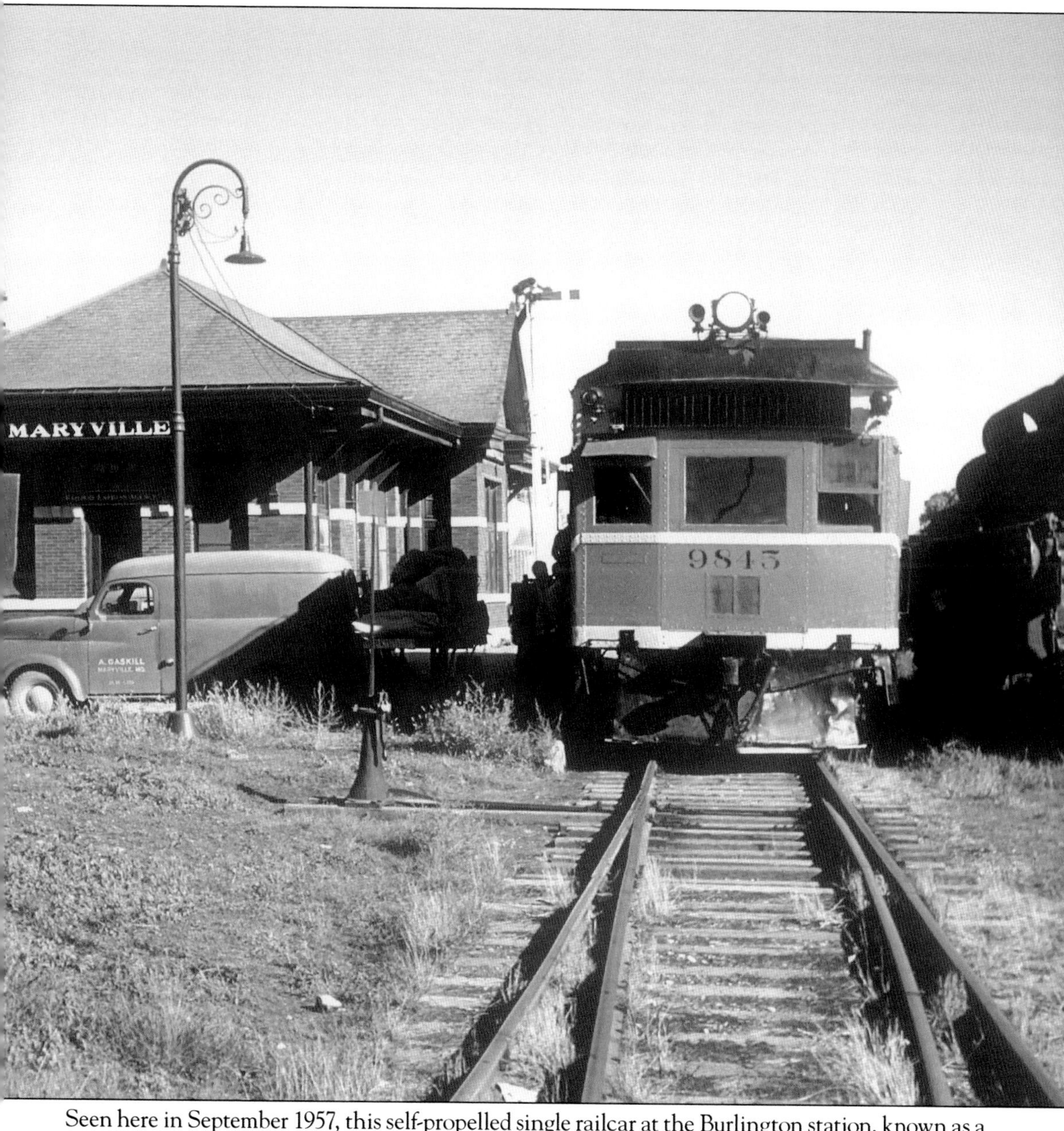

Seen here in September 1957, this self-propelled single railcar at the Burlington station, known as a "doodlebug," transported passengers and mail through Maryville after World War II. As passenger traffic began to diminish in the 1940s and 1950s, they served as a cost-effective alternative to full passenger trains. CB&Q doodlebugs, like this one built by EMD-Pullman, used gasoline or diesel engines to power generators that sent electricity to traction motors. They stayed in service as late as 1967. (Courtesy of Chuck Zeiler.)

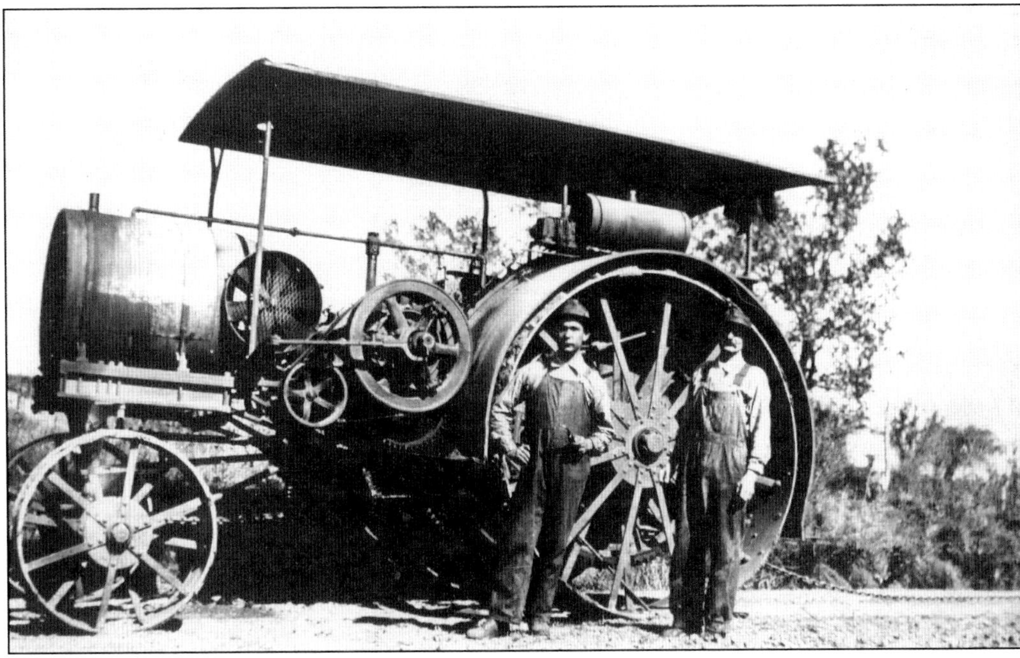

Humphrey and Wilder Horde show off their Aultman-Taylor 30-60 gas tractor in 1915. Farmers and city-folk alike were amazed by the power of the assortment of new machines that ran on steam, kerosene, and gasoline. The Hordes were no doubt proud that their model set pulling power records at the time.

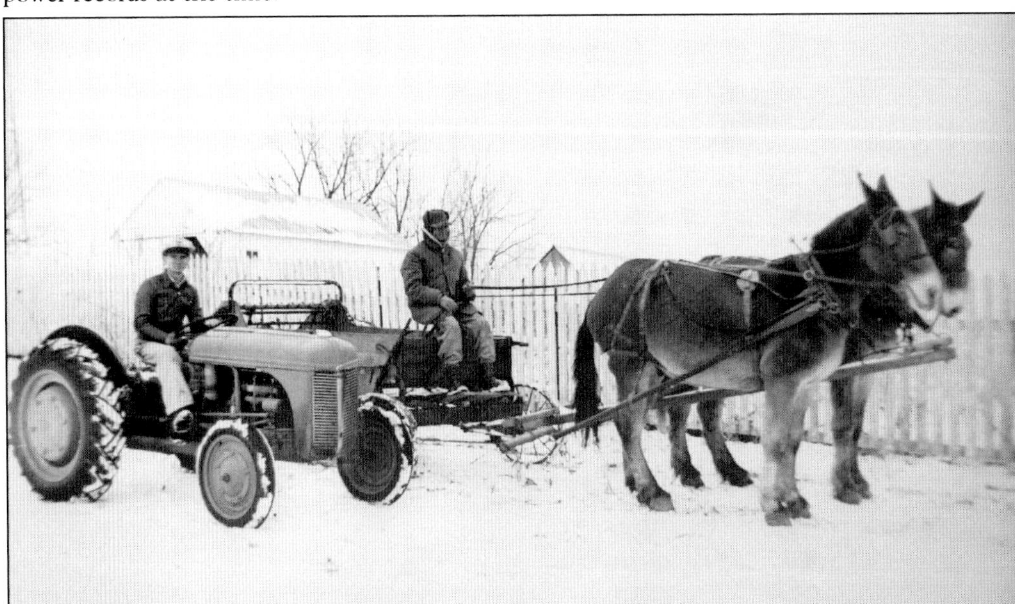

Spreading manure during the winter was a great way to prepare fields for the new season. While tractors became stronger and more affordable by the mid-20th century, many farmers clung to their animal power, particularly when the ground was snow-covered or wet. In a community closely tied to agriculture and surrounded by fields, residents have long been accustomed to the animals and equipment of farm life.

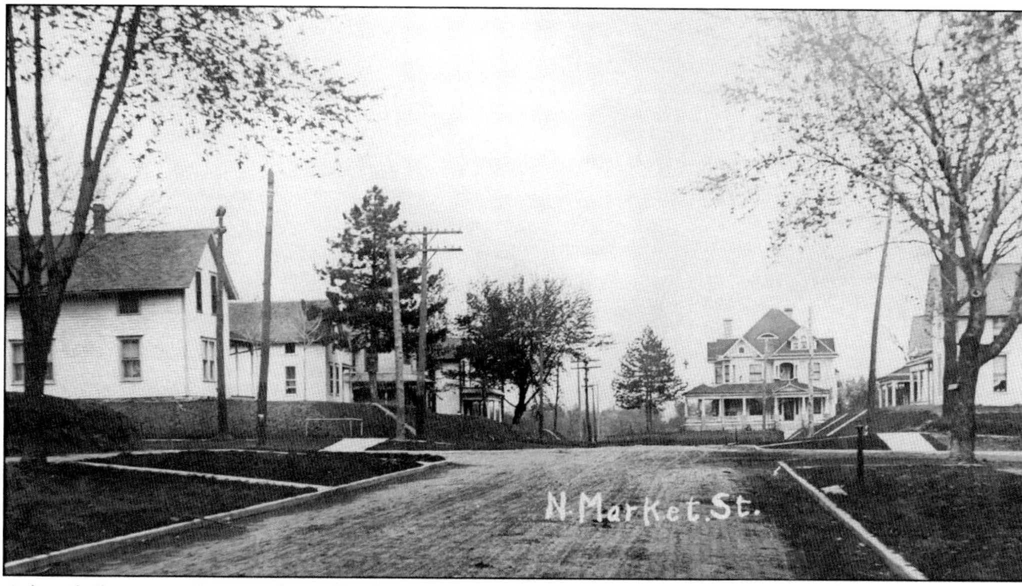

A local photographer surely wished to capture town pride in the transition from the 19th century to the 20th century in this view of North Market Street. Freshly poured sidewalks allowed for clean hems while strolling along an avenue of fine homes ranging from modest to spectacular. Newly laid concrete curbing not only helped to maintain the dirt road but also prepared the way for the brick paving that was soon to follow.

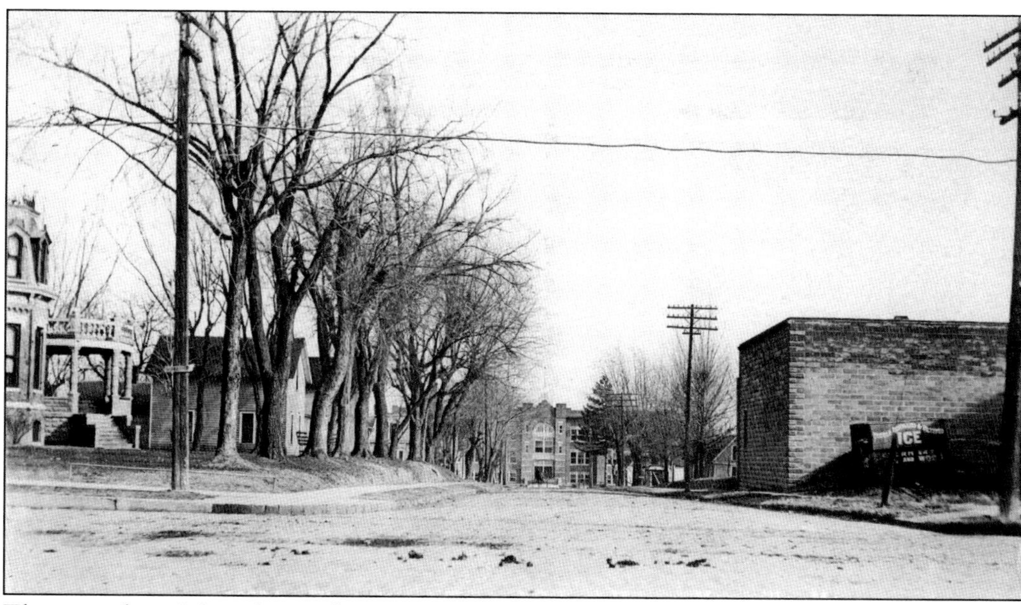

The view from Main Street down East First Street towards Washington School shows the hallmarks of the transition era in a prosperous community. Well-laid brick streets paved the way for automobiles at the turn of the century, but unfortunately could not absorb the waste left by horses still being widely used. The ice wagon parked on the right marks another transition from one century to another. By this time, W.M. Everhart's ice company no longer packed ice from ponds in straw, but used Ruemmell machines that by 1920 could produce up to 30,000 cubic feet of ice per year.

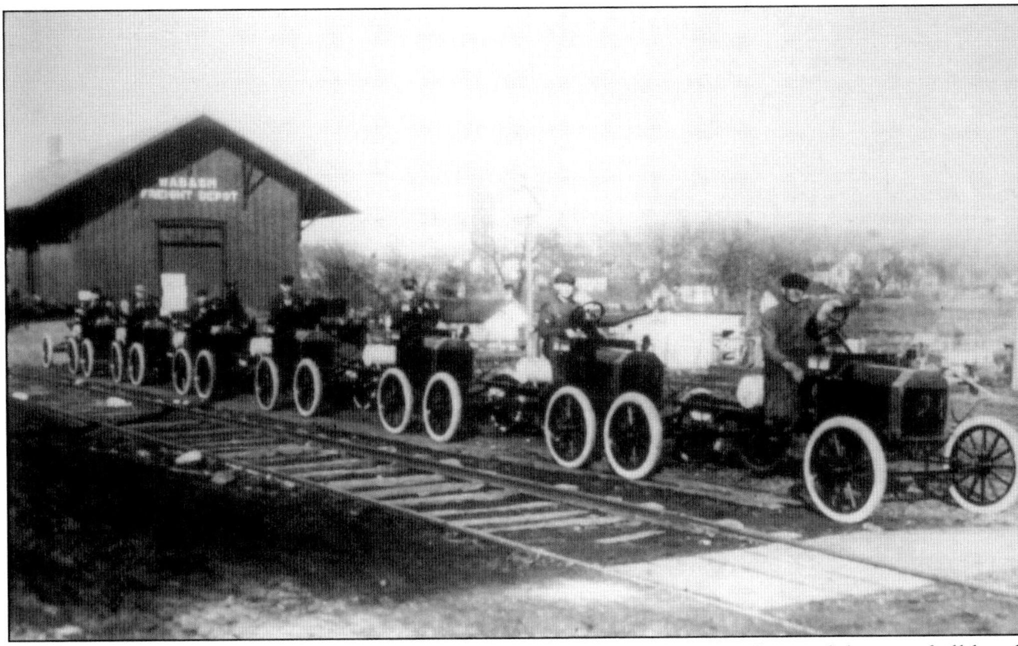

The Wabash freight depot, on a siding south of the passenger terminal, saw delivery of all kinds of commodities including these brand new Ford trucks around 1915. The autos were delivered to Frank Barmann's dealership on Main Street, where they were finished with the bodywork and beds and customized to local preference.

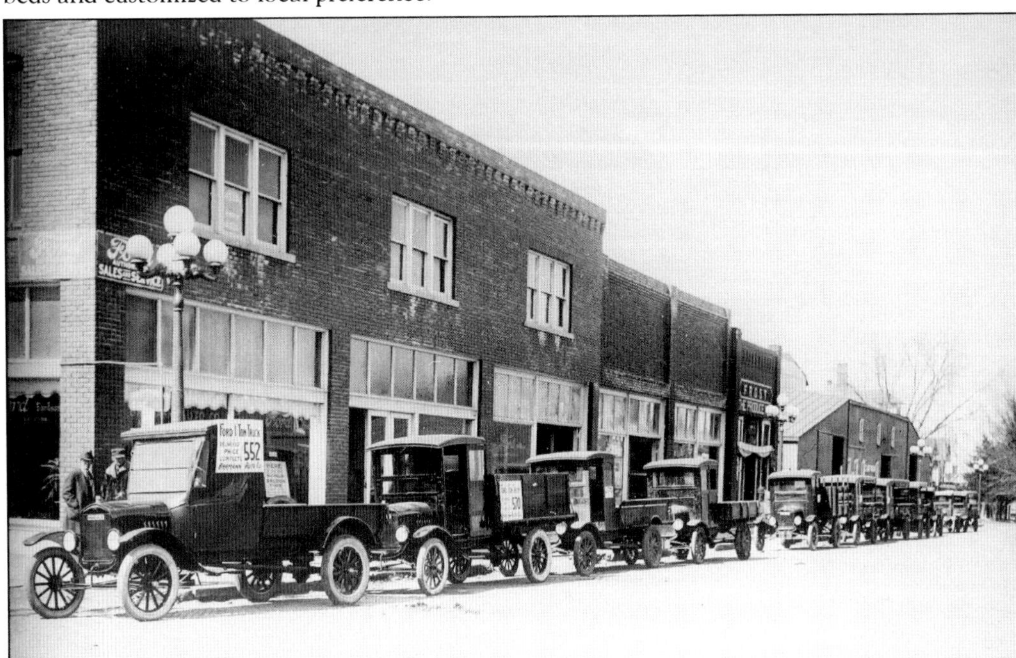

New Ford trucks line North Main Street in front of Barmann Auto Supply Company with a handsome 1925 one-ton Model T at the front. The trucks came in different bed configurations to fit the needs of the driver, in prices ranging from $500 to $600, including the innovative new balloon tires. Fullerton Lumber Company anchors the opposite end of the block.

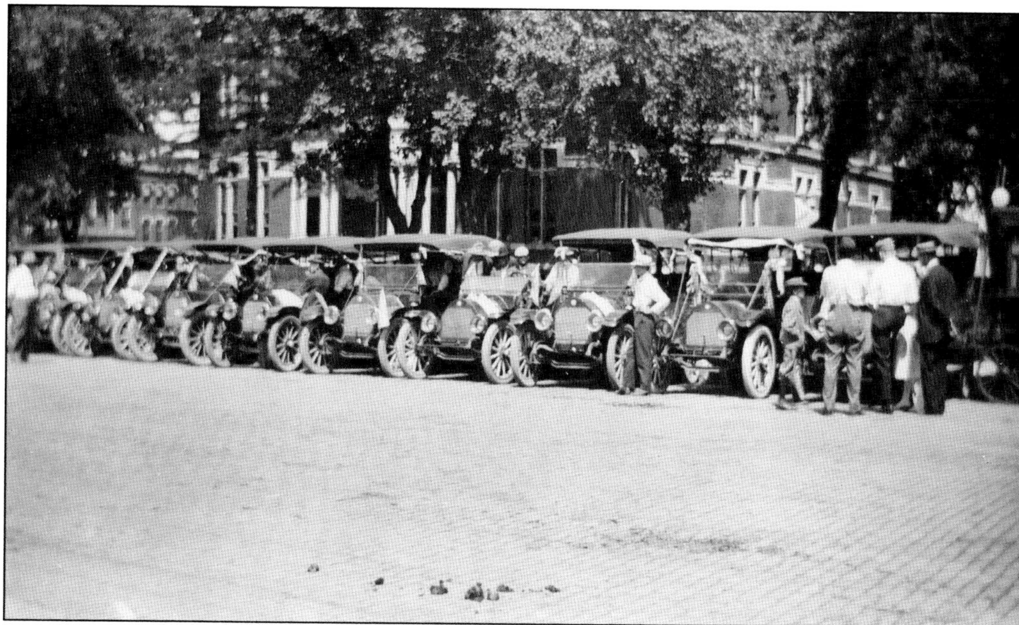

By the advent of World War I, cars appeared on the square in impressive numbers, though not in considerable variety. Henry Ford's apocryphal offer that "you can have any color as long as it's black" was rooted in the truth that his assembly lines turned out affordable cars that in any single year were all much the same. As the manure in the street testifies, however, these men waiting for a parade would see time and styles pass by quickly.

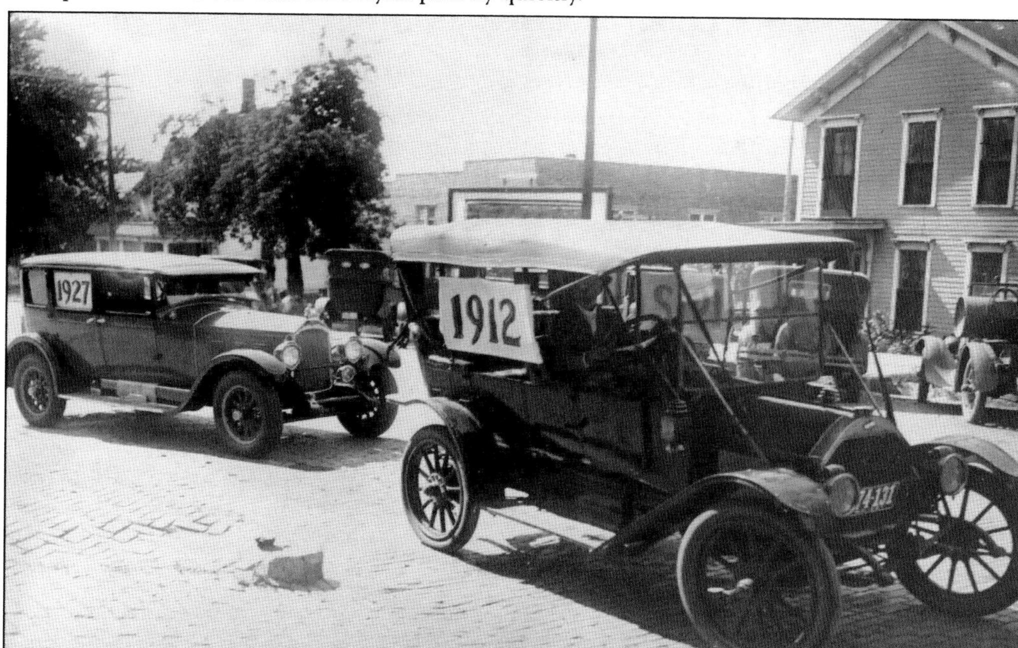

Automobile technology changed rapidly during the 20th century. Shown here is the vast difference between cars sold by the Sewell Auto Company when it was first established in 1912, versus the 1927 Willis Knight that sold for $1,200 that year. Evidence of the changing roles and consumer power of women, the advertising campaign focused on explaining why women liked driving this car.

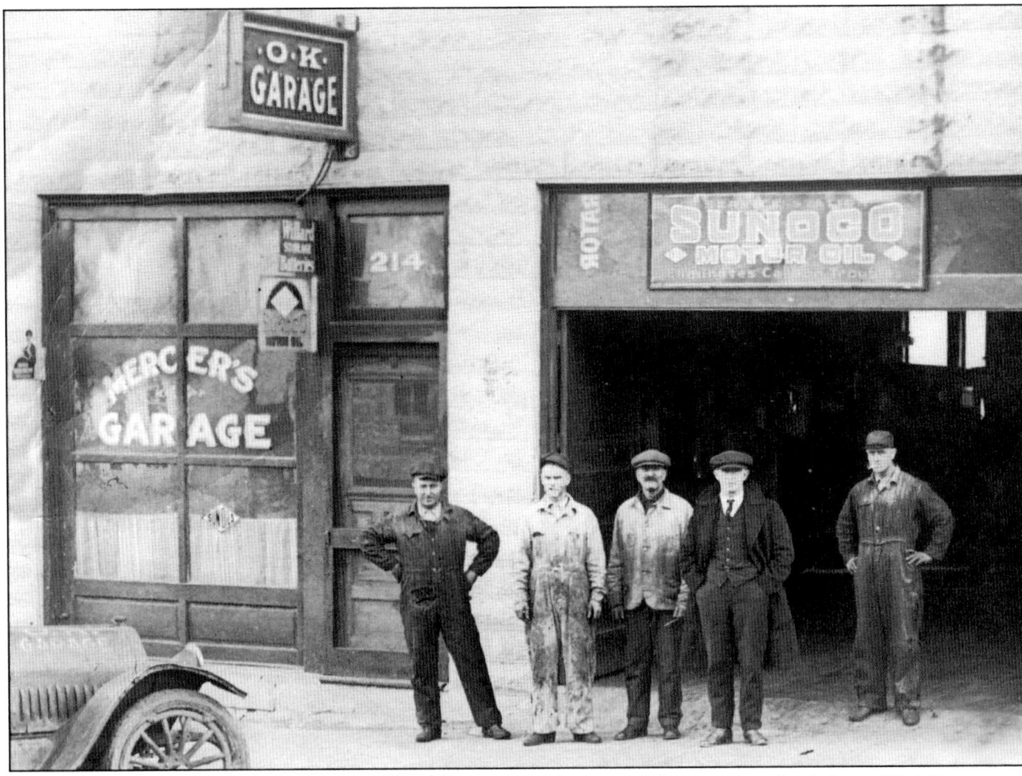

Albert Mercer's OK Garage on East Third Street, on the site of the present-day Maryville Typewriter Exchange and seen here in the early 1920s, provided service to local motorists from the start of the automobile age. The numerous ancillary products that accompanied automobiles found advertising space on the fronts of such garages for decades to come. Willard Storage Batteries and Sunoco Motor Oil are featured here. The interior of the garage, shown below, offers evidence that early engines were not particularly reliable, with this relatively young car already getting torn down. Most early mechanics started in carriage repair or work on small engines for other uses. Using poorly-drafted manuals, trial-and-error, and a good deal of shared advice, engine tinkerers repaired automobiles and quickly professionalized their trade. (Courtesy of Coby Lamb.)

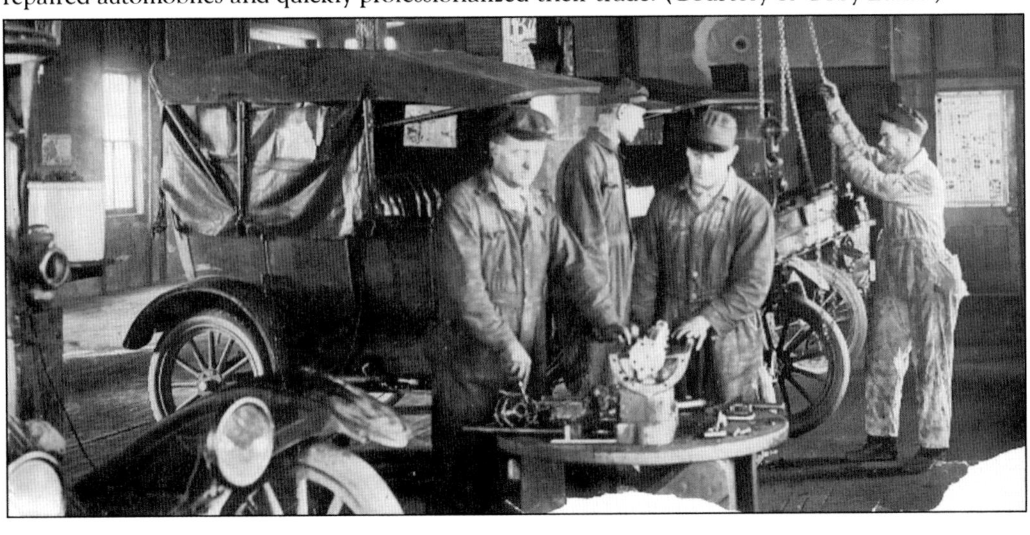

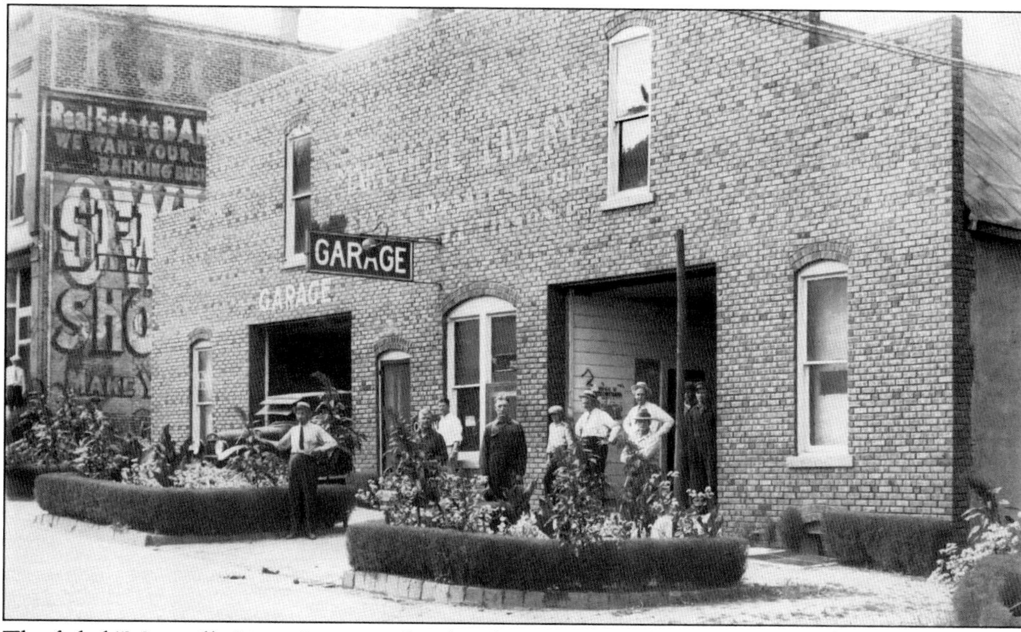

The faded "Maryville Livery" sign on this façade in 1926 testifies to the passing of the livery stable to a modern automobile garage on East Fourth Street. Livery and carriage businesses that did not make the transition generally did not make it past 1915. A sign inside advertises the impending arrival of the 1926 Chautauqua. (Courtesy of Coby Lamb.)

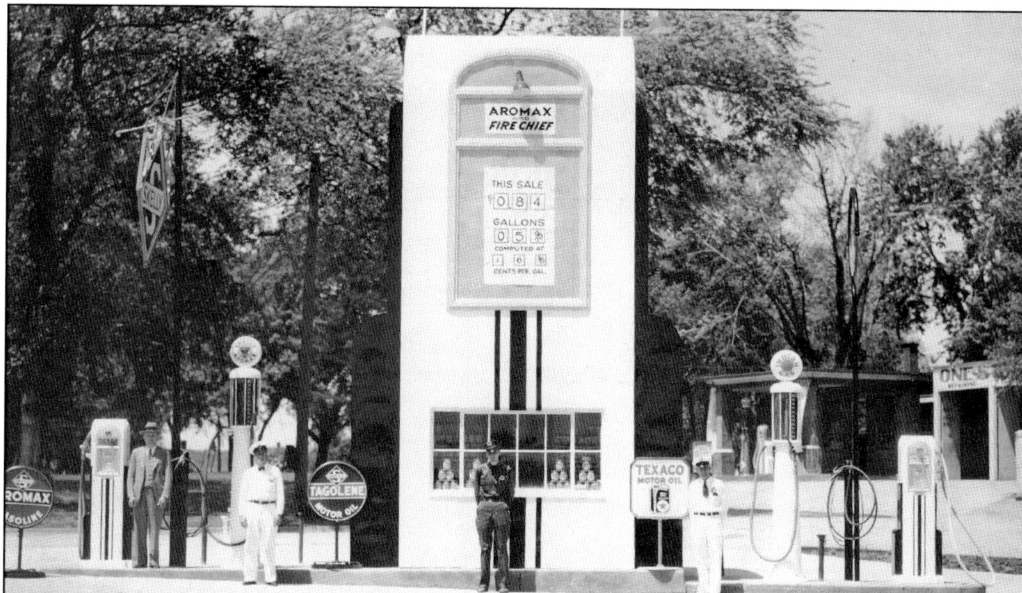

Originally on South Main Street at the corner of West Lincoln Street, this unique gas station, shaped as a giant gas pump, was built by Foster's Construction in 1937 for Kyle Phares' Oil Company. Initially a provider of non-brand discount gas, the station later served several different brand names. The station, listed in the National Register of Historic Places, fell into disuse, was moved to a private lot at the north end of town, and then moved 40 miles east, where it is preserved by the Tri County Museum in King City, Missouri.

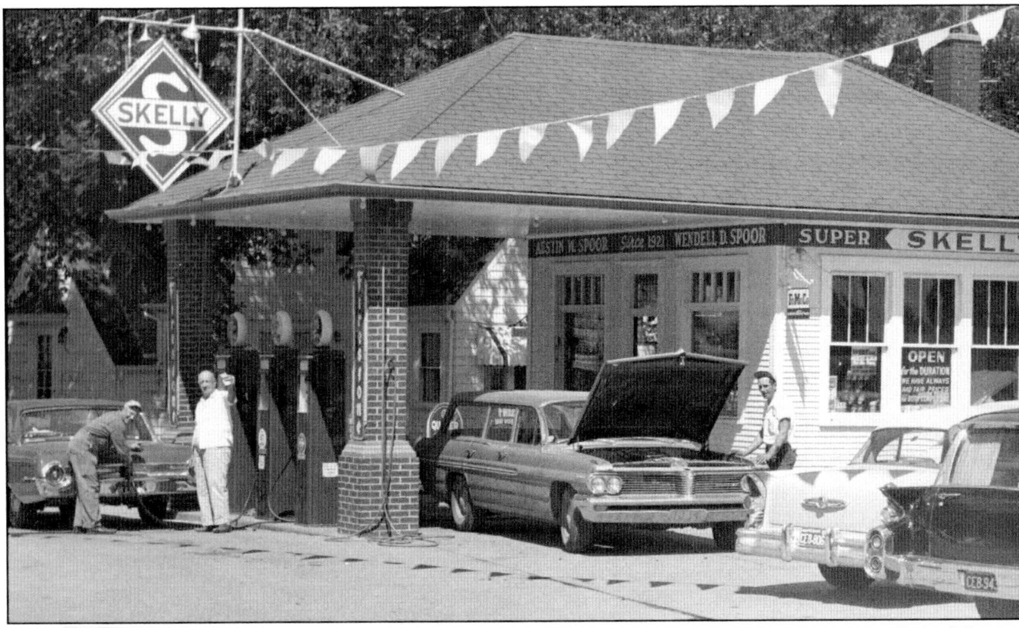

The Spoor Skelly Station, shown here in 1967, features the owner Austin Spoor, at left, filling a 1962 Ford for customer Glen Bradley, center, while Austin's son Wendle, right, checks a Pontiac for smooth operation. The station was originally built in 1935 and expanded to feature a full service shop in 1938. Today, the gas station still stands at the corner of West Lincoln and South Main as an auto dealership. (Courtesy of Virginia Spoor.)

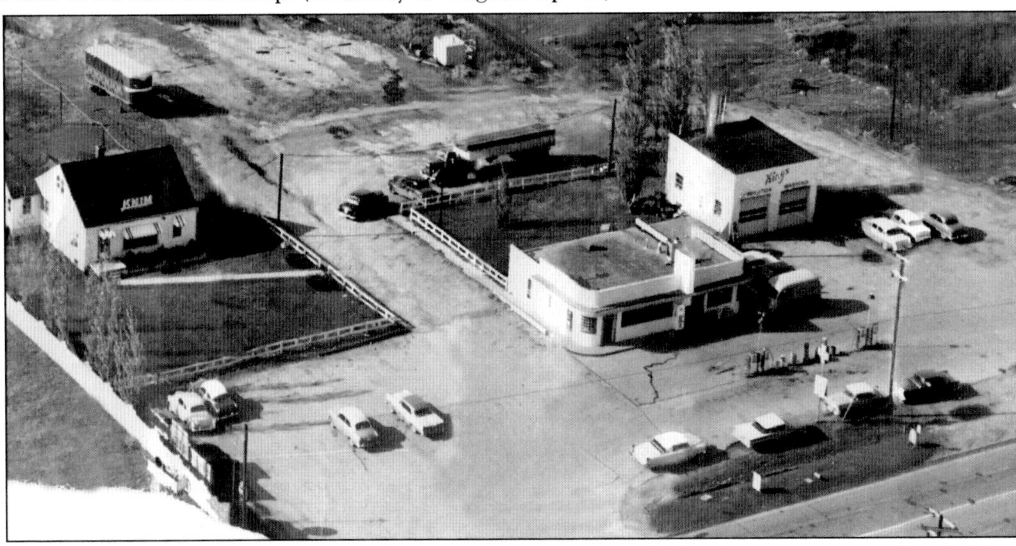

This image shows an aerial view of the Conoco station and King's restaurant on South Main Street/Highway 71, with the original KNIM radio station building to the left. Increased truck traffic in the 1930s and 1940s called for service stations with space and facilities to accommodate the large vehicles and provide them with the diesel fuel not available at most gas stations. The creation of the interstate system in the 1950s encouraged truck transportation further, and even those not on the interstate highways saw significantly increased truck traffic. King's offered fuel, food, a wash and lubrication station tall enough to accommodate trucks, and all-night service. (Courtesy of Suzi Schneider-Anderson.)

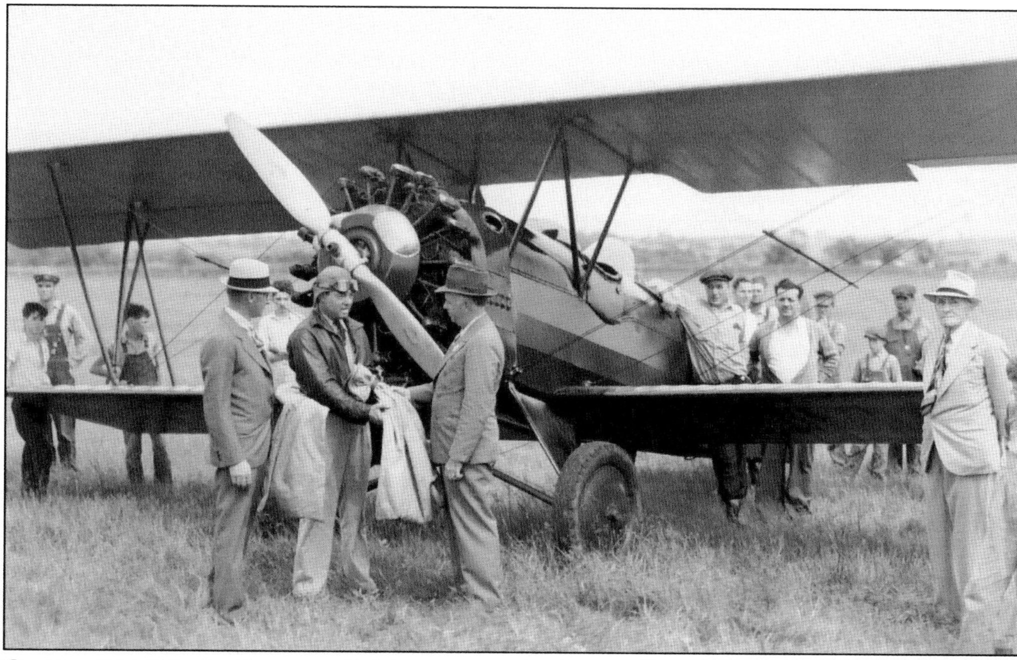

On May 19, 1938, the first airmail delivery arrived in Maryville. Pilot Joseph Holly Boyd, working for an unknown contractor for the US government, is greeted by postmaster Theodore Robinson. Against the plane leans local mail deliveryman Charles Kalstrup. The first mail took to the air in 1918 and by the late 1930s became rare for local service, making Maryville's brief receipt of the service a mystery. Below, young men two decades later found the biplane more of an exciting novelty visiting town than a workhorse connecting them to the outside world. The pilot in his white jumpsuit looks mildly amused by the mixture of poses surrounding him on his stop in Maryville. (Bottom image courtesy of Northwest.)

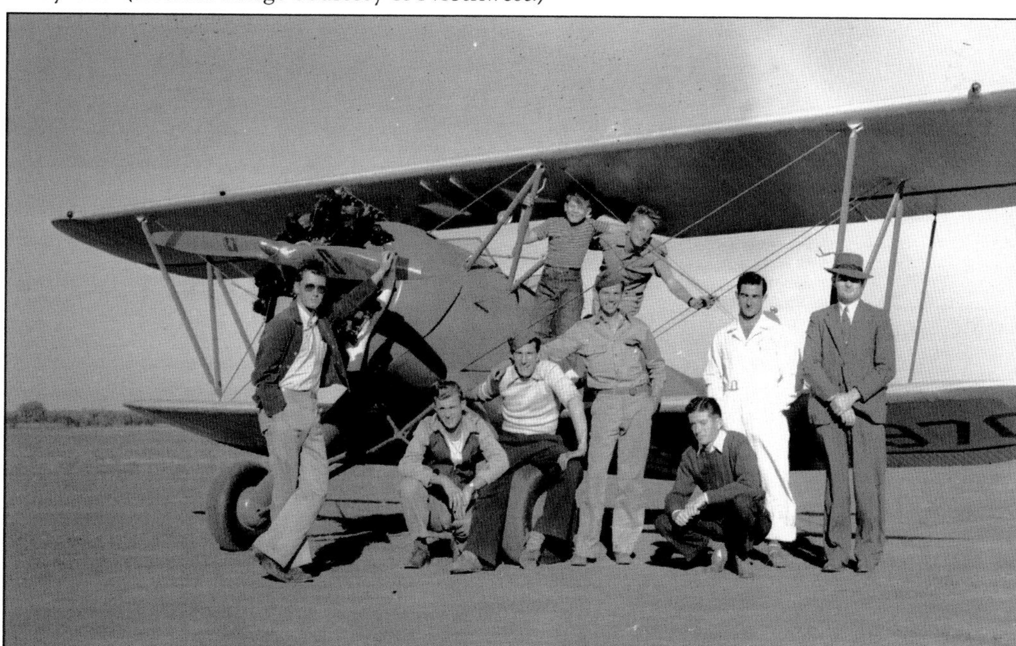

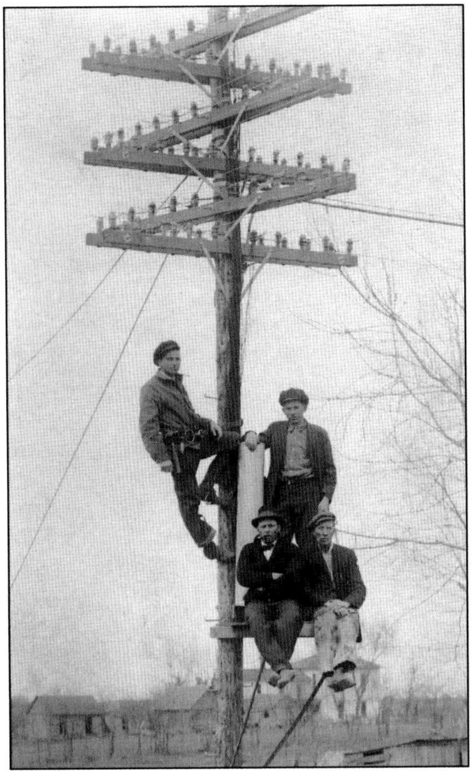

The advent of telephone service in the 1890s brought a complex system of poles and wires to businesses and homes across the community. The dizzying array of wires carried signals directly to a business phone or to groups of residential receivers on "party lines" that were directly connected to a plug in a board at the operator's station at an exchange. These workers carried only a hammer and a pair of side-cutting pliers while working in Maryville on the Hanamo Company service that dominated the local telephone market. (Courtesy of Michael Steiner.)

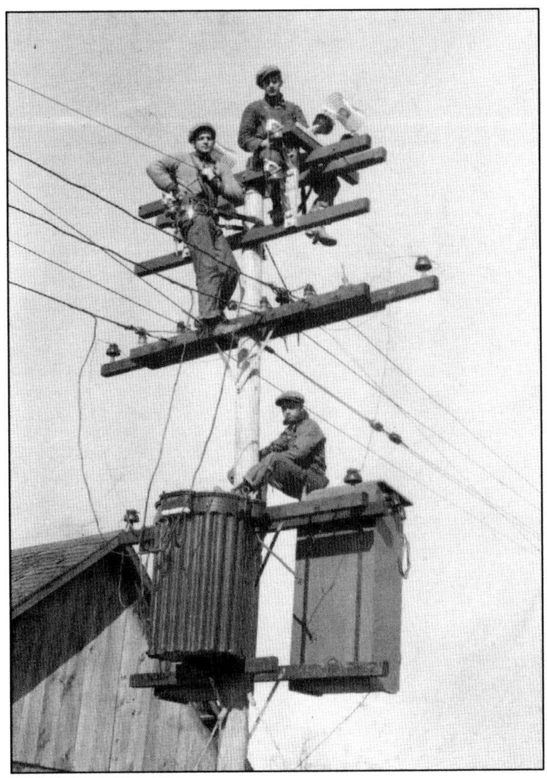

While linemen of all sorts, like this crew perched on a pole in Maryville, faced the similar hazards of height and weather, the new breed of electrical line workers that emerged in the 1890s faced the considerably greater danger of electrocution. Apprenticeship served from the start as the principal means by which technical knowledge and safety were transmitted to new workers, guided by the International Brotherhood of Electrical Workers based in St. Louis. Nonetheless, prior to the 1930s, at least one in four of these brave workers died on the job. (Courtesy of Michael Steiner.)

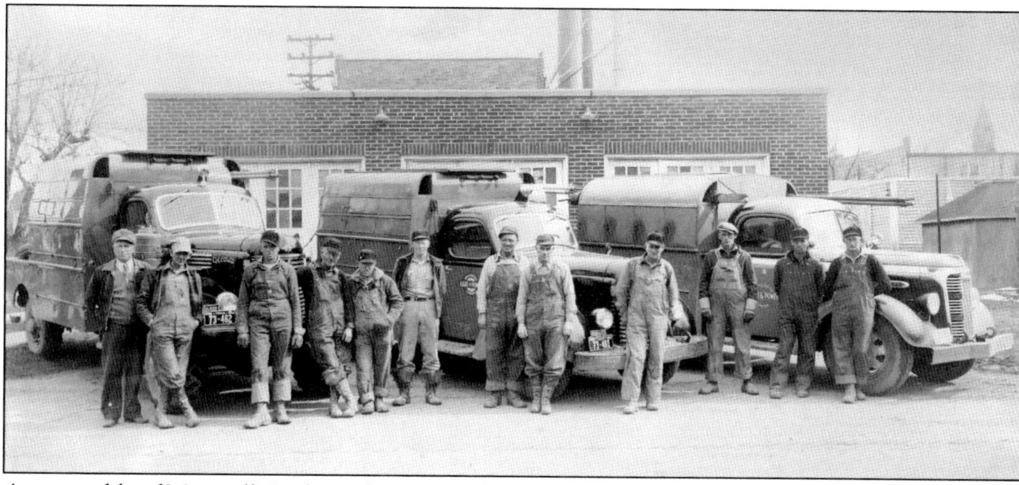

An assembly of Maryville Light and Power workers gather in front of their work trucks around 1940. Two of the vehicles bear the logos and tags of the parent company, Iowa-Nebraska Light and Power Company. Rugged vehicles and even more rugged men were required to take on the dangerous work these crews faced. The first power station, built near the Burlington line in 1887, was replaced by the brick structure that still stands at the corner of North Buchanan and Fifth Streets—originally a livery stable converted with the addition of a boiler and generator engines. The power company ran its business for many years out of an office in the Empire Theater building on Main Street.

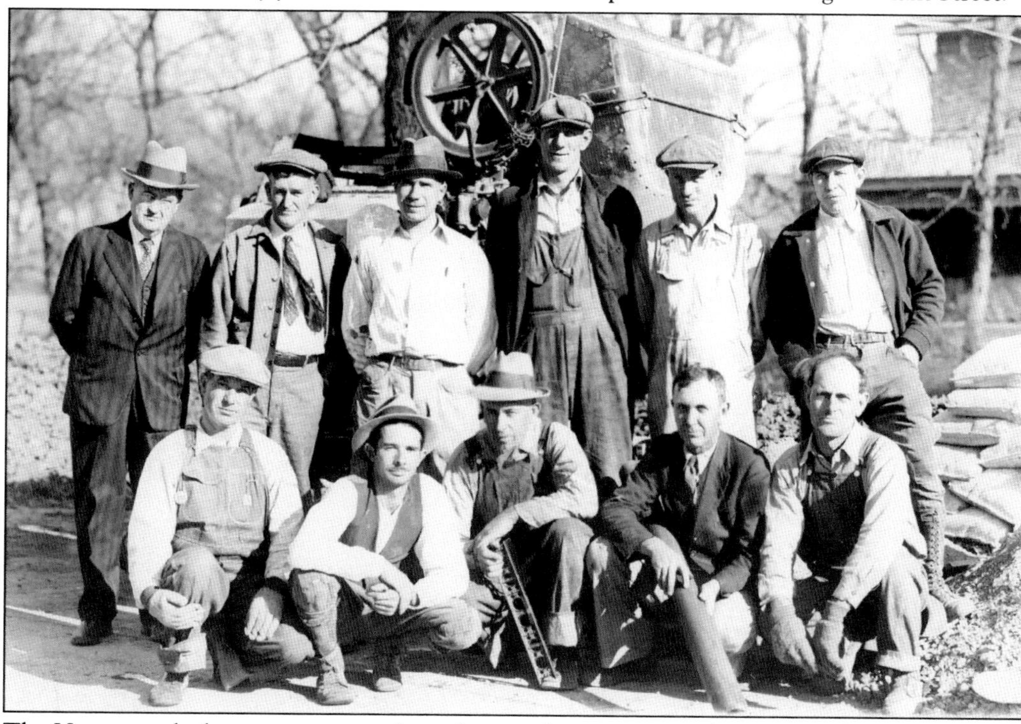

The Hanamo telephone crew pauses from their work sometime in the 1920s. Bill Price (front row, left), who appears in other photographs from the time in costume as a member of a local vaudeville troupe, wears his work bibs and a more serious expression than usual. E.H. Ralston, J.C. Donnell, and H.E. Ralston incorporated Hanamo in 1897 in Maryville and purchased lines from the Missouri and Kansas Telephone company to considerably expand its coverage after the turn of the century.

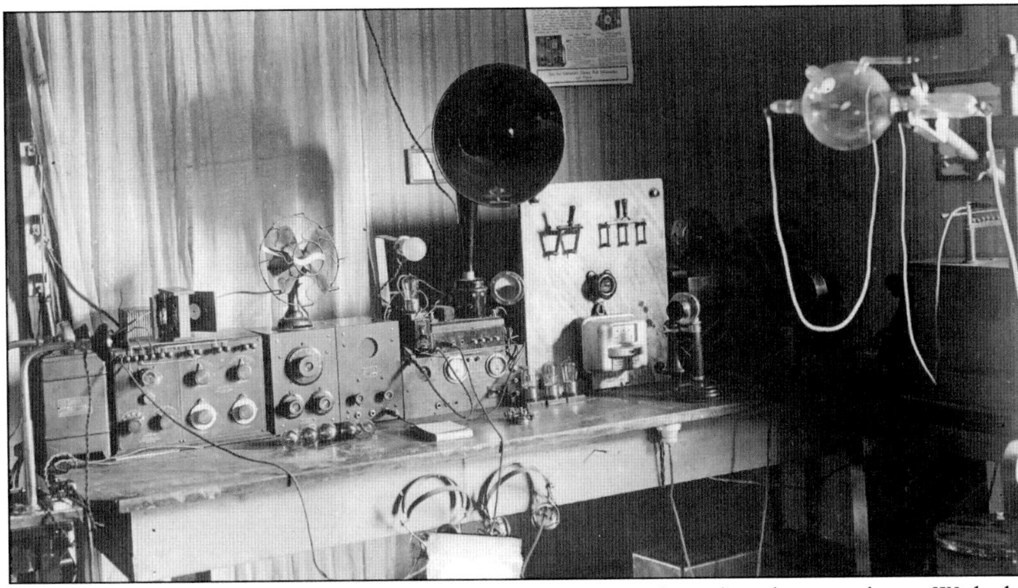

During the early 20th century, amateur "ham" radio stations skyrocketed in popularity. With the advancing technology of the vacuum tube, equipment to transmit radio signals became increasingly affordable. During World War I, the government forced many stations to close, but following the end of the war stations multiplied. The origin of the term HAM is highly debated, either used as a pejorative by professional radio-telegraph operators to describe rank amateur status, or to represent the call signs of Harvard's radio club, Hyman-Almy-Murray. From 1921, as shown above, to 1924, below, the technology and transmission distance of these Maryville operators greatly increased. IDs posted on the wall for quick reference indicate regular contact with stations in Hopkins, St. Joseph, and Omaha, though the equipment was capable of covering much farther distances.

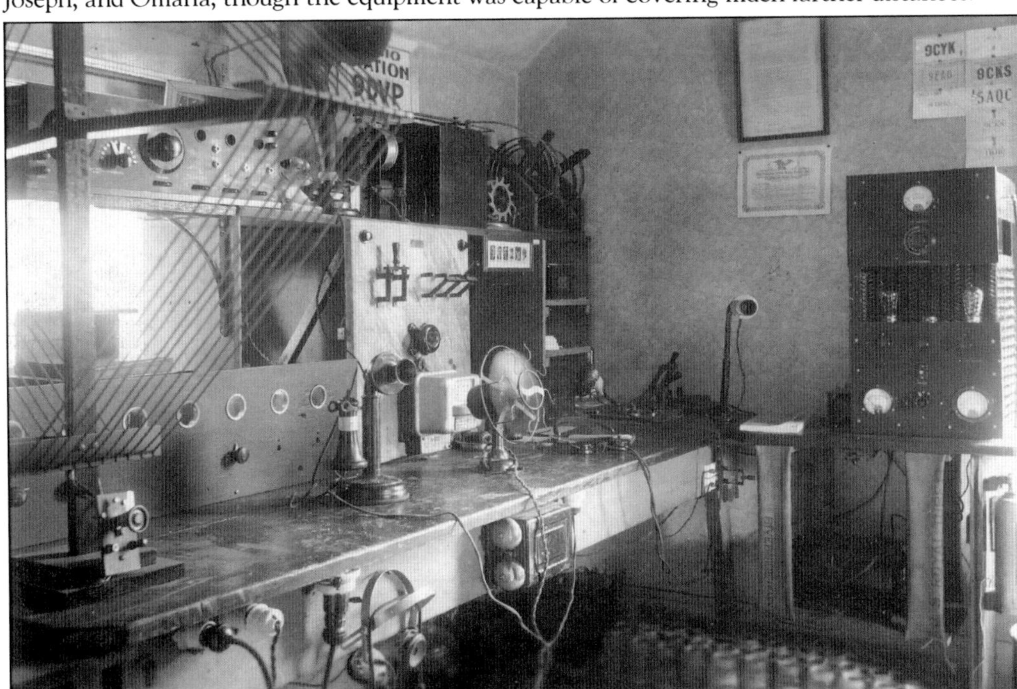

Dredge boats spent several years, beginning in 1915, dredging and straightening the One Hundred and Two River through Nodaway County from Hopkins to Arkoe. Well after serving as a useful transportation route and power for mills, the One Hundred and Two continued to provide water for Maryville and other communities along its course. (Courtesy of Michael Steiner.)

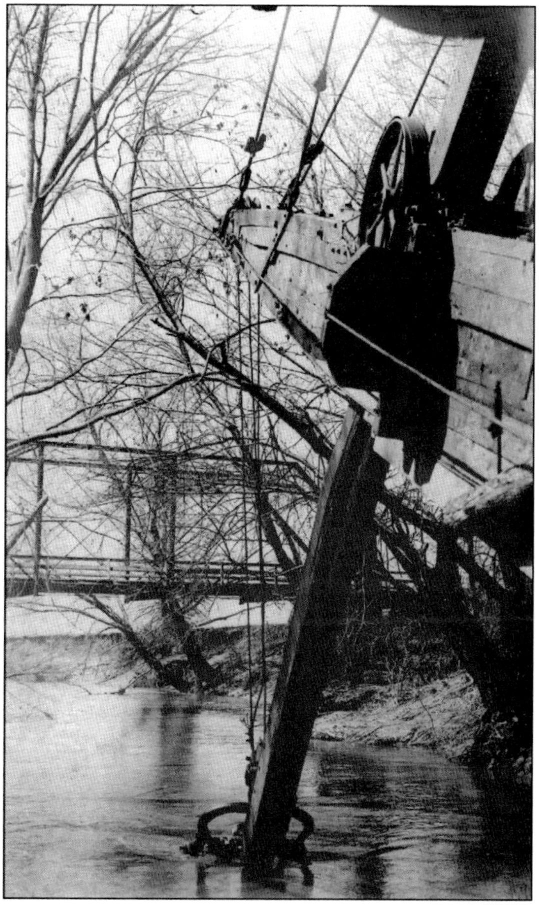

The concrete dam on the One Hundred and Two River was designed by engineer H. Phillips of St. Louis in 1913 to fulfill the need to make improvements to the Maryville Water Works by adding a $30,000 high-quality concrete structure to coexist with the old dam. Workers are seen here 20 years later, making further improvements to the dam and its connections to the water works.

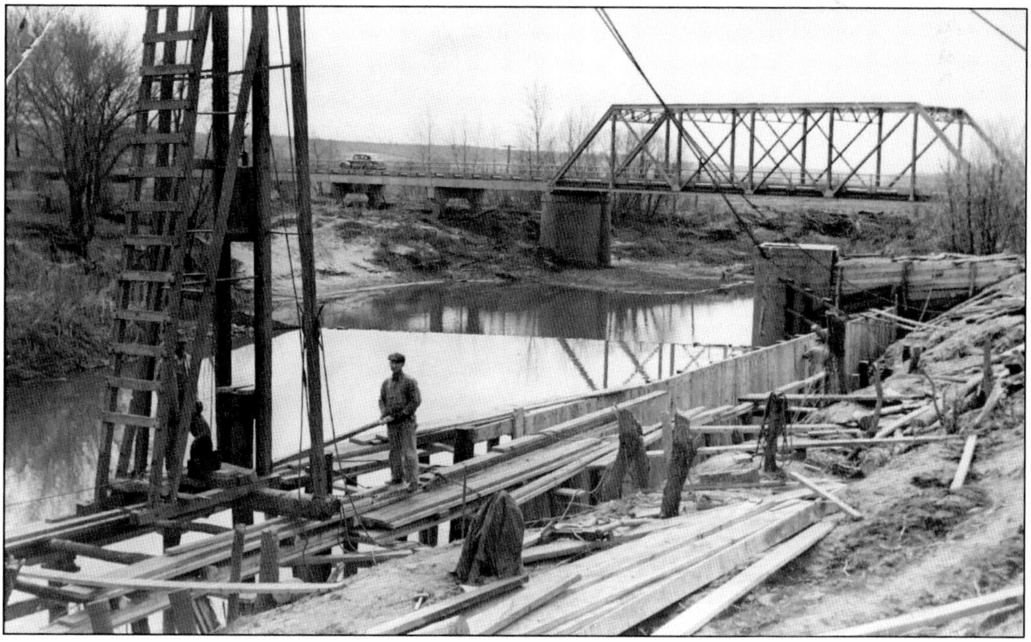

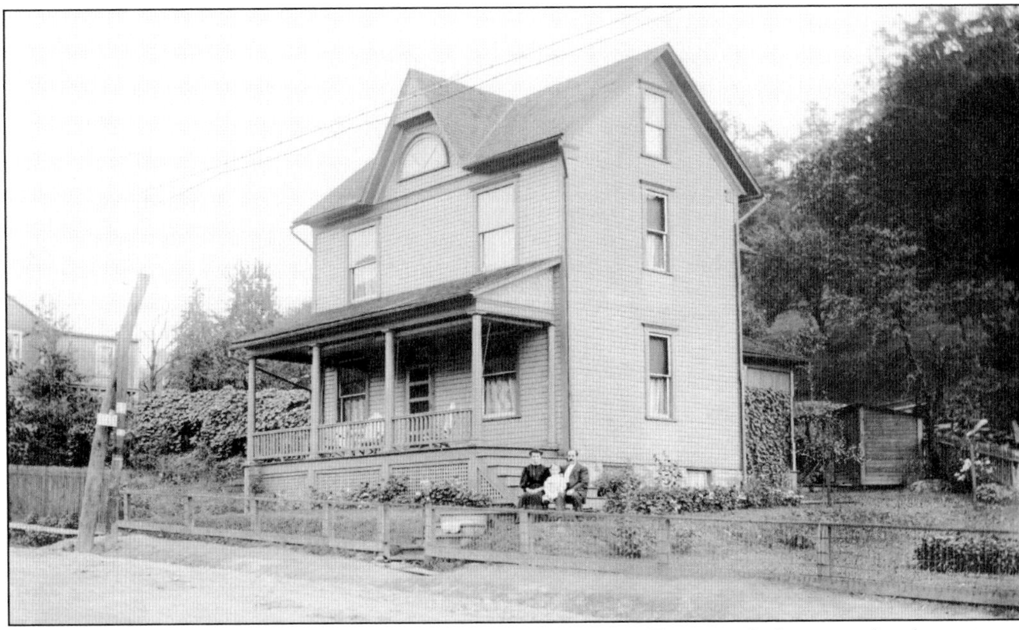

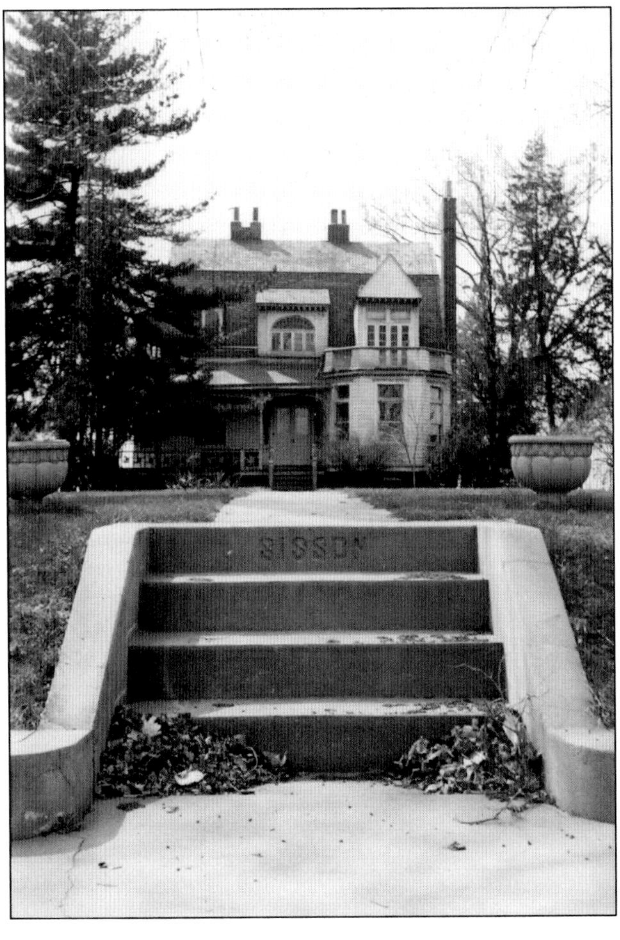

Tours and photographic histories of communities typically feature grand homes, with justifiable pride and interest. The vernacular homes of ordinary residents, however, say far more about the experience of most people in small-town life. Here, a common home displays the standard "I-house" design, with four rooms on two floors divided by a central hallway. One can just see at the rear a kitchen likely added to the original home.

Local real estate and banking entrepreneur Nathaniel Sisson had this home built in 1889 on the western edge of town at the end of Third Street. The home contains 22 rooms, including five baths and four fireplaces. The eclectic style of the home, seen here in 1940, was modified many times over the years including the addition of the porch. The esteemed Sisson, a Civil War veteran, served as a bugler and is credited in local lore with sounding the last bugle charge before Lee's surrender at Appomattox.

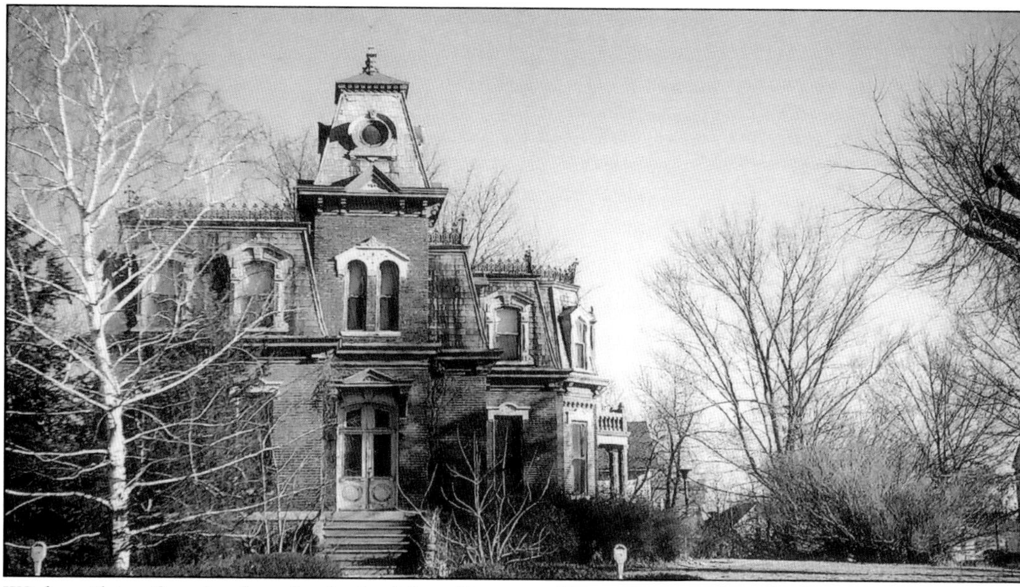

With striking façades from both the Main Street and First Street sides, the home built for Albert Ellis, known as the "The Landmark" and later the Forsyth place, was among Maryville's earliest and finest showplaces. Built in 1883, the French Colonial home was designed by J.M. Gile. The brick and sandstone structure featured six bedrooms, two bathrooms, kitchen, dining room, parlor, and sitting room.

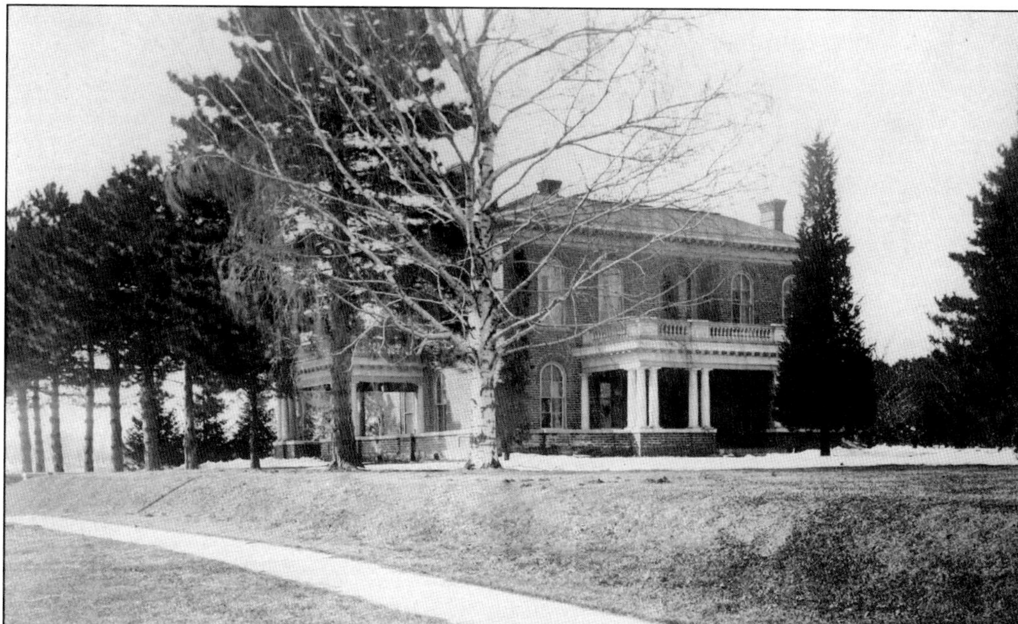

English immigrant Thomas Gaunt established in 1857 a nursery on the grounds surrounding this home. Gaunt's brother-in-law, Joseph Castillo, built the home out of bricks produced locally along the banks of the One Hundred and Two River. Among the home's many interesting features was a bucket lift that drew water from a well and cistern in the basement into the kitchen. The home has served as the residence of every president of Northwest Missouri State University since its inception in 1905 and is now listed in the National Register of Historic Places.

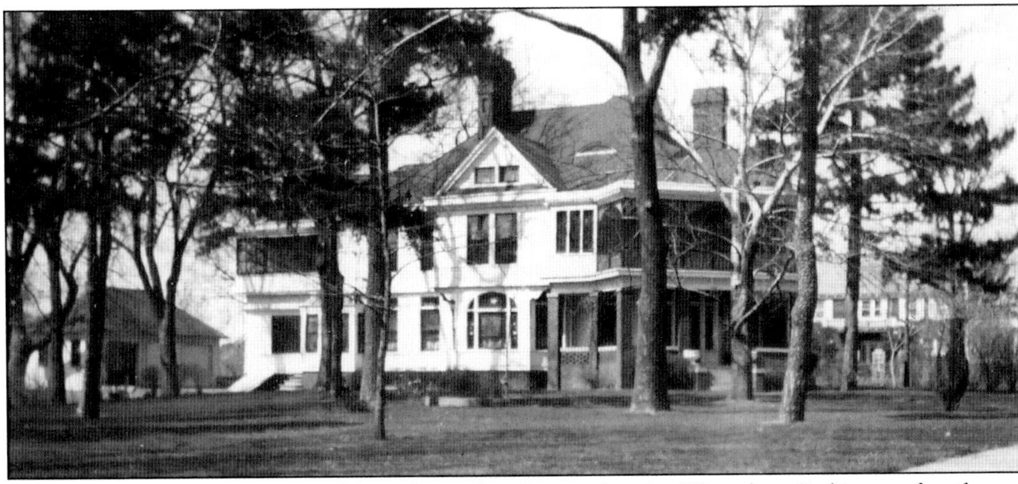

The impressive home designed by Alexander Searcy for the Theodore Robinson family was completed in 1888 on West Third Street. Seen here in 1940, the asymmetrical Queen Anne home graced the row of fine homes along West Third Street from Dunn Street to North Grand Avenue. Still standing, the home was constructed with six fireplaces, one of which has a flue that divides and rejoins to accommodate a stained glass window in the center.

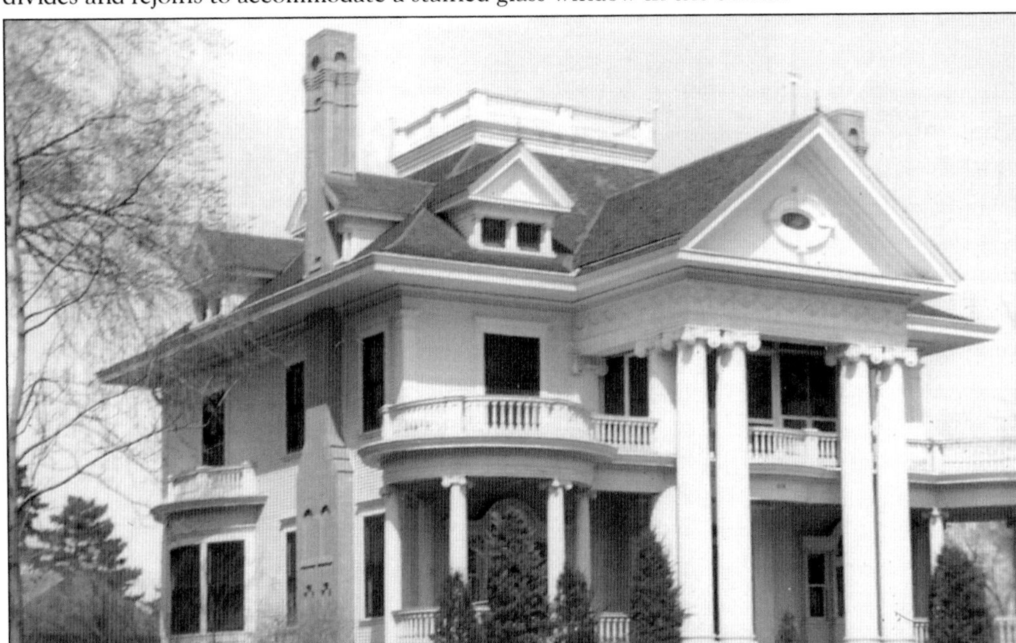

James B. Robinson, president of the Nodaway Valley Bank, contracted Fred Faye to construct this Alexander Searcy design, completed in 1904. The Georgian style recalls the height of colonial-era architecture in an expansive structure. Designer Searcy was educated at College Springs College in southern Iowa and designed and built numerous homes, businesses, and churches in the region. Searcy also designed Maryville's Washington School, the Elks Club Building, and the Nodaway County Infirmary.

Four

TOWN AND GOWN

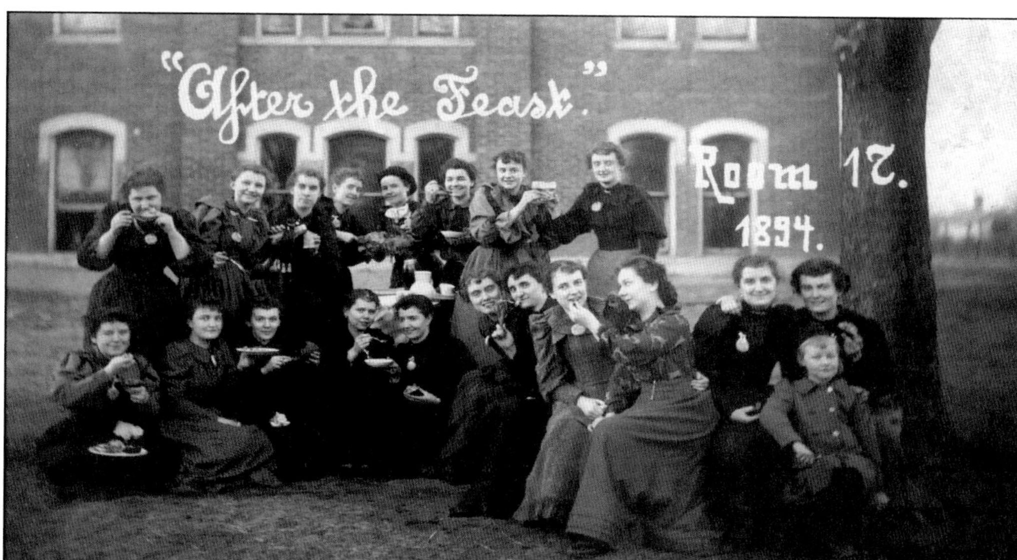

Young women enjoy a chance to frolic and mug for the camera on the lawn at the Maryville Seminary. Opening in 1889, the seminary operated under the auspices of the Methodist Church and brought teacher training to northwest Missouri in what came to be known as the "Old Seminary Building" at the end of West First Street in Maryville. While the school must have seemed permanent to them at the time, only 16 years after its opening the creation of the state's Fifth District Normal School closed the doors on the faltering seminary.

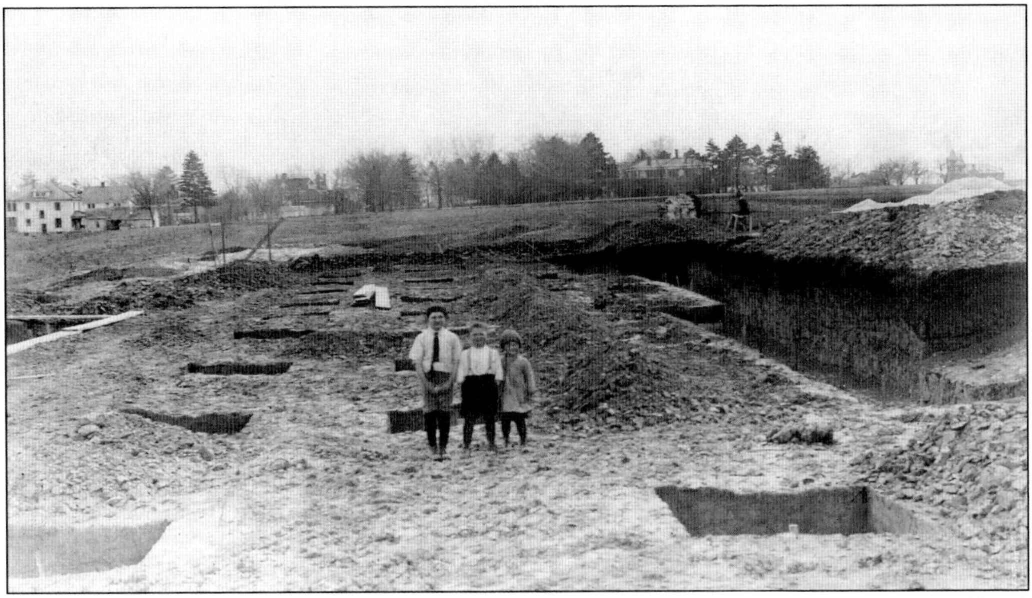

The construction of the "Academic Hall" (hereafter referred to as the Administration Building) of the Fifth District Normal School was plagued with financial difficulties and several work stoppages from its start in October 1906 until completion in September 1910. With excavation of the foundation complete, the delays may have been a source of great anxiety for school officials, but local children surely found it fascinating. On the distant horizon at right, the old seminary building watches its much grander successor arise. (Courtesy of Northwest.)

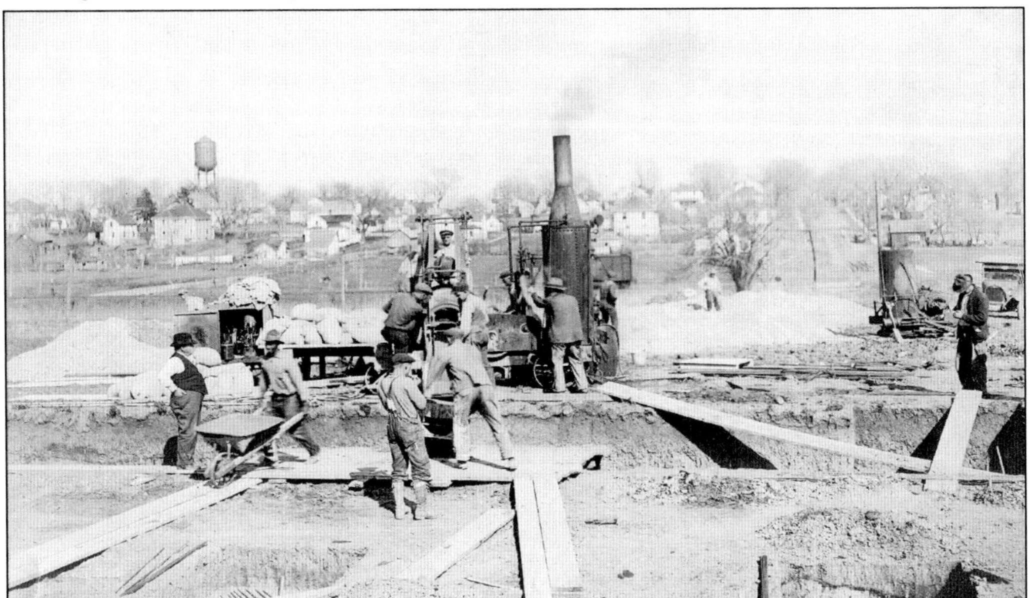

Shown here in 1907 is the construction crew operated by J.H. Sparks, whose bid the Fifth District Normal School Board of Regents approved for the excavation and construction of the new Administration Building. With the help of a steam-powered concrete mixer, the crew was able to excavate and pour the foundation of the school just in time for the October 12 cornerstone laying event. (Courtesy of Northwest.)

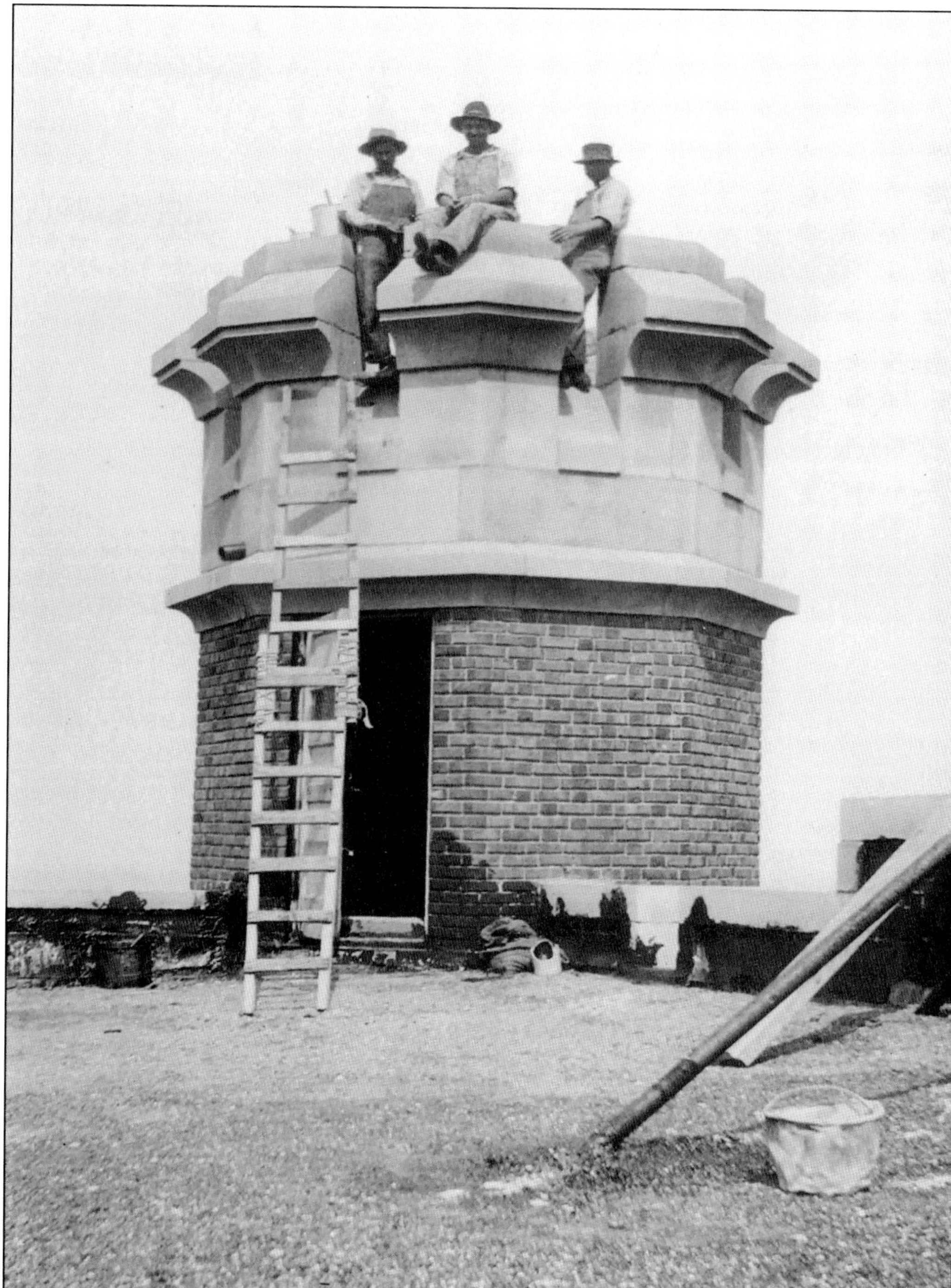

Most likely taken in 1910, some of the roof workers take a quick moment atop the Administration Building's turret to pose for posterity. The four turrets successfully survived decades of inclement weather, but eventually one needed repair following the fire of 1979. While the front two turrets, which exemplify Collegiate Gothic Architecture, are purely decorative, the rear two serve as airshafts. (Courtesy of Northwest.)

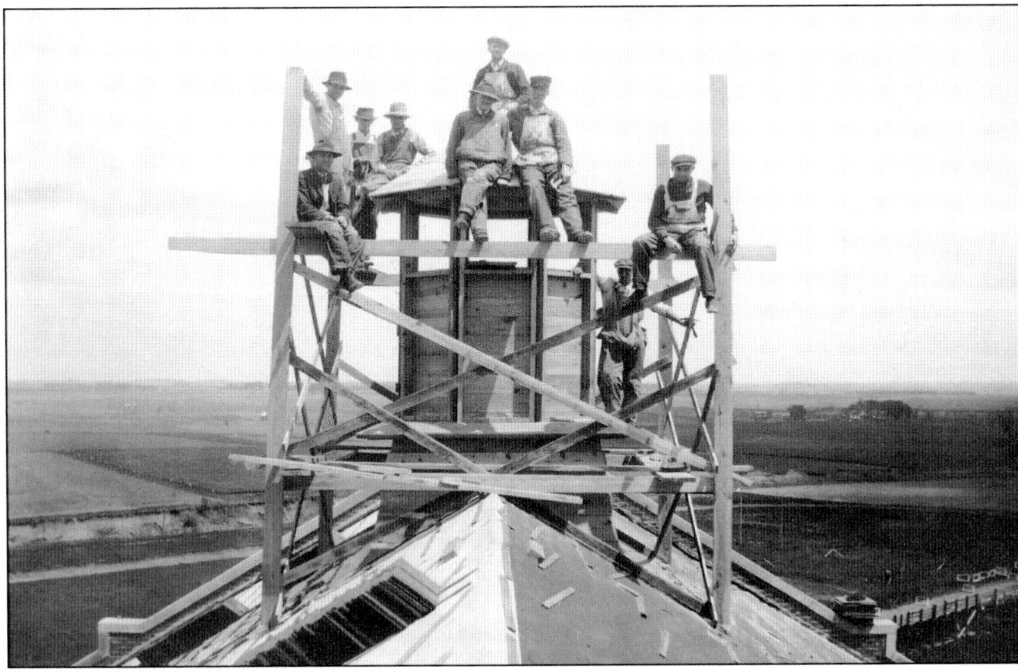

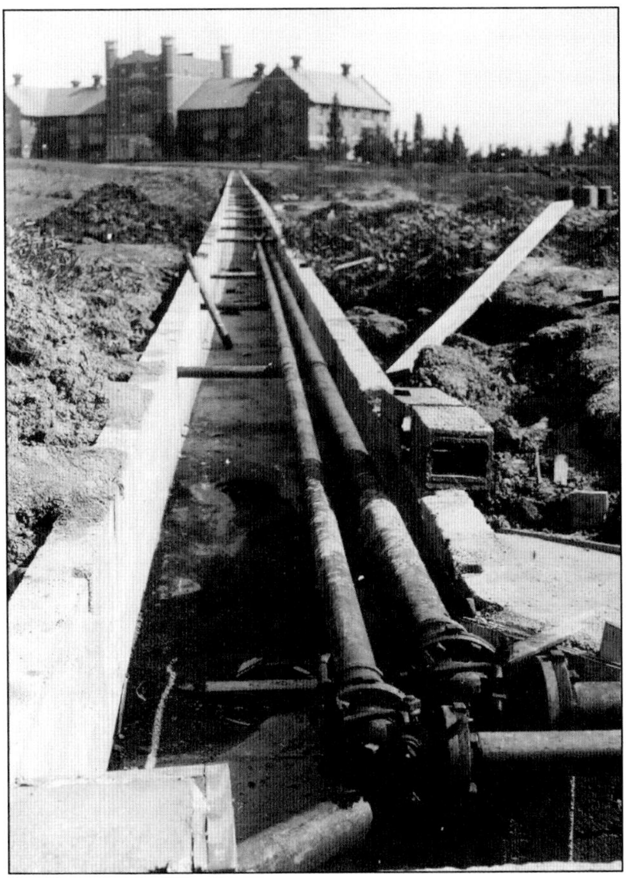

In 1910, before finishing the Administration Building, roof workers on the north wing of the building above the theater take a break from laying shingles to pose around one of the roof air vents that rest at the peaks of the gable roofs. These vents circulated air throughout the building during hot Missouri summers. Originally crafted out of wood, these were later replaced by copper cupolas. (Courtesy of Northwest.)

In 1919, the State Normal School became a state college and began to expand outward from its single building. With the addition of new facilities, including a separate gymnasium, the steam system from the power plant that heated the Administration Building spread outward in the 1920s through a system of steam tunnels, still used today by the university and its innovative energy system. (Courtesy of Northwest.)

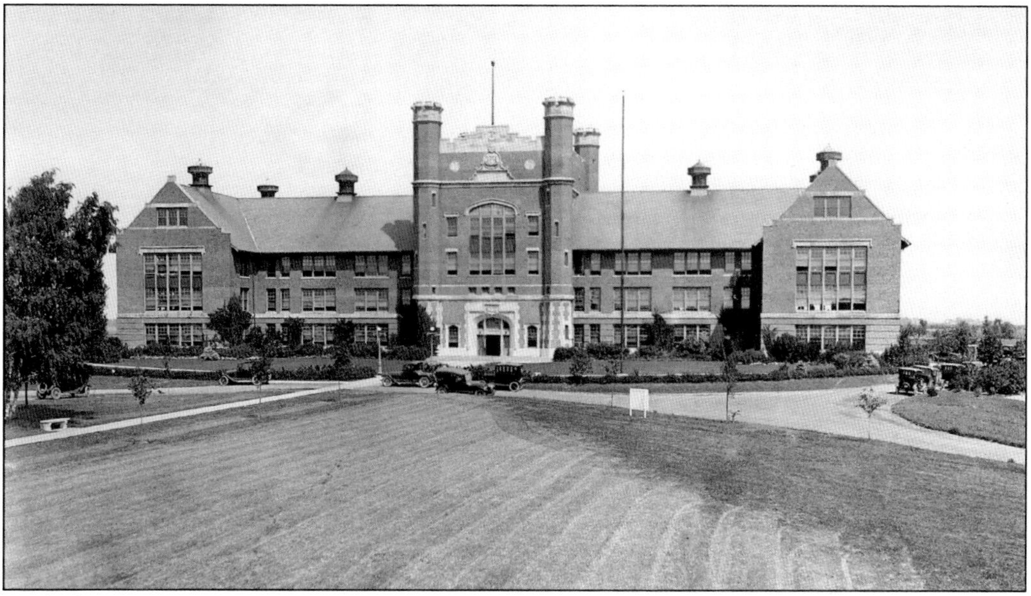

With the cornerstone set in 1907 and the building opening for operation in 1910, the impressive Administration Building struck a commanding presence on a high knoll on the northwest corner of town. In addition to the usual stresses of weather, time, and heavy use, the building also persevered through a tornado in 1919 and a massive fire in 1979. The Tudor Gothic building was designed by J.H. Felt and Company and is among those in Maryville listed in the National Register of Historic Places.

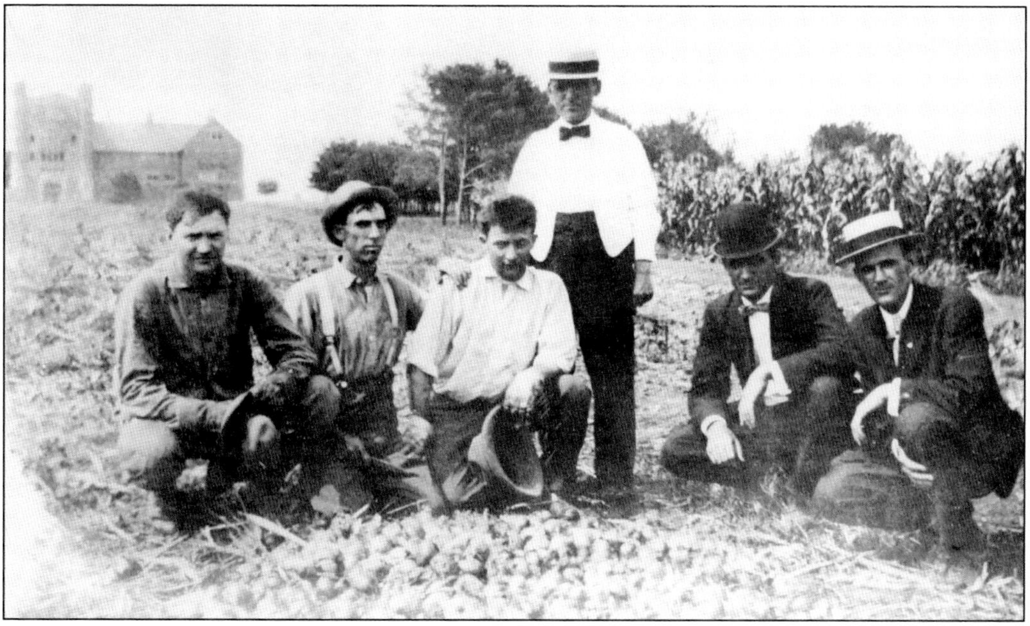

The location of the college in northwest Missouri quickly brought agricultural training and experimentation to the school. President Henry K. Taylor's enthusiasm for agricultural opportunities led him to launch an experiment, at his own expense, in growing vegetables on the land in front of the Administration Building to raise funds for the school. Taylor, shown standing here, surveys in 1910 his first, and only, onion crop, which proved not worth the effort.

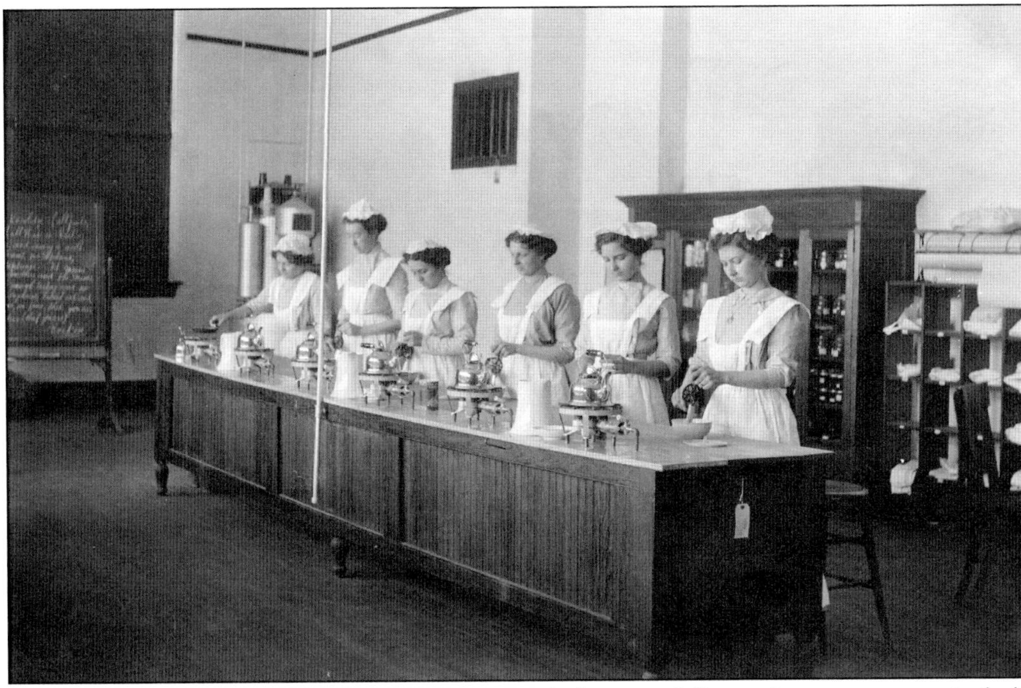

In 1911, the school received funding for new materials for many different departments, particularly home economics. Here, the girls are learning to master an iron egg beater. Home Economics was an important department in early normal school history. Hettie Anthony, on the right, spent a long career teaching home economics at Northwest after graduating. (Courtesy of Northwest.)

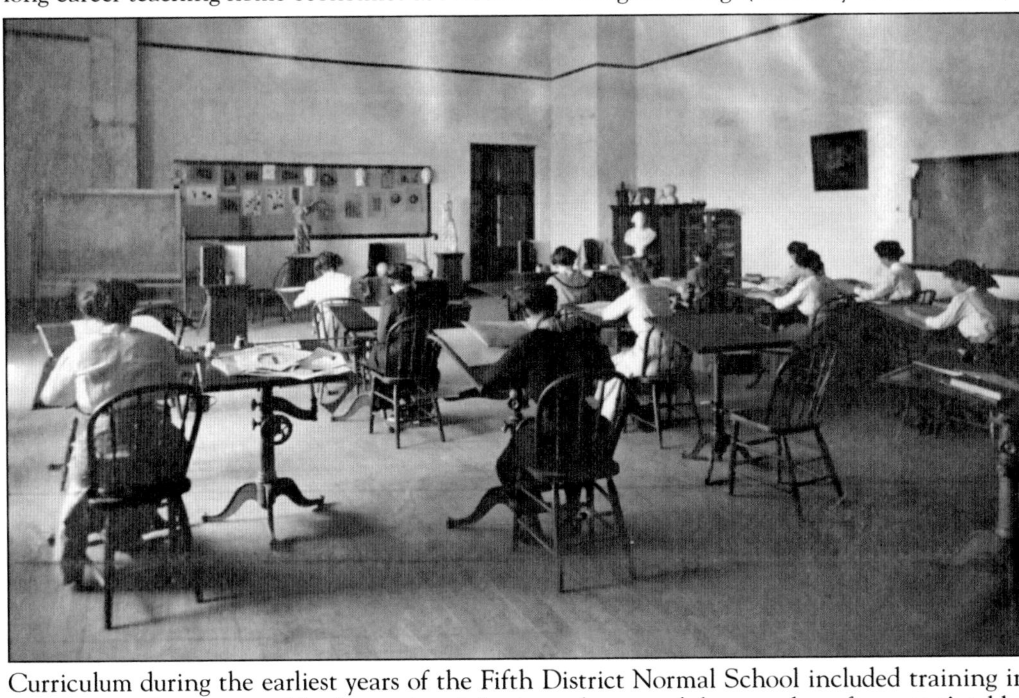

Curriculum during the earliest years of the Fifth District Normal School included training in art. Here, students inspired by the copies of classic works around them work on fine artist's tables manufactured by the Dietzgen company in Chicago. (Courtesy of Northwest.)

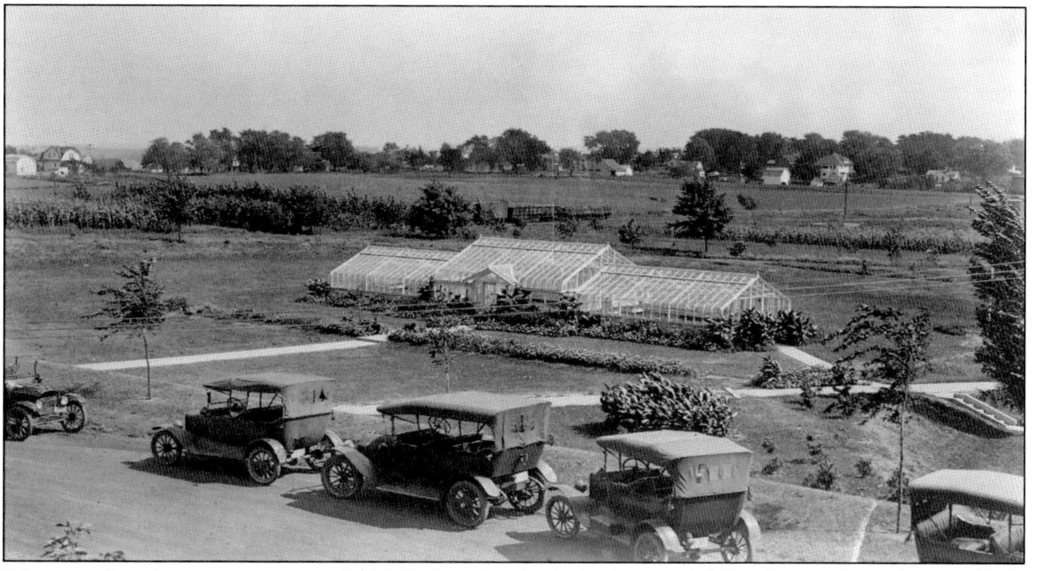

The state legislature appropriated $10,000, with which the Normal School was allowed to establish a farm and greenhouse on the grounds. An excellent greenhouse was erected on the current site of the Facilities Services building north of the power plant. Behind it, rail cars of the Wabash line sit on a siding and, farther to the northeast, houses appear around the land owned by the Prathers, on what became Prather Avenue. (Courtesy of Northwest.)

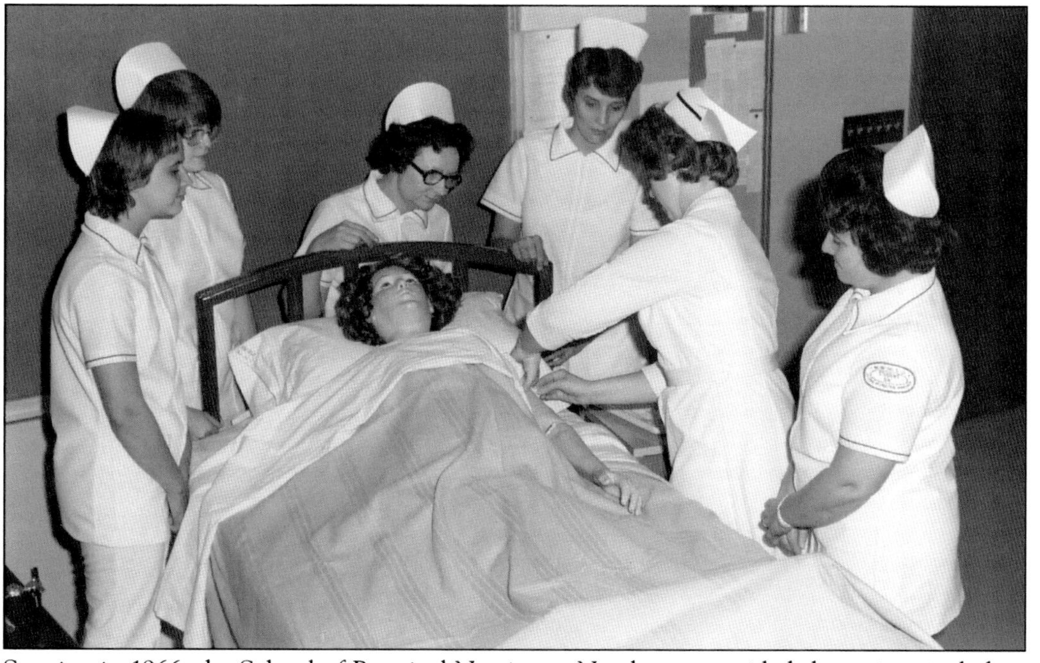

Starting in 1966, the School of Practical Nursing at Northwest provided the region, including the local St. Francis Hospital, with a Licensed Practical Nursing program. In 1974, a bachelor's degree in nursing was added to the program. These were ceased in 1986 under an agreement with Missouri Western State College. The university continued to provide pre–nursing school preparation, and in the fall of 2009 resumed serving nurses with a bachelor of science degree. (Courtesy of Northwest.)

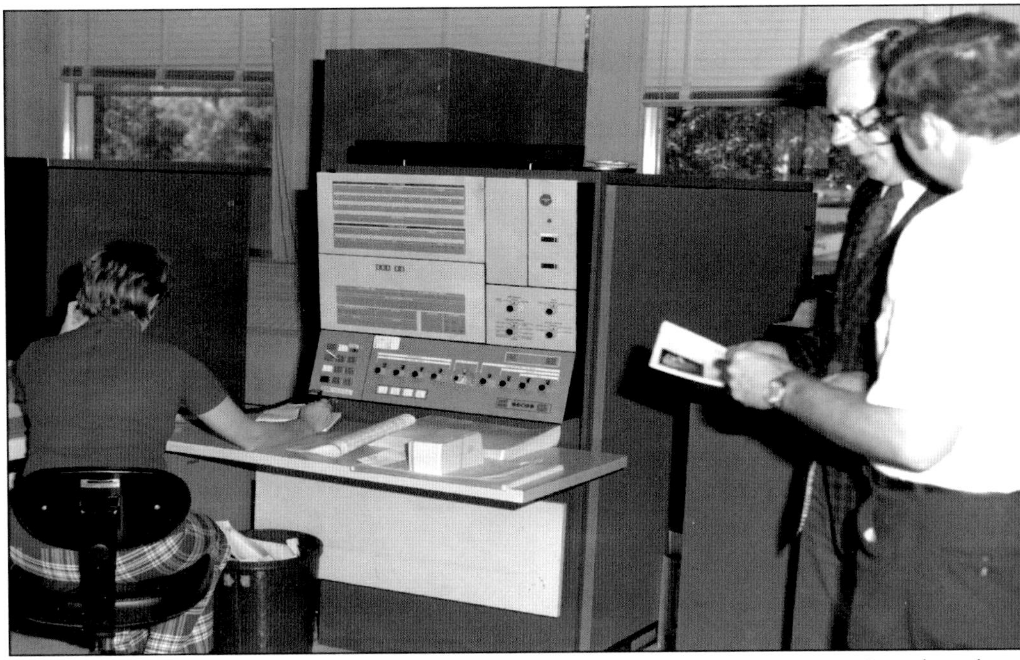

Known as one of the first electronic campuses in the nation, Northwest Missouri State has always integrated technology into education. The IBM 360 Model 30, shipped in 1965, was one of the most powerful small-scale mainframe processing units that combined over ten machines into two. Retailing brand new at $133,000, the unit was considered a bargain. (Courtesy of Northwest.)

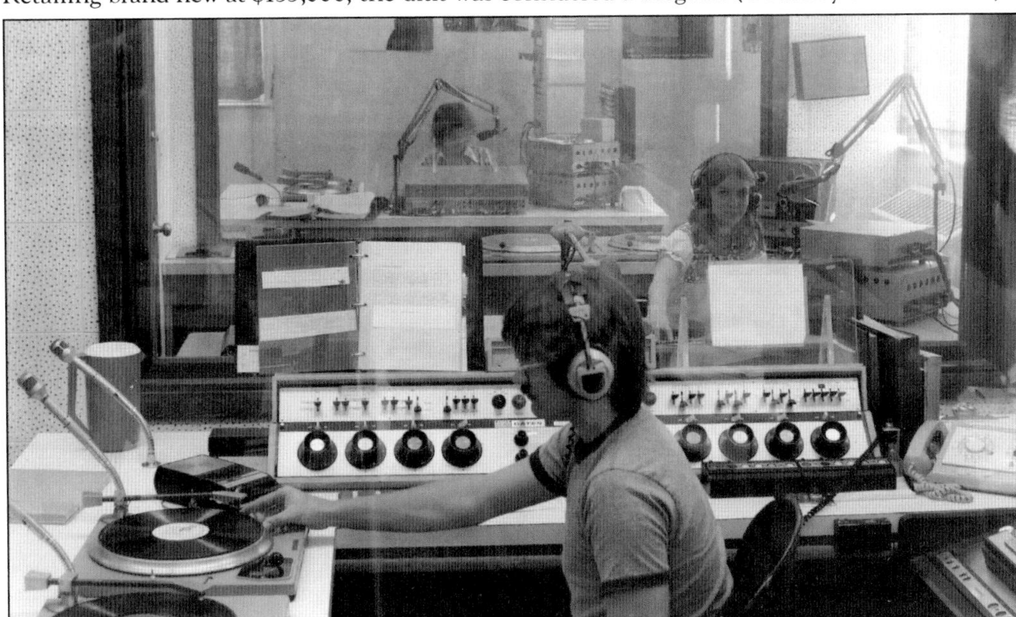

KXCV campus radio has been on the air since 1971. Originally stationed in the Administration Building, the fire displaced operations to a temporary location before it moving to its new home in Wells Hall. The KXCV station rotates between blocks of student programming and news-related segments. The primary mission has always been to educate students in radio broadcasting while serving a large listening area. (Courtesy of Northwest.)

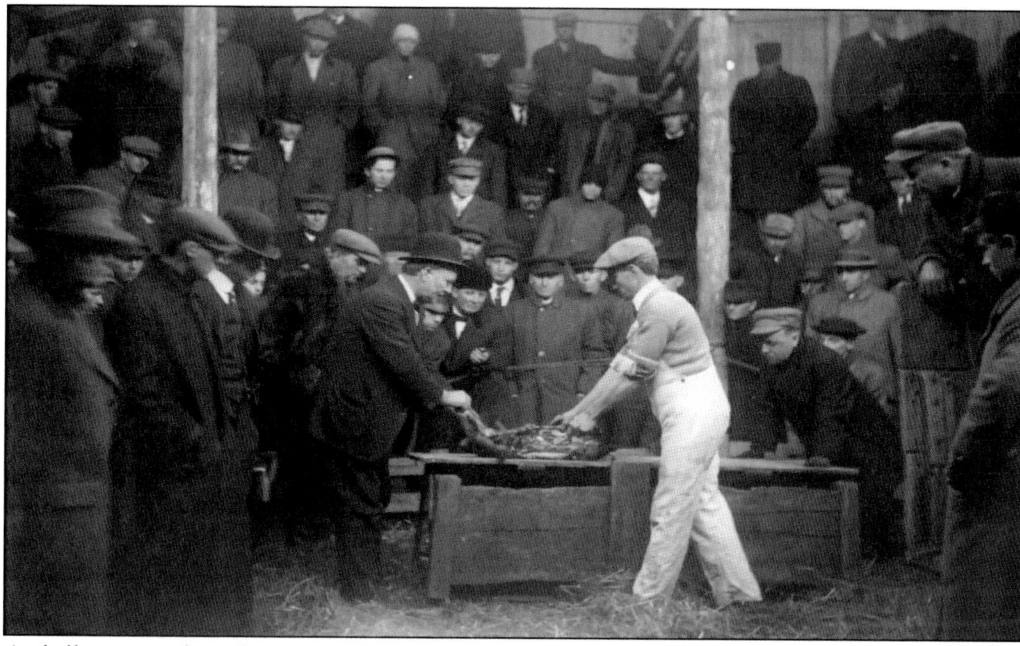

A chilly group of gentlemen watch with keen interest as an expert clad in butchers' bibs, joined by another teacher under the auspices of the college, offers a demonstration to local gentlemen in either animal anatomy or the cleaning of game. (Courtesy of Northwest.)

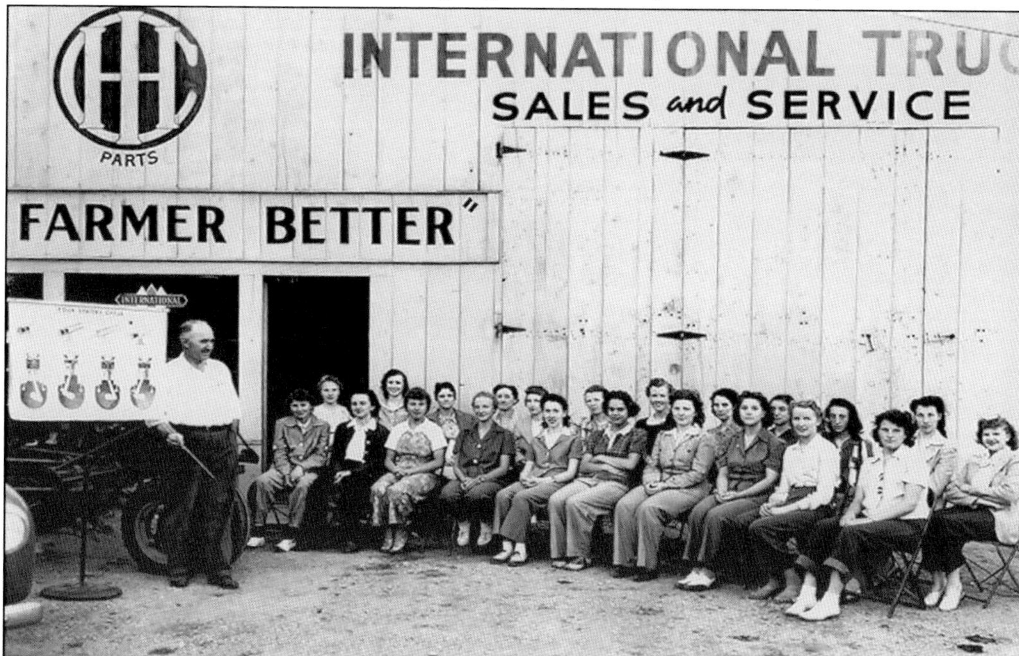

To combat the farm labor shortage created by men serving overseas during World War II, International Harvester developed the Tractorette Program. Here in 1942, John Schneider, owner of the Nodaway County Implement Company, instructs local women in the operation of the four-stroke tractor engine. Other lessons included transmission operation and service care, all leading to effective farm operation.

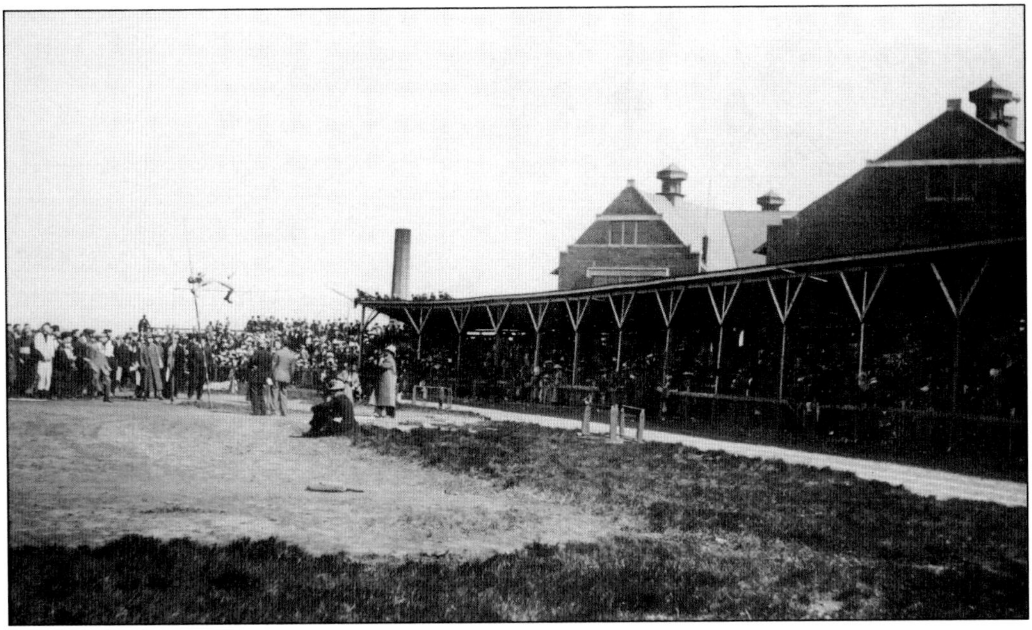

Normal School president Henry K. Taylor hoped to shift interest away from the popular but controversial and dangerous game of football by building a track and inviting 14 high school teams to a meet in 1910. Participants engaged in running and field events on a day that started chilly and was soaked with rain. Youngsters peered from the roof of the packed stands as brave pole-vaulters hurled themselves over the bar and back to a thin layer of sawdust on the ground. The event was a grand success, and by 1912, the normal school fielded a track team itself for intercollegiate competition.

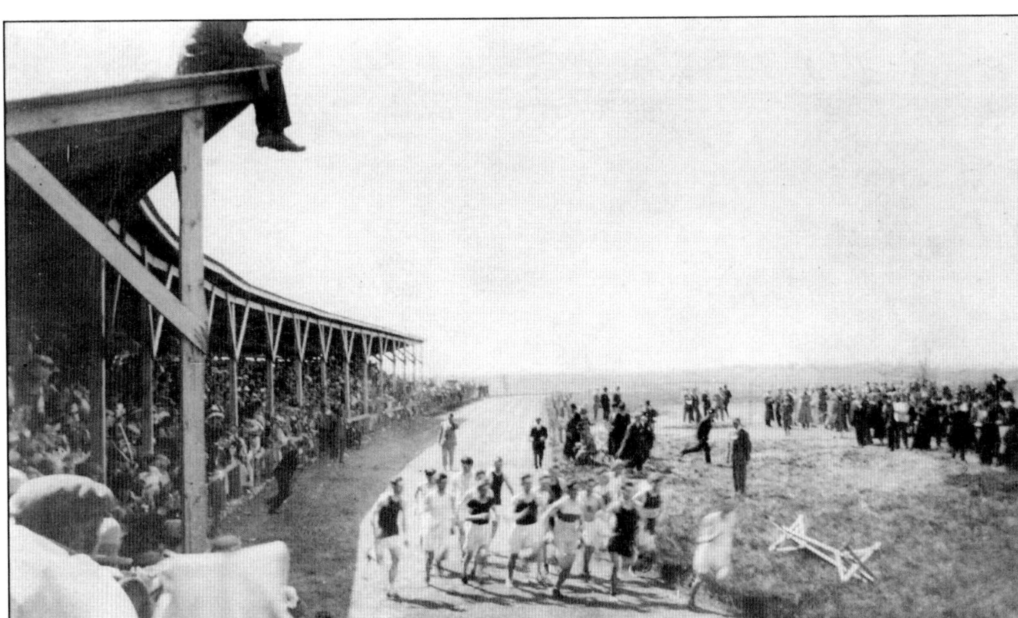

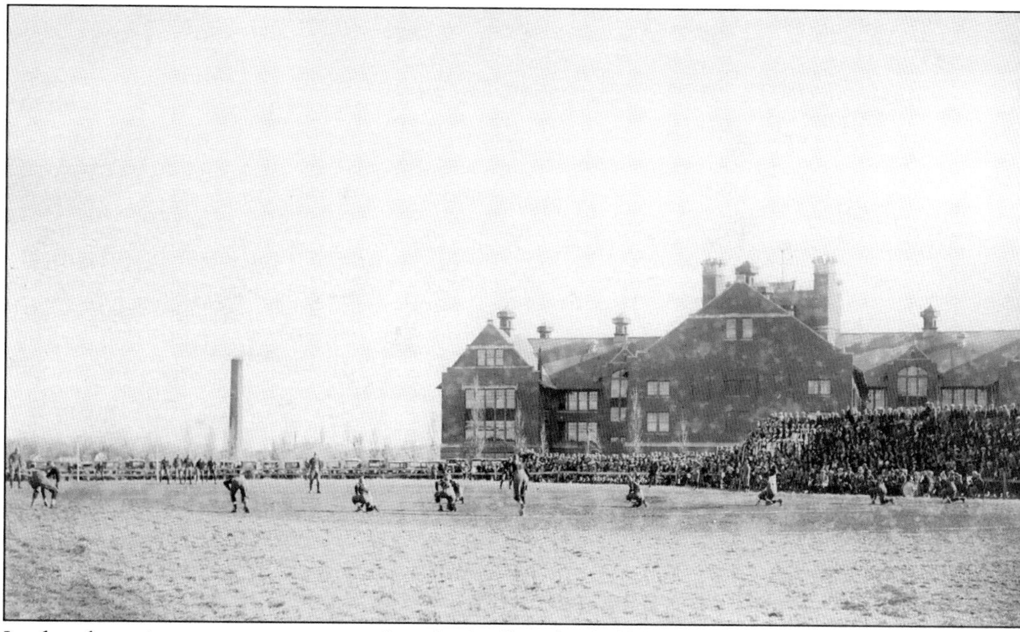

In the above image, teams prepare for a kickoff at the field behind the normal school. The first matchup for the school was October 2, 1908, against Amity (Iowa) College. The home team won its first-ever game, with assistance from a seated band and an ad hoc marching troupe that called themselves Zimmy's Zobo Zouaves, playing kazoo-like zoboes, and led by the head of the Art Department. 50 years later, the equipment had changed considerably; the football field chalked in the middle of the track was replaced by a track surrounding the football field on the west side of campus, and the band took the field at half-time in proper uniforms. (Courtesy of Northwest.)

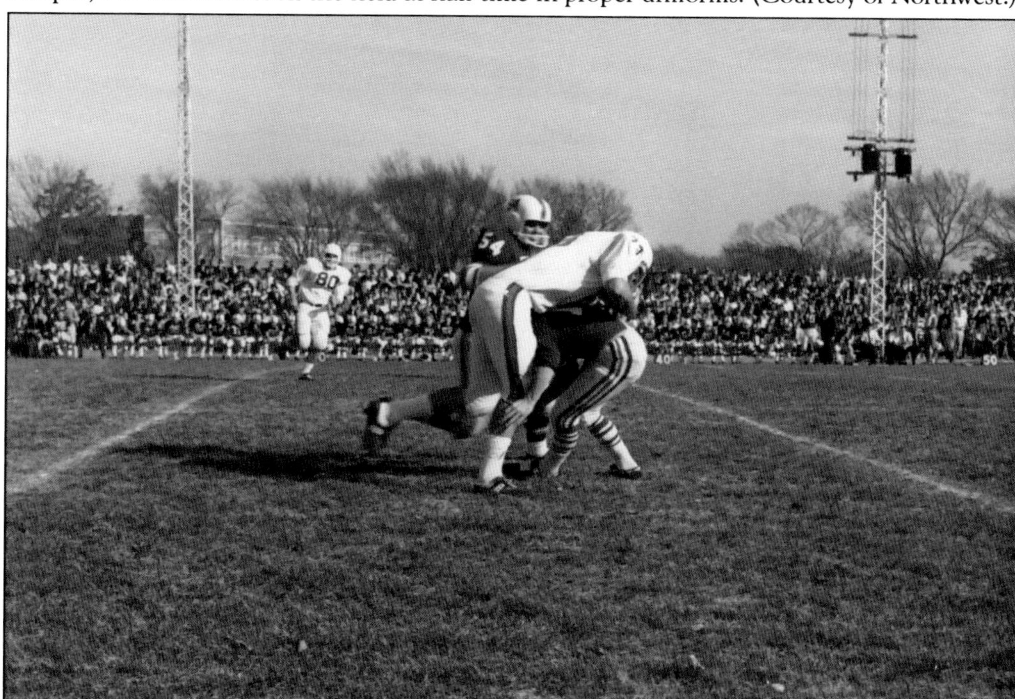

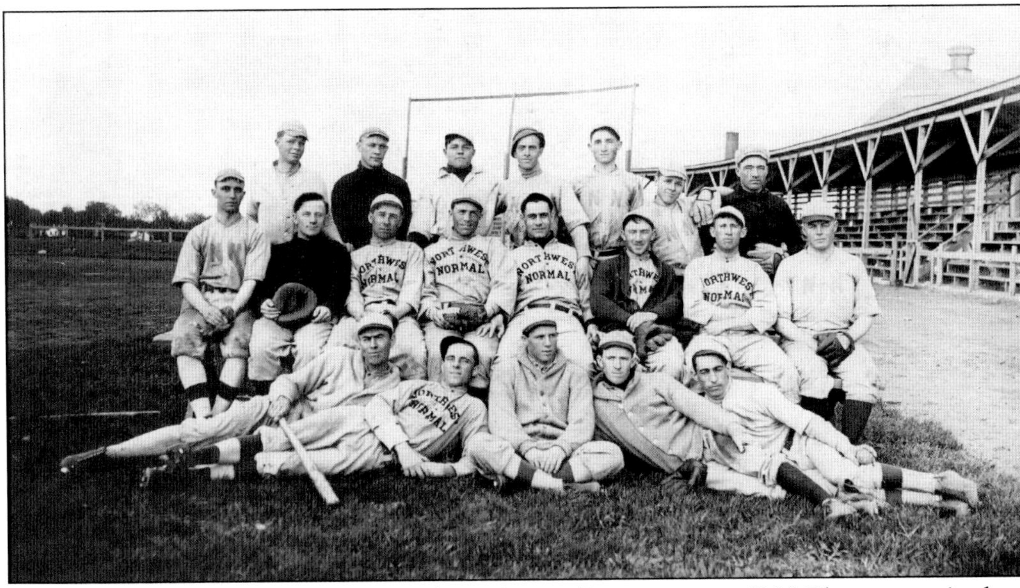

The first Normal School baseball team took on a Maryville town team in 1906. The next year's school bulletin boasted of an athletic field to promote health and encouraged students to improve themselves through baseball. The team shown here still sports the jerseys of the "Normals" worn through the 1910s, until the school achieved official designation as a college in 1919. (Courtesy of Northwest.)

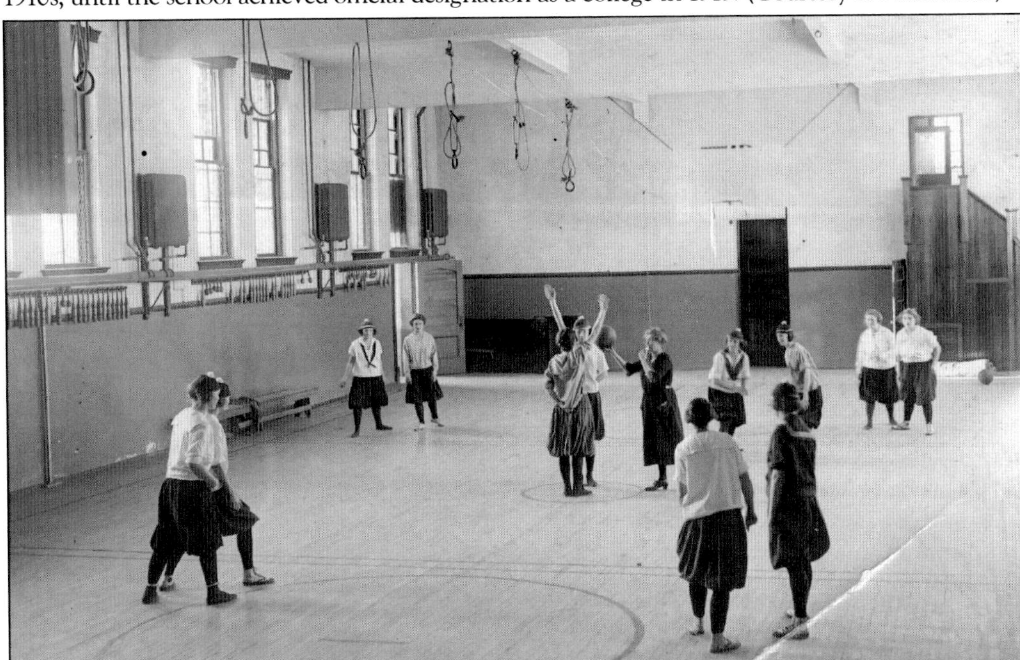

Women's physical education took place in the gymnasium under the Academic Hall theater in the administration building, next to a separate gymnasium for the men. The freshmen are seen here wearing their bloomers and beanies for a game of basketball. On the ceiling hang ropes for a kind of suspended calisthenics, and on the wall to the left are the bowling pin–shaped "Indian clubs" that were popular in the period for choreographed group exercises with young women. (Courtesy of Northwest.)

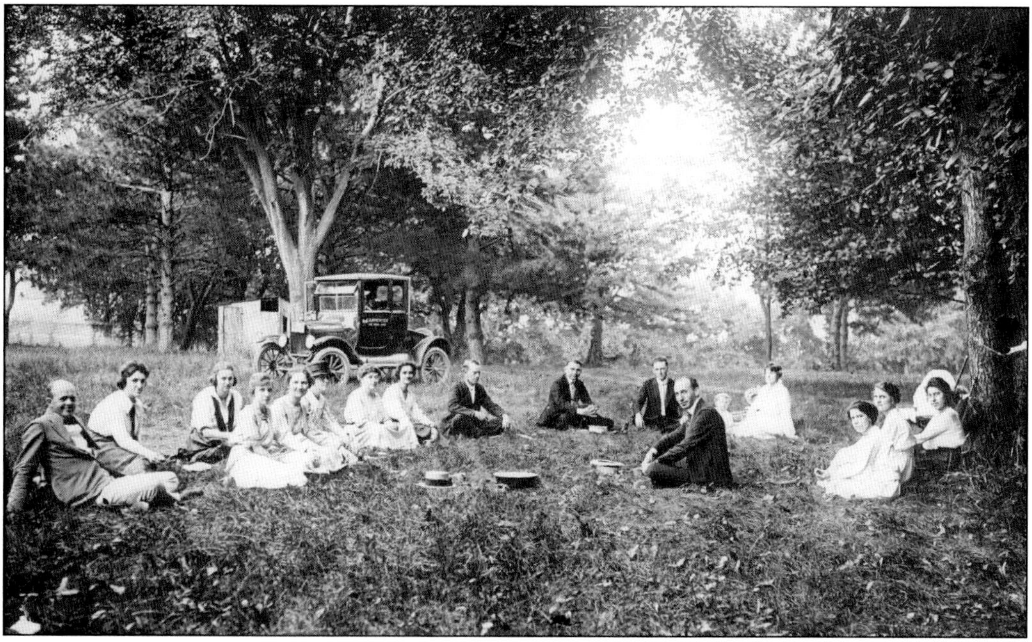

It was a beautiful day for a picnic in 1913 at the College Park, when Normal School president Ira Richardson took some of the students and staff out for a picnic. Accompanying them is Jim "Kodak Man" Carpenter, famous for traveling around Maryville to capture the grins of nearly every student in the area.

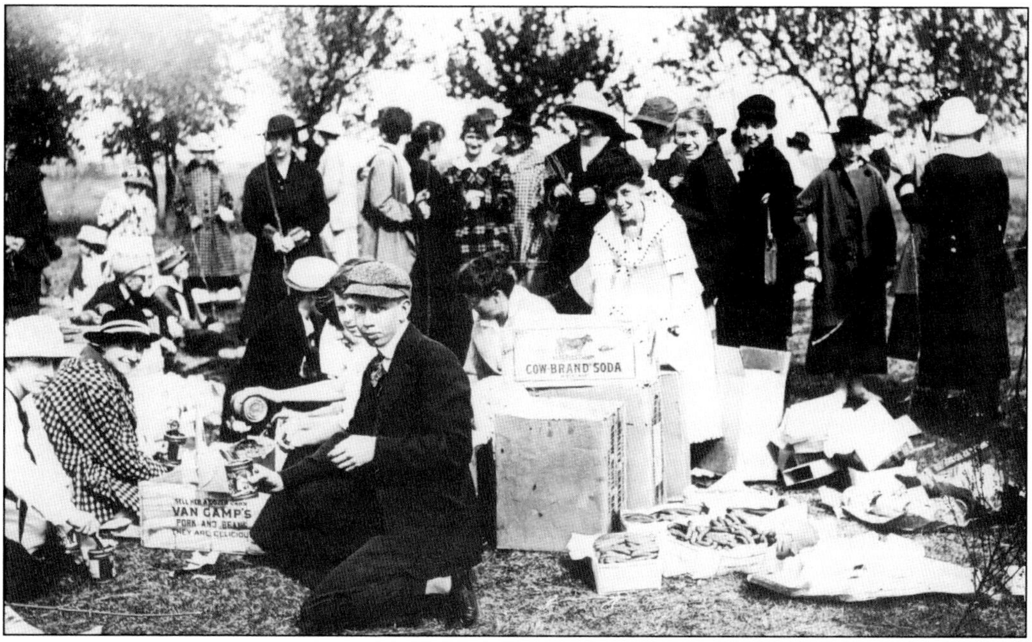

Started by the literary societies of the Normal School, Walkout Day began as a spontaneous act of celebration through rebellion. On October 18, 1916, the third Walkout Day, seen here, featured a morning walk to the picnic grounds and a wonderful lunch featuring Cow Brand Soda, Van Camp's pork and beans, and roasted wieners. For dessert, the Bee Hive Shoe Store sent several cartons of oranges. The students put up rope swings and young men dared to push the young ladies.

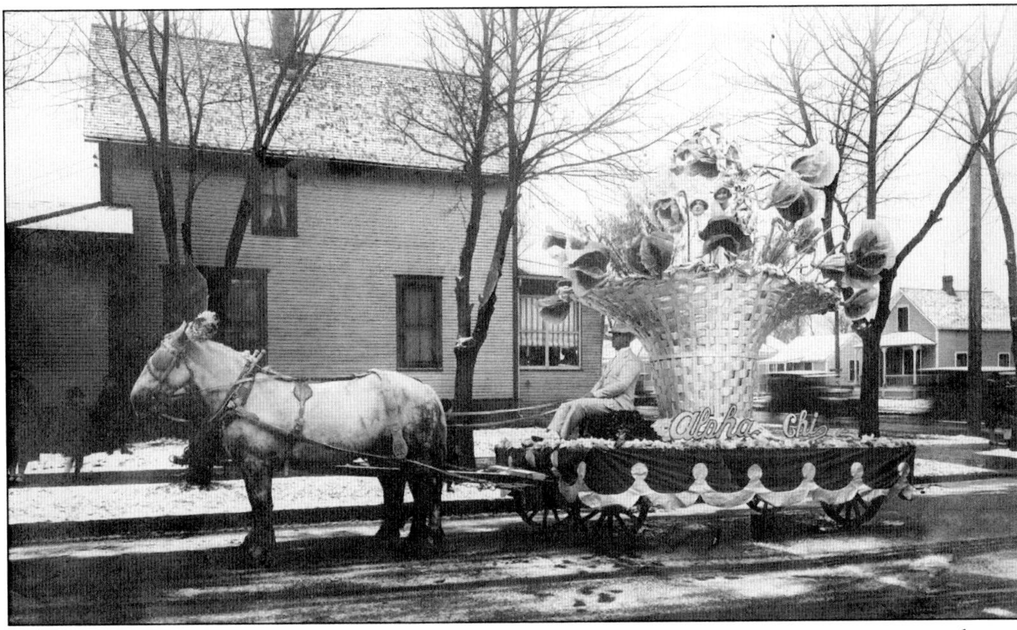

Local parades provided opportunities for school and community organizations to join together on display. Local fraternal orders and societies mixed with college fraternities, sororities, and honor societies. Above, children in the 1910s marvel at the Apha Chi (Omega) float, representing a sorority first founded nationally in 1885 as a women's professional society to promote music among college women and to "cultivate those principles that embody true womanhood." By the early 20th century, it tacked toward designation as a social sorority. A fortunate town youngster, below, in proper knickers and cap, gets the honor of carrying the banner for the State Normal School, but likely looks forward nonetheless to ageing into his first "longie suit" for public occasions. One can guess that the large flag the college women carry for the parade normally flew on the pole on the Normal School campus. (Bottom courtesy of Coby Lamb.)

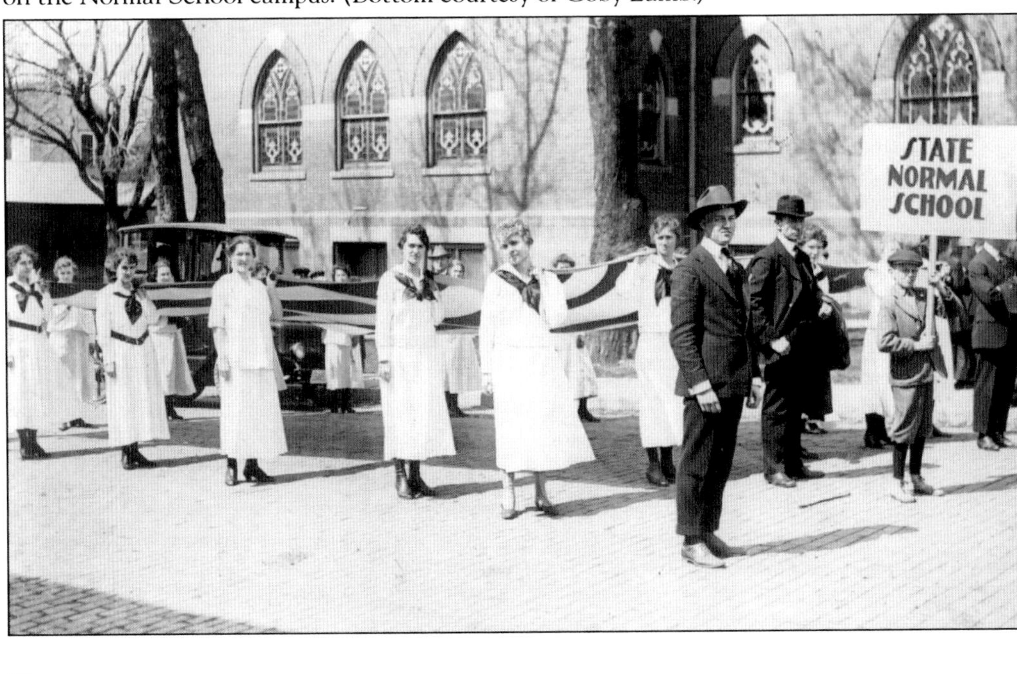

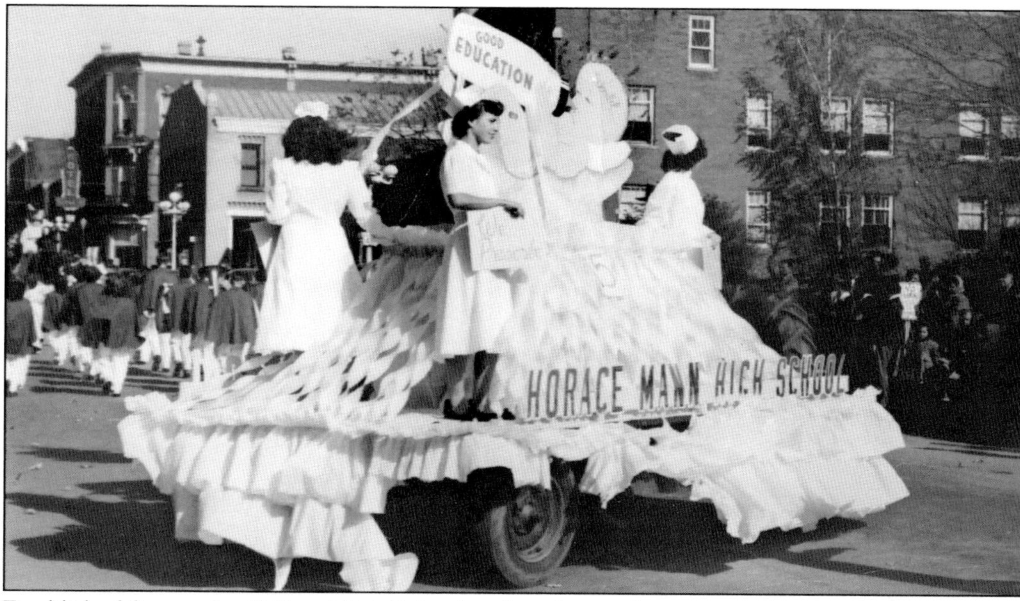

Established first as the College High School within the single structure that was the Fifth District Normal School, secondary students moved into a separate building in 1940, known as the Horace Mann High School. The school served high school students until 1960. The junior high grades were eliminated in 1968, and Horace Mann School has remained since a laboratory school for elementary grades. Many members of the Maryville community today call Horace Mann High School their alma mater. (Courtesy of Northwest.)

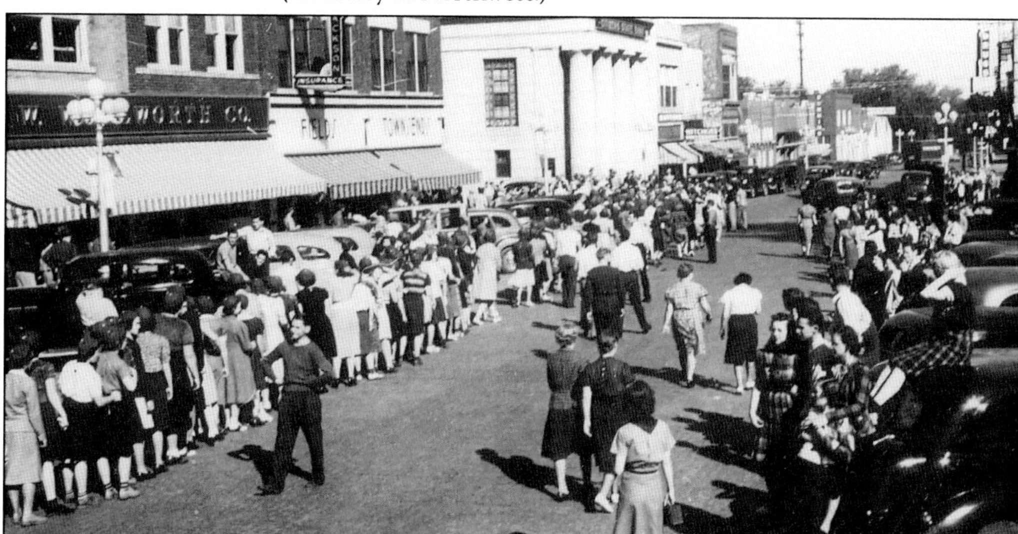

Among the events that weave together the life of the college and community, the many events surrounding homecoming are preeminent. Homecoming activities on Main Street in the 1950s still involved the mild hazing that freshmen endured at the hands of upperclassmen. The line of young ladies on the left are all wearing their green freshmen beanies, and at several points during this day's events will be cajoled into "buttoning," in which they kneel deferentially before upperclassmen strutting the Main Street and touching the button atop their beanie. (Courtesy of Northwest.)

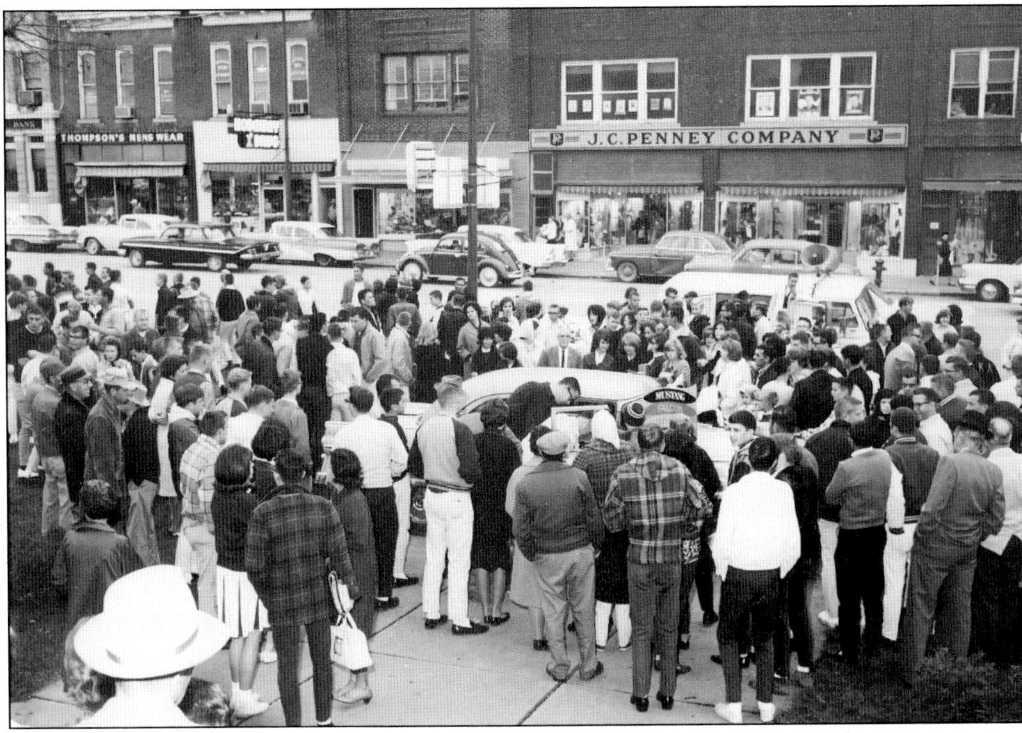

When the Ford Caravan of Music arrived in Maryville in 1965, it offered not only big name concerts to the college crowd, but fun contests. To promote the company's new four-door Fairlane sedan, Ford offered a $100 prize to the team of college students that could fit the most people inside the car. Students, faculty, and town folk watched as the girls from Northwest Missouri State's Hudson Hall successfully piled 37 coeds into the vehicle, winning the prize. The ladies' effort remained a record for the contest until Central Missouri State's Lambda Chi Alpha sorority bested it the following year. (Courtesy of Northwest.)

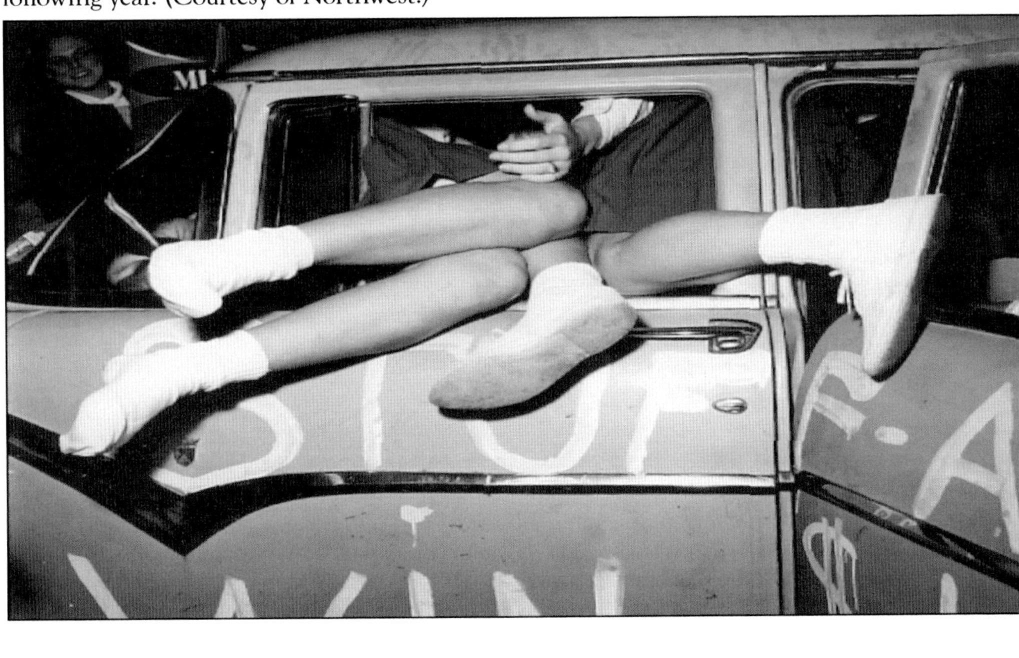

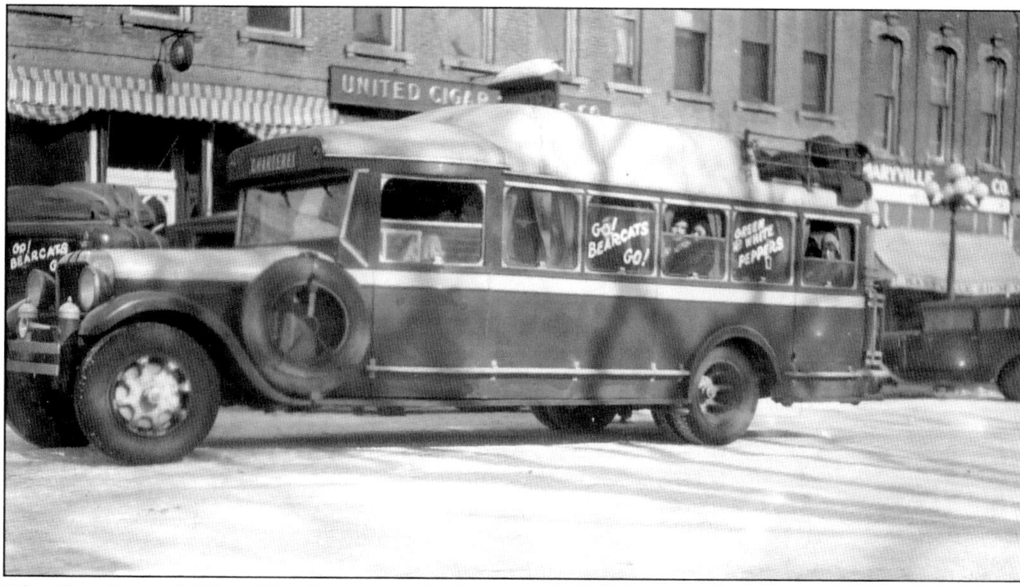

The first "pep club" at Northwest might be considered the conglomeration of musicians and kazooists who attended the 1908 football game. From that date forward, athletic events drew students who were more than mere spectators, and the expansion of college athletics through the first half of the 20th century offered an array of opportunities. Seen here in 1930, the Green and White Peppers head off to a contest. Today, the motor coaches that transport students to national championship football games find their roots in these intrepid "peppers." (Courtesy of Joyce Miller Holt.)

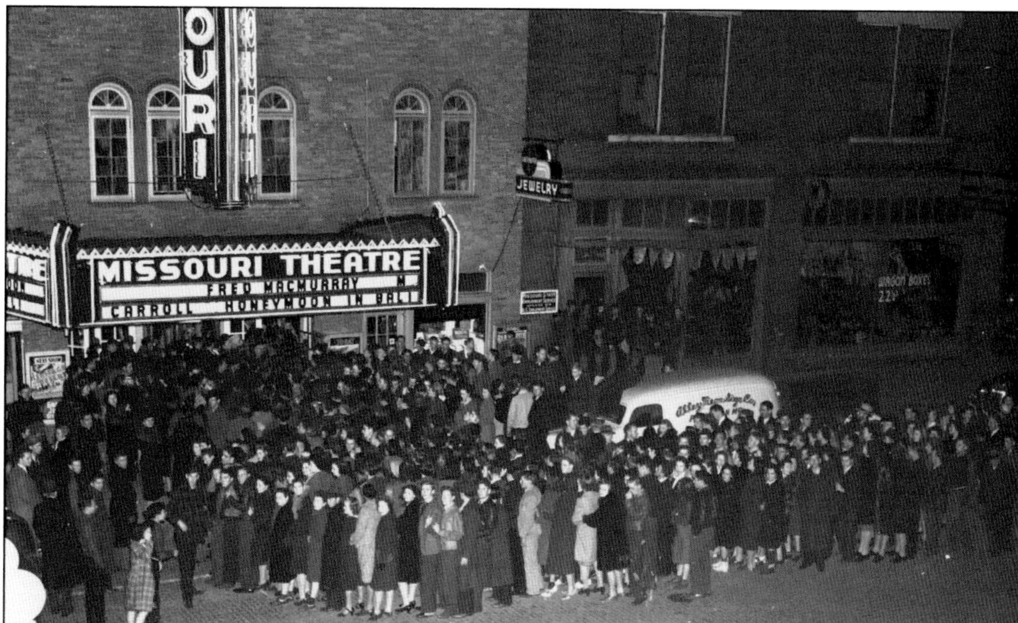

Local businesses have thrived throughout the century on entertainment dollars spent by students. Restaurants and theaters that advertised and catered to students in particular have enjoyed the benefit of the migrant population of youngsters looking for a break from their studies and life on campus. (Courtesy of Northwest.)

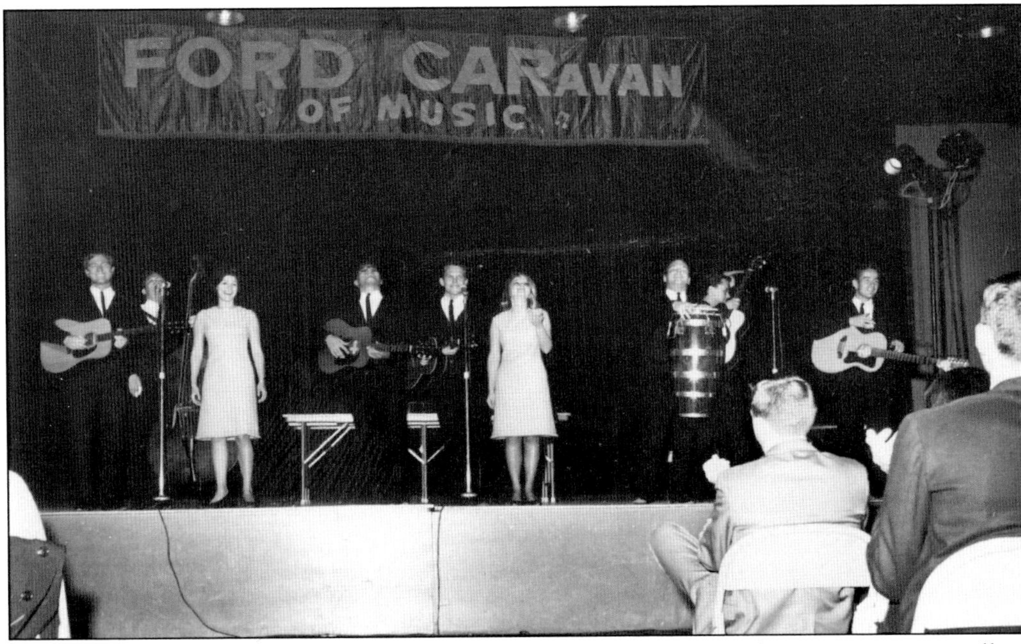

The Ford Motor Company designed the Ford Caravan of Music to advertise its cars to college students. The Caravan toured college towns across the nation, providing students with access to well-known musical acts and sideshow contests. Shown here around 1964 are the Serendipity Singers performing in Maryville. Besides a fun night out with music and friends, many students walked away with free records, hats, and other promotional items. (Courtesy of Northwest.)

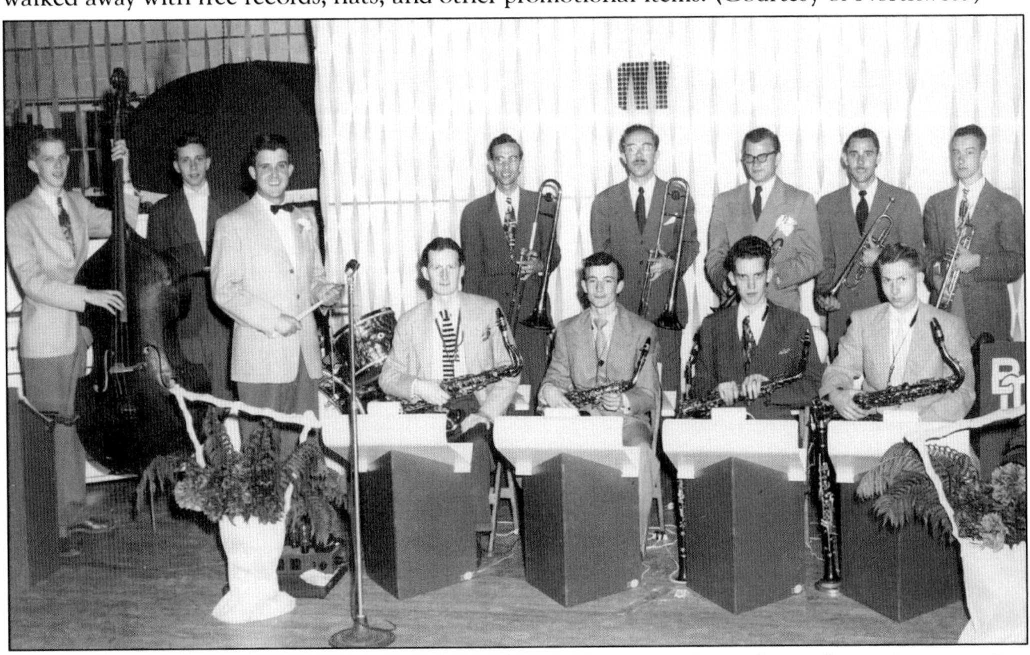

Dance bands born out of college ensembles played for events throughout the region, earning talented students a few extra dollars, professional experience, and a good time. Long-time musician Harold Hall, the trombonist on the left, provided this image from his sophomore year at Northwest in 1947. (Courtesy of Harold Hall.)

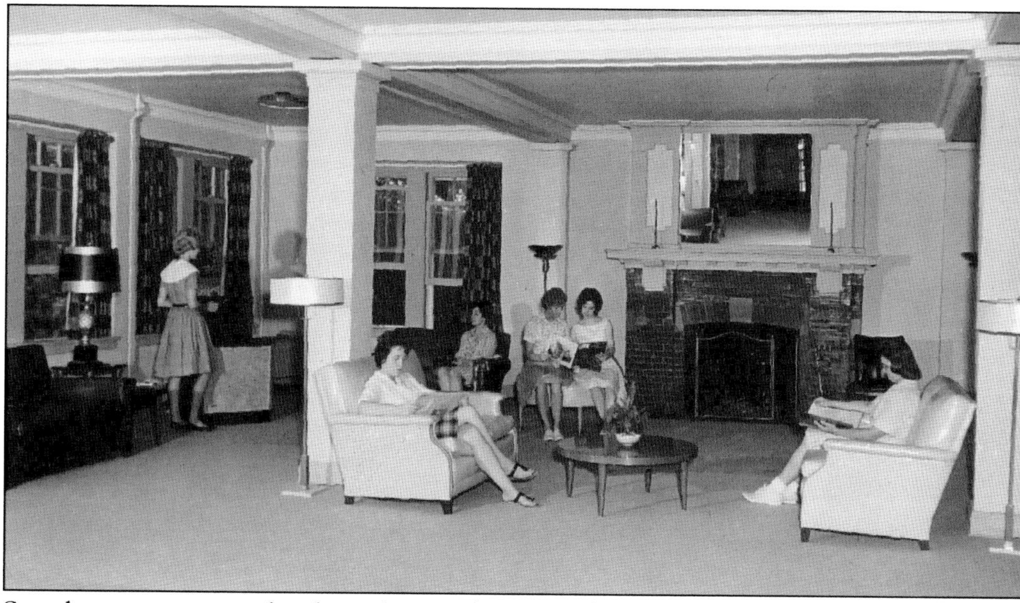

Seen here are a group of undergraduates relaxing in the community living room of Residence Hall (now Roberta Hall) in 1951. Opened as the only residence hall in 1923, it has, with a brief exception during World War II, housed only women since. The hall featured finely appointed dining rooms and parlors in which to greet guests, particularly gentlemen visitors. The building underwent significant remodeling after the explosion that struck the hall, likely within a month of this photograph. (Courtesy of Northwest.)

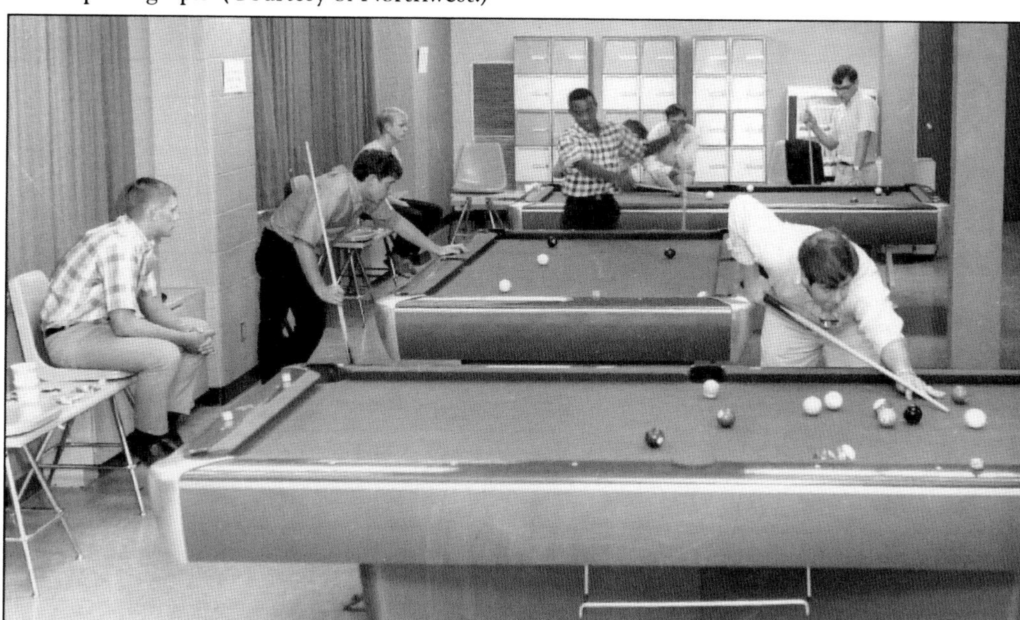

Though the pose over the table with a cigarette hanging loose invokes a seedy pool hall somewhere, these college students are never far from the more sedate environment of books, classes, and study. The growing population of students on campus has required the university throughout its history to entice new students with recreational opportunities that make life on campus enjoyable and help relieve stress. (Courtesy of Northwest.)

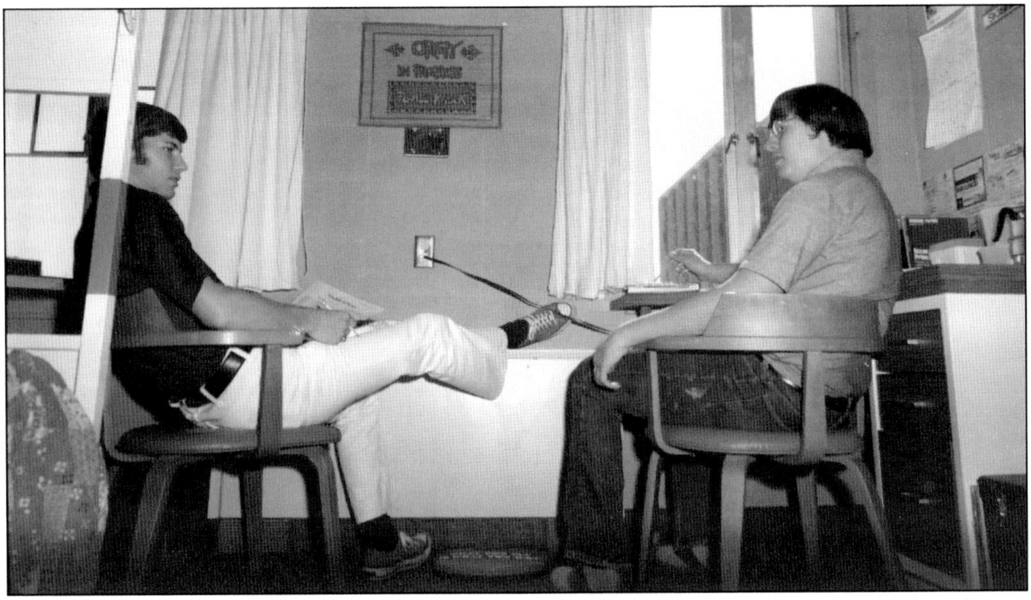

Dorm life for students at Northwest Missouri State expanded their horizons and introduced them to new friends. Dieterich Hall residents compare class schedules when they were still made by pulling cards and printed on paper. Despite the orgy warning on the gentlemen's wall, residential life remained relatively sedate under the watchful eye of resident assistants and hall directors in gender-segregated accommodations. (Courtesy of Northwest.)

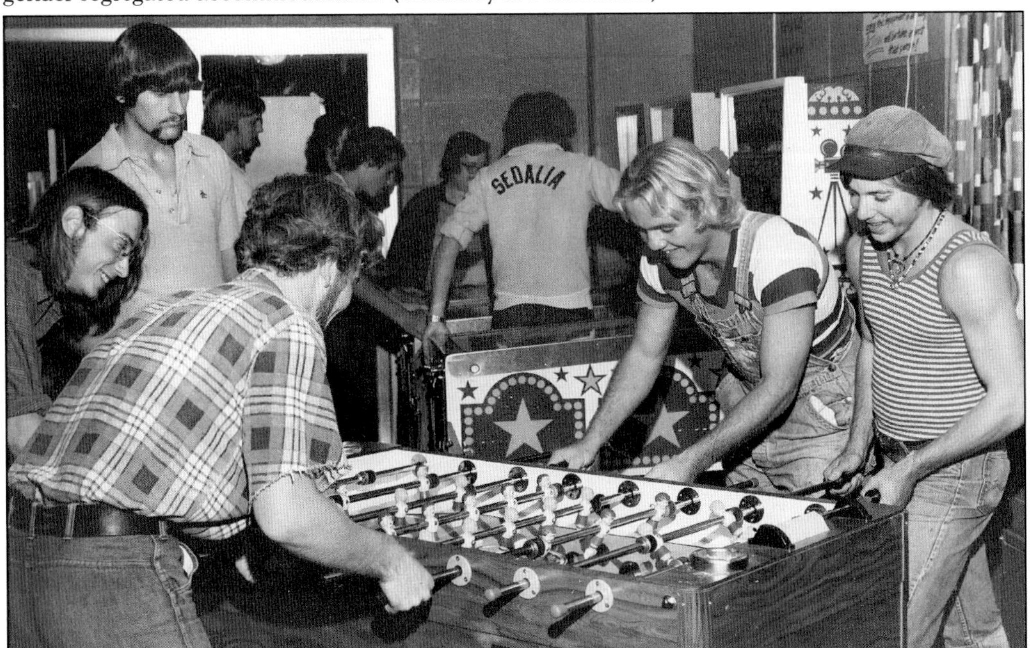

Rapid expansion in the 1960s under Pres. Robert Foster included doubling the size of the student union and adding a recreation area, bowling alley, and a barbershop. Students in the early 1970s enjoyed the wildly popular foosball, introduced to Americans by trademark holder Lawrence Patterson in 1962. Within the decade, the pinball machines on the west wall would be replaced by video games in the space today occupied by J.W.'s Grille. (Courtesy of Northwest.)

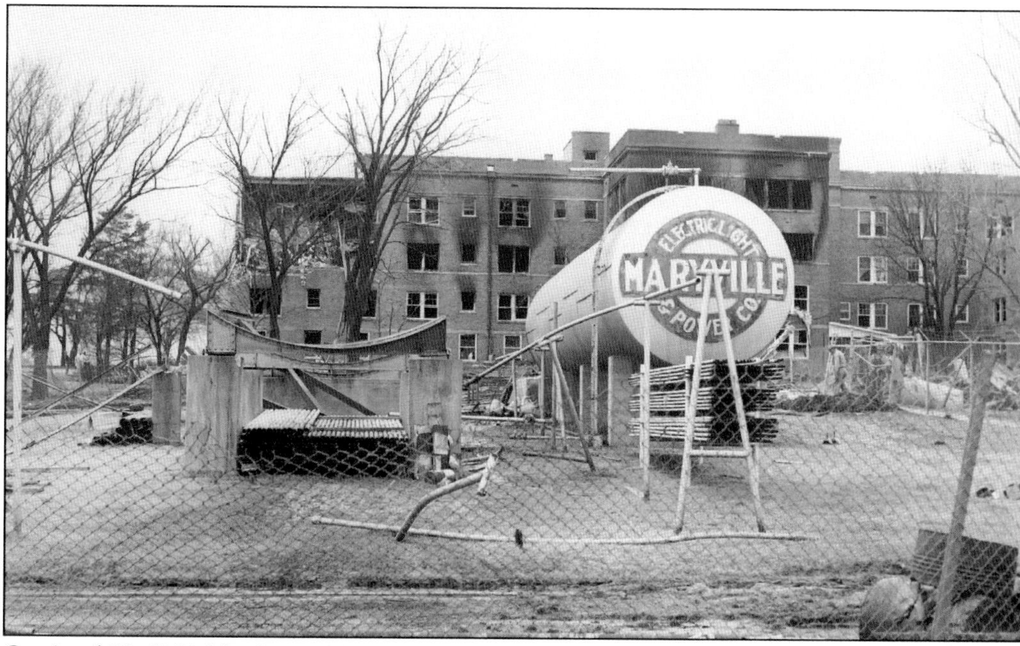

On April 28, 1951, Northwest Missouri State Teacher's College was shaken by a gas storage tank explosion and ensuing fire that engulfed a portion of the Women's Residence Hall. The disaster critically injured four women, and one of those, Roberta Steel, died from her injuries over a year later. The university later renamed the dorm Roberta Hall in her honor. In a show of the strong bond between the university and community, local families took into their homes many of the girls that were displaced, and many others pooled resources to restock some of the girls' wardrobes. Debate continued for months over the level of wisdom in the location of the tanks so close to the dorms, with the outcome being the clearing of the old industrial rail siding that now serves as a parking lot east of Roberta Hall. (Courtesy of Northwest.)

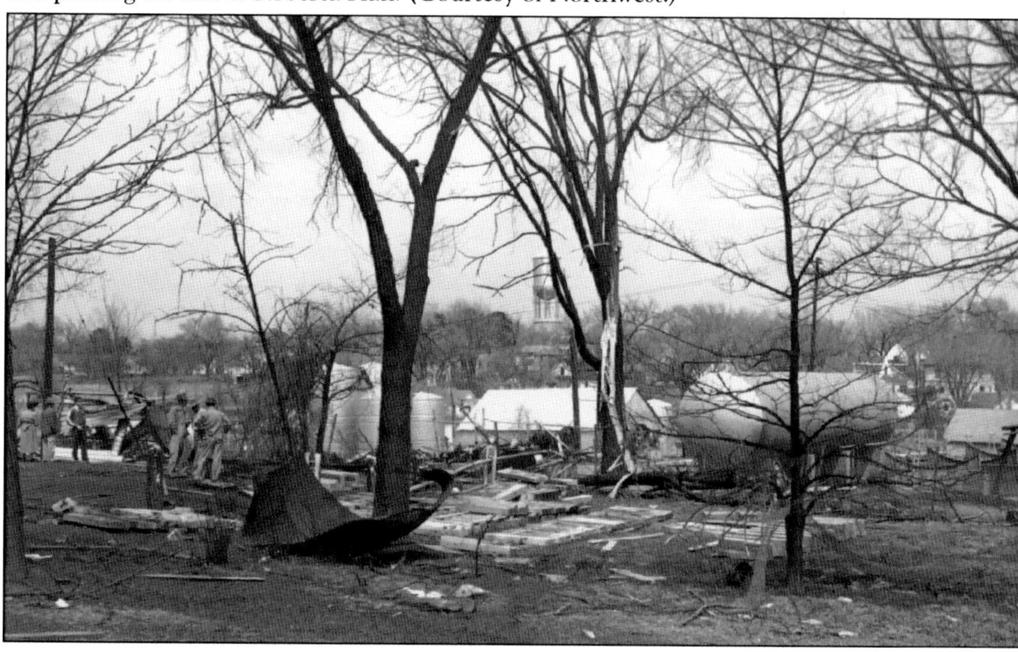

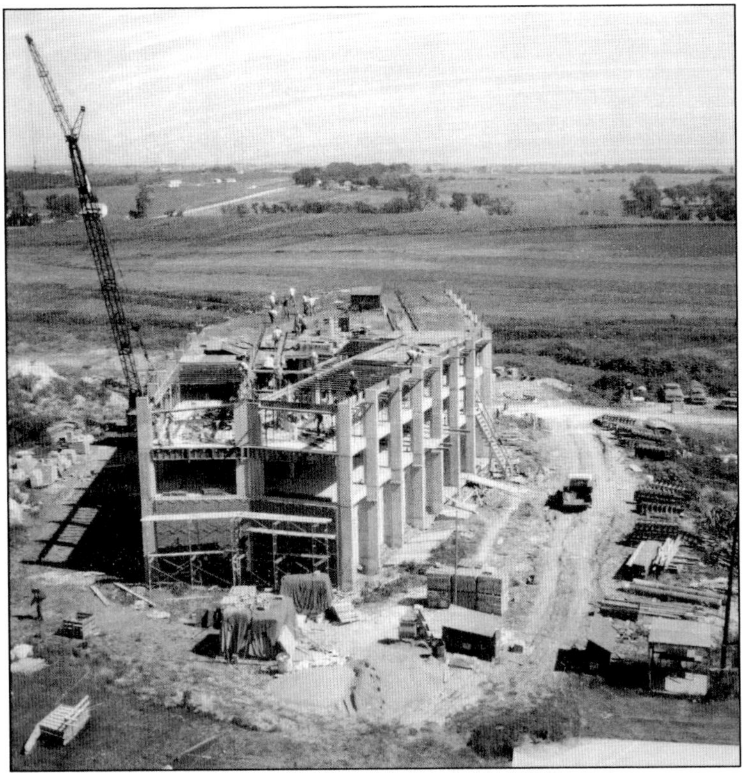

The population of Maryville grew significantly as a result of tremendous growth in the college from 1945 to the 1970s. The G.I. Bill and other factors filled colleges, with Northwest seeing its population grow from 750 students in 1950 to around 5,000 in 1970. From 1965 to 1971, the school built four high-rise dormitories, the last of these being Millikan Hall, seen under construction here from its neighbor Phillips Hall. Four more high-rises on the original architect's drawings were never built. (Courtesy of Northwest.)

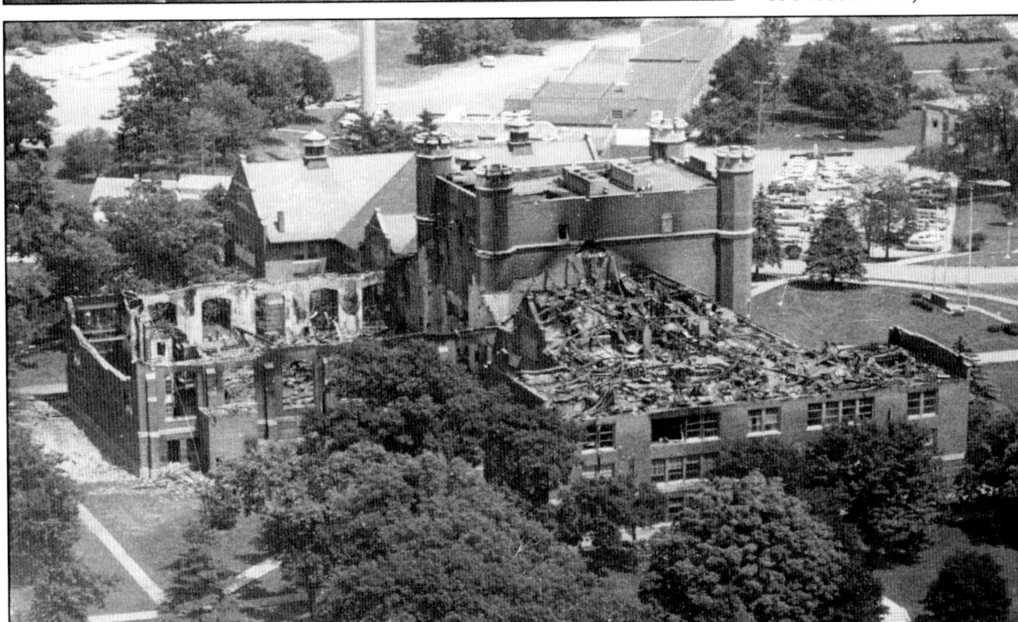

On July 24, 1979, an electrical fire spread through the iconic Administration Building and destroyed at least 60 percent of the facility. The fire ravaged the theater inside the north wing, and destroyed the third and fourth floors of the west wing. The fire displaced multiple academic and administrative departments, but the spirit of Northwest persevered and returned to the building in 1981 with a renewed sense of hope. (Courtesy of Northwest.)

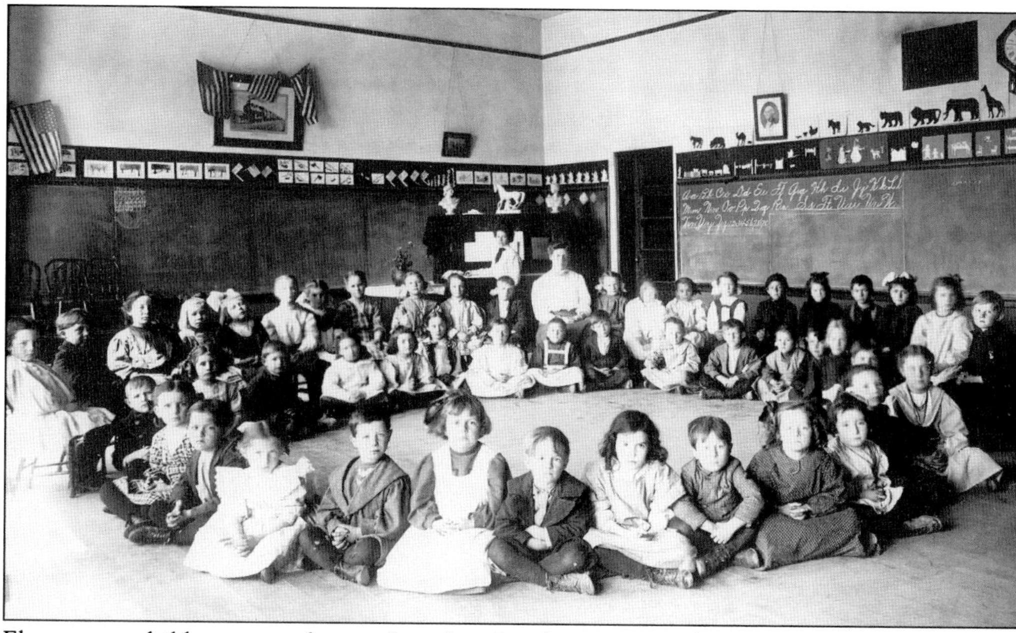

Elementary children pause from a day of studies for a unique class portrait. The room tells of a balanced curriculum of art, music, and the "three Rs." At the turn of the century, Maryville supported elementary classes in its central public school, three ward elementary schools, two Catholic schools, and a separate school for black children that operated from 1870 to 1921. The advent of the Normal School initiated an additional elementary lab school on the college campus.

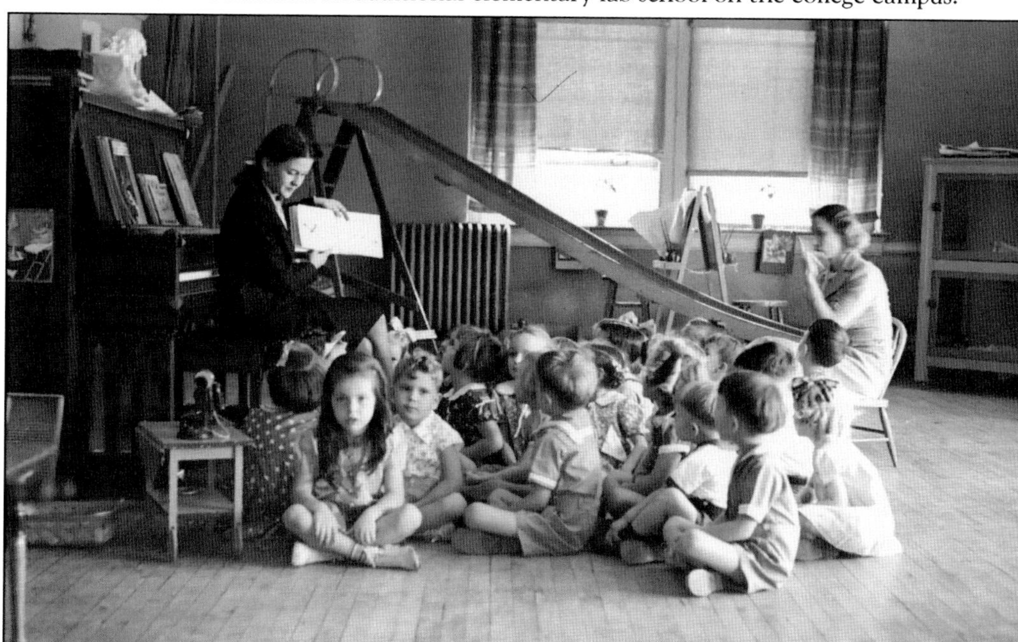

An elementary class is seen here in the central Washington School building in 1939. This wonderful room allowed for a piano, an outdoor slide brought inside, and enclosures for small class pets. Torn between a good story and the photographer's camera, the children exude the timeless nature of life under the age of eight.

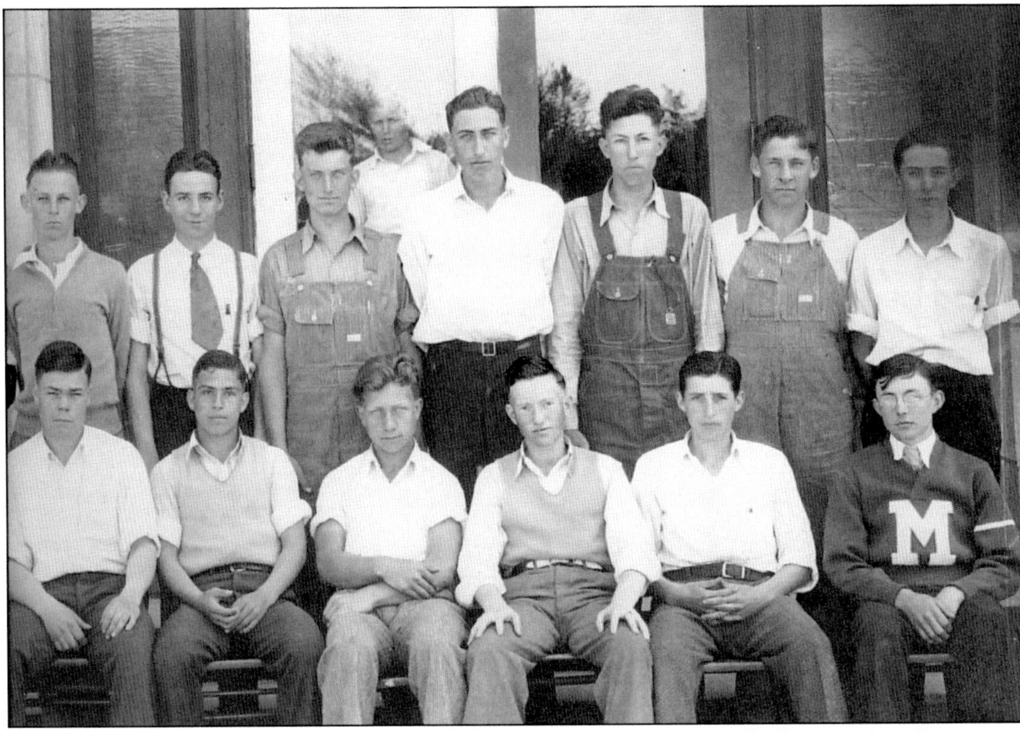

The 1935 College High School yearbook commented of its boys "kittenball team" that, "composed chiefly of inexperienced players, it suffered a disastrous season, losing three games and failing to score in the win column. Bad weather hampered practice somewhat but Glenn Marr and Gerald Stigall, the coaches, were turning over a promising group for next year." Though generally displaced by the term "softball" by the early 1930s, the variant of baseball that used a larger ball and a smaller playing field dates to a Thanksgiving Day game invented at the Farragut Boat Club in Chicago.

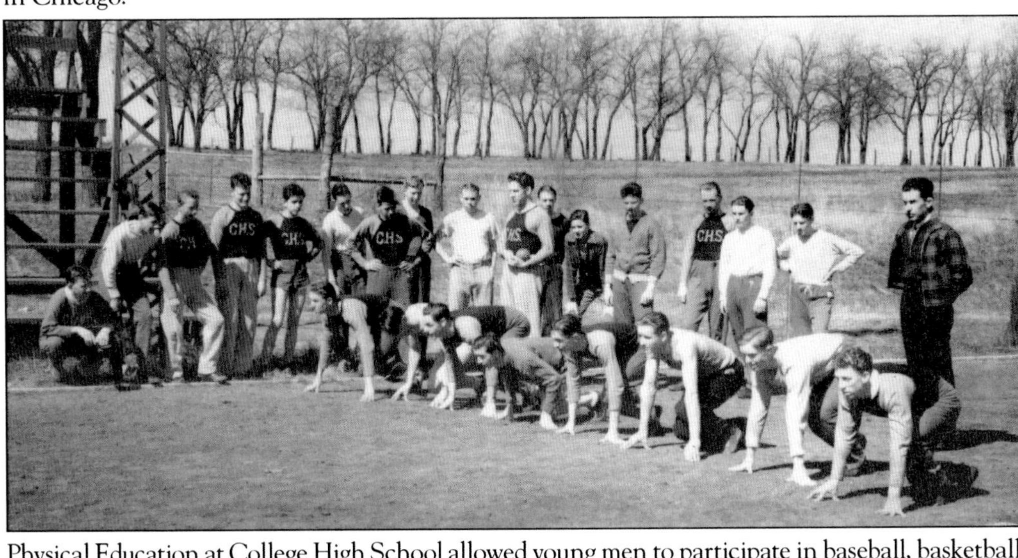

Physical Education at College High School allowed young men to participate in baseball, basketball, track, social dancing, swimming, and tennis. Young women could choose to participate in volleyball, soccer, basketball, general gym, rhythmics, social dancing, and swimming.

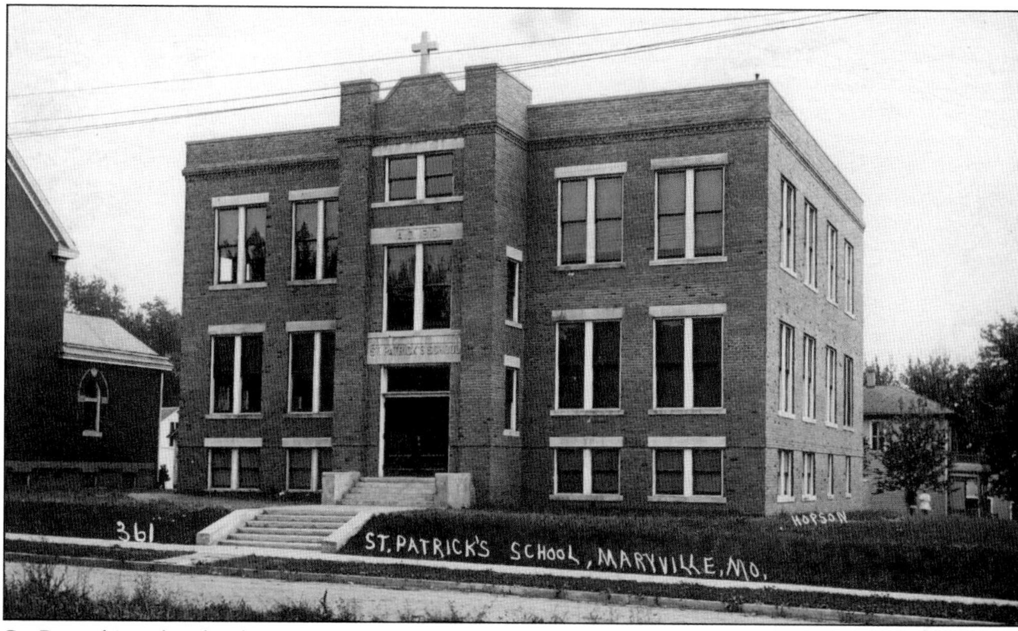

St. Patrick's School, adjacent to St. Patrick's Catholic Church at the corner of First and Fillmore Streets, was conducted by the Benedictine Sisters. The school housed grammar grades, high school, and "commercial courses" that included shorthand and typewriting.

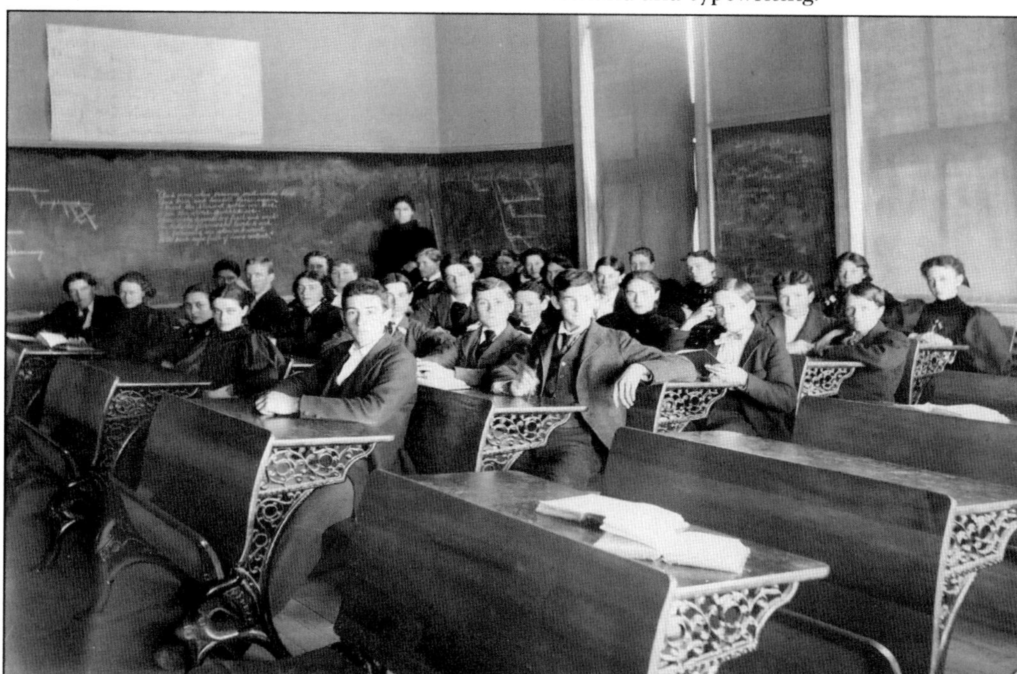

An early view of life at Maryville High School brings us Miss Pratt's class in 1897. Young men and women, dressed in their finest, sit stiffly for the photographer. One can imagine as soon as hearing "got it!" a rapid return to their original seats and restless motion beginning in earnest again. Heavy wrought iron double desks offered stability and efficient use of space, but little comfort for the users.

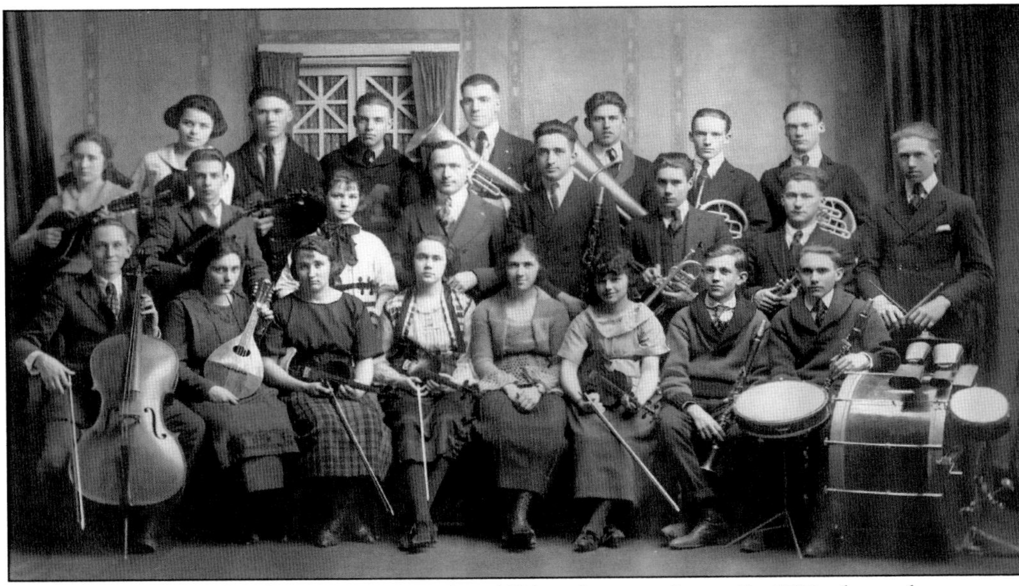

The first high school orchestra was started in 1914 with six students. By 1922, the orchestra grew to 35 members, but then suffered a period of lapse. College faculty re-instituted the orchestra, and in 1934 Maryville High graduate William Gaugh, with degrees from Northwest State Teachers College and graduate studies at Columbia University, the Chicago Musical College, Northwestern University, and Iowa State, returned to his alma mater to teach music. Seen here is one of his orchestras from the 1930s. (Courtesy of Coby Lamb.)

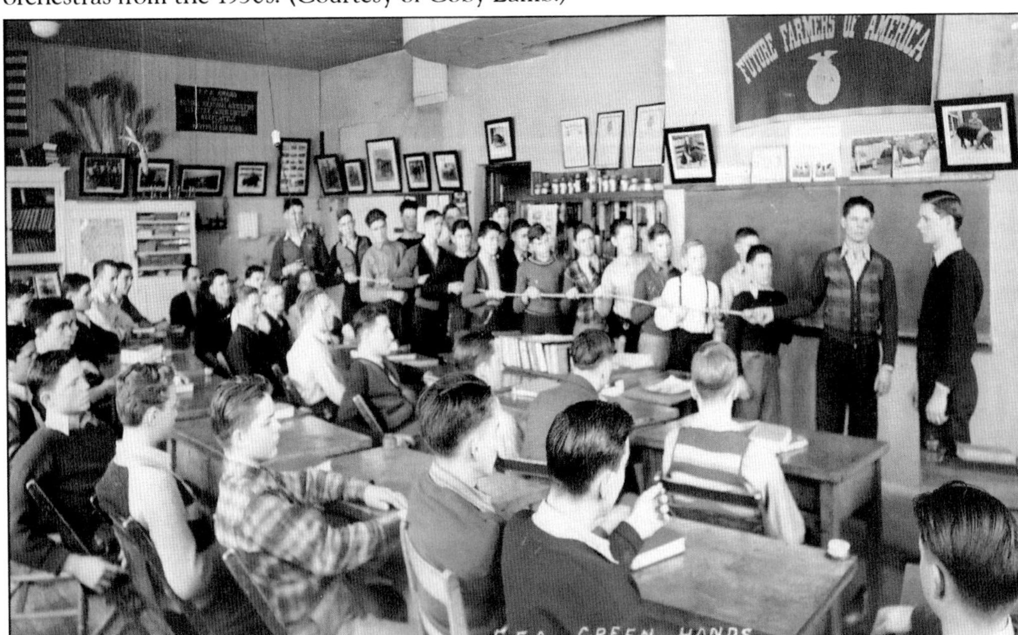

Future Farmers of America was founded in 1928 as a youth organization for those in rural communities who were interested in farming or livestock. The Maryville High School Chapter through 1939–1940 earned a substantial $11,836 in income from its projects. Members traveled to events around the region, including livestock judging, grain judging, dairy judging, and entomology team events in Kansas City and Columbia.

Perhaps hearkening back to the Washington High School tradition that on the last day of school the climb be made, and the bell be rung, seniors celebrate the last day of school and the journey they face ahead in life. The school was founded in 1908 and later became Maryville Middle School in 1965. This building was erected in 1908, after the prior Washington School had deteriorated.

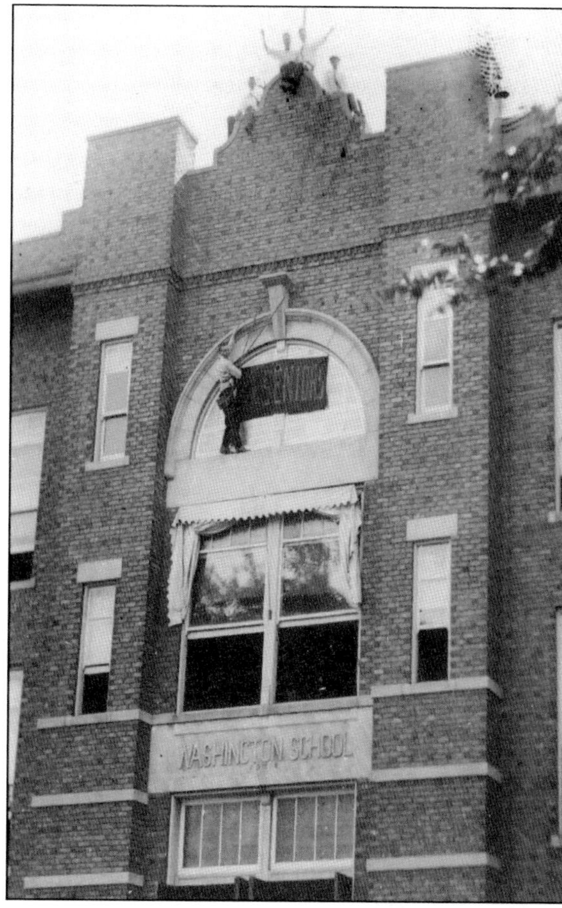

High school yearbooks often provided opportunity for the high-jinks and clowning around to gain a place in history. A standard bit in the 1930s was writing on the bottom of shoes. No one needed to know why—it was just funny.

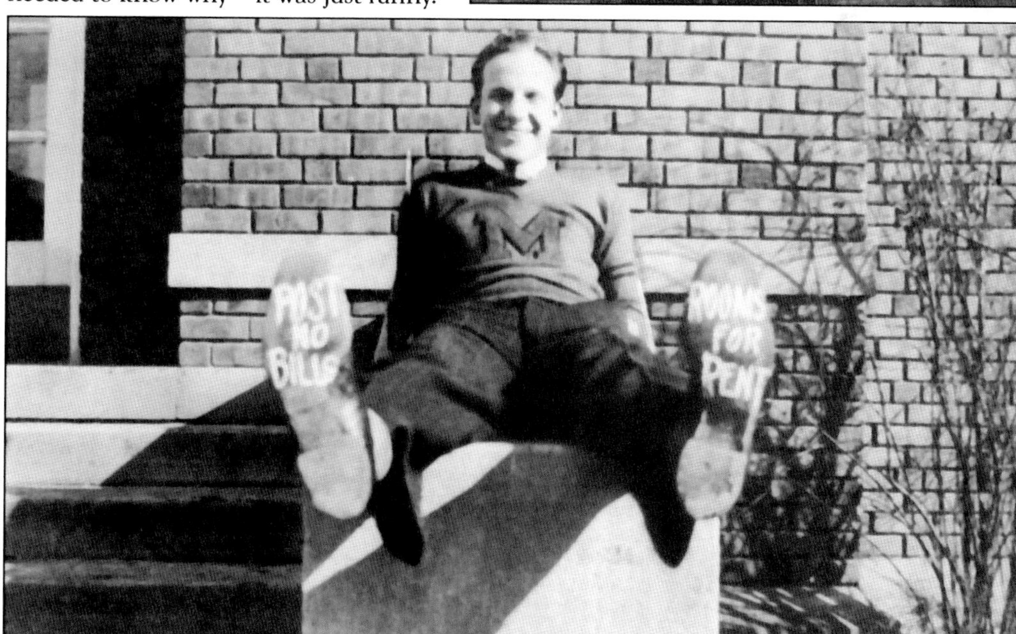

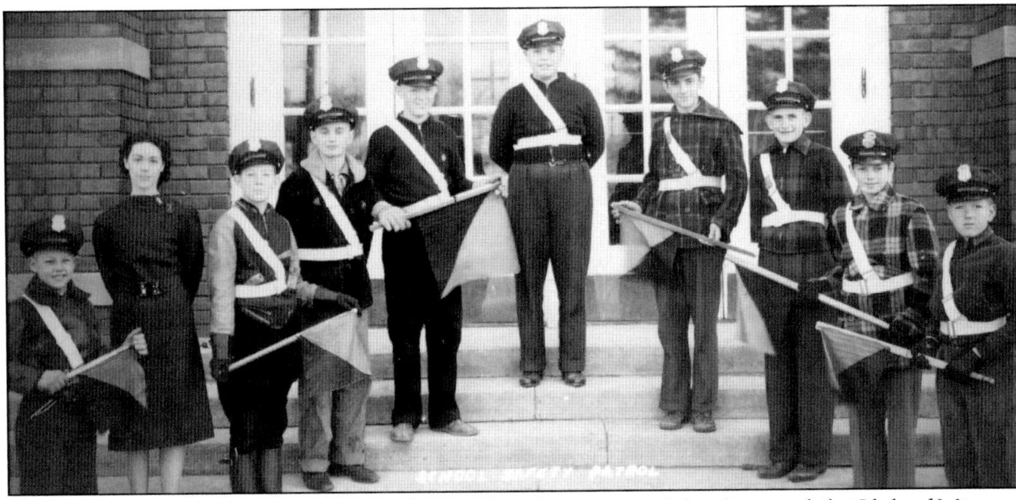

The school's "Boys Patrol," established in 1930 at the urging of the Automobile Club of Missouri and seen here in 1938, was stationed in a three-block radius around the high school to direct traffic and assist students. At the time of this image, the patrol could boast seven years of accident-free work. The Chamber of Commerce bought this crew a set of all-weather coats to get them through Maryville's fickle conditions.

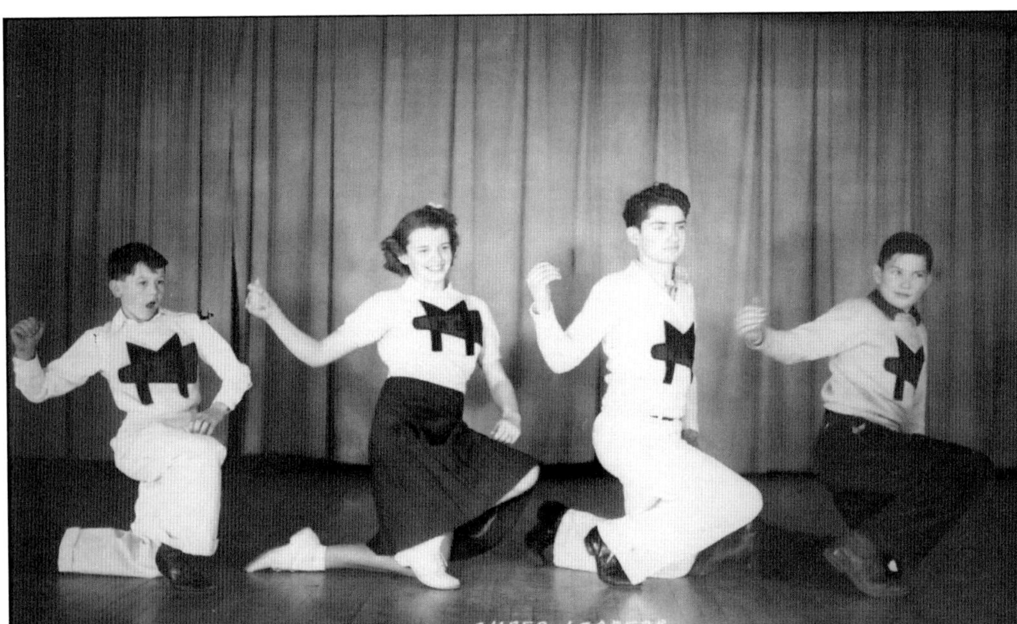

The cheerleaders of Maryville High School in 1940 hearken back to the days when boys could outnumber the girls on the high school "yell squad." The cheerleaders were assisted by the girl "Spooferettes" and boy "Spoofers," who offered assistance from the stands.

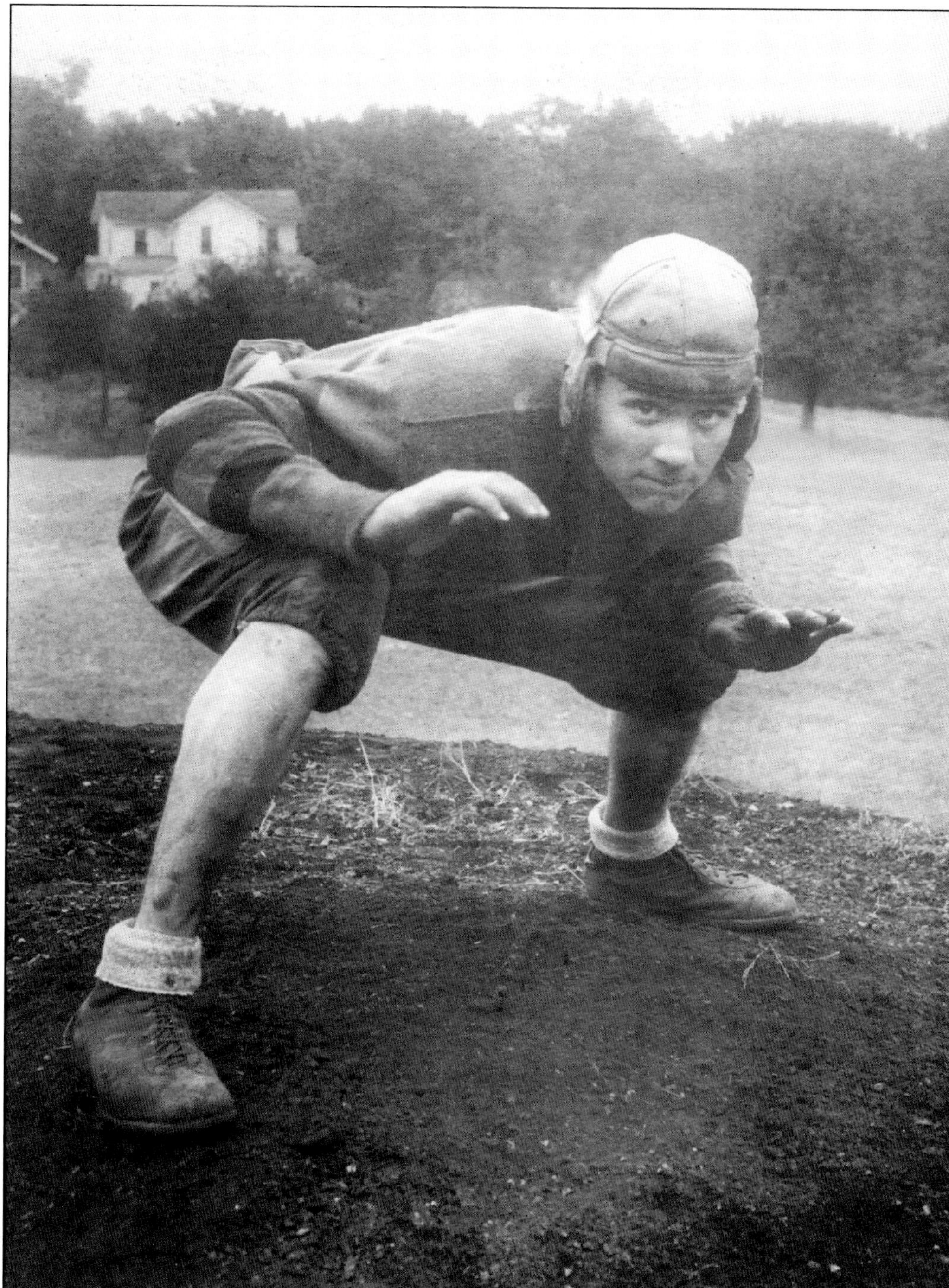

A Maryville High School football player, guard Curtis "Cutter" New, strikes a classic pose in 1926. Around the country parents and school officials debated whether the relatively new sport, given its propensity for serious and sometimes even fatal injuries, should be banned. No such controversy seems to have dampened enthusiasm in Maryville, save perhaps college president Henry Taylor's attempt to stir a preference for track and field.

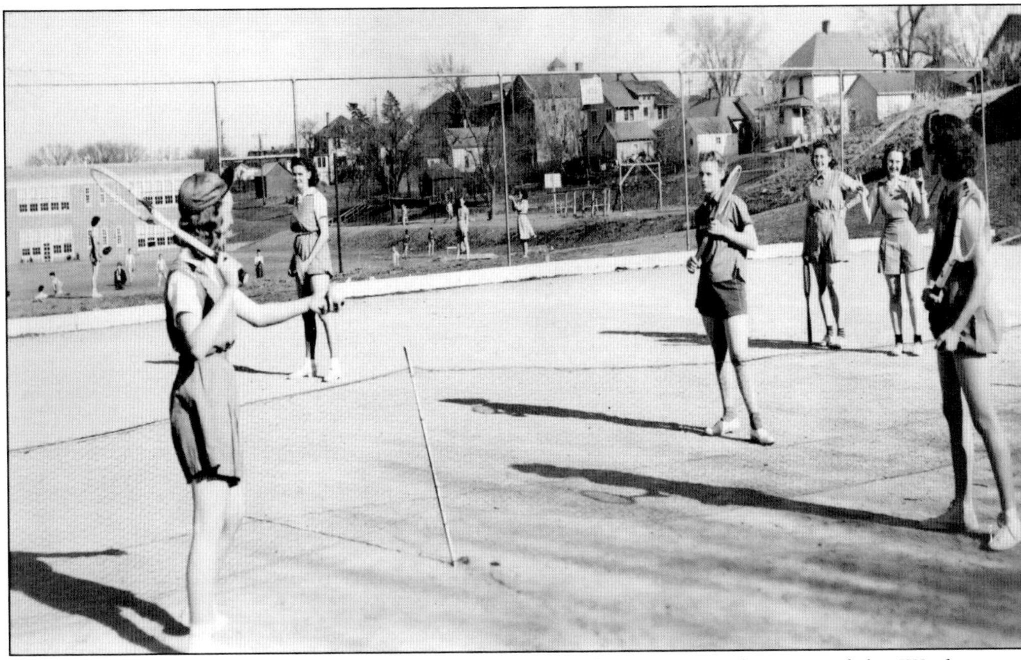

The Maryville girls' tennis team practices in 1940 on the courts to the west of the Washington School. Senior high girls' sports that year included tennis, volleyball, basketball, softball, relays, kickball, and Indian club drills. Girls also participated in an archery club. The new elementary building, now Eugene Field Elementary school, can be seen further down the hill.

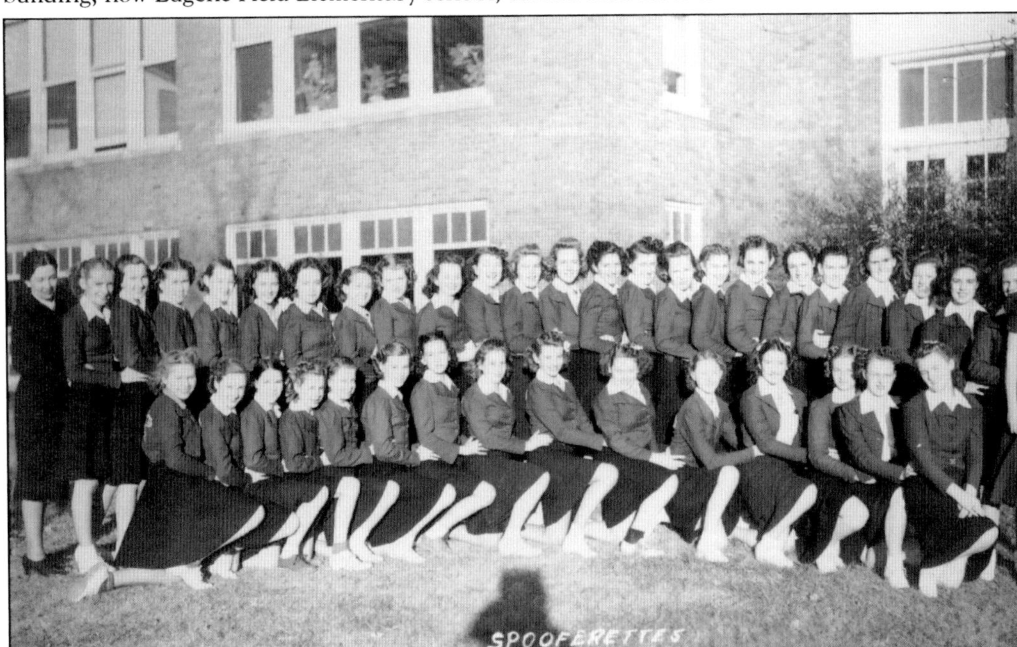

The Spooferettes were organized in the fall of 1928 for the purpose of instilling more pep and enthusiasm in the student body. The team cheered and performed "stunts" at basketball games, football games, and assemblies. An all-male team of Spoofers started performing in 1929. Both groups had 25–40 members through the 1930s.

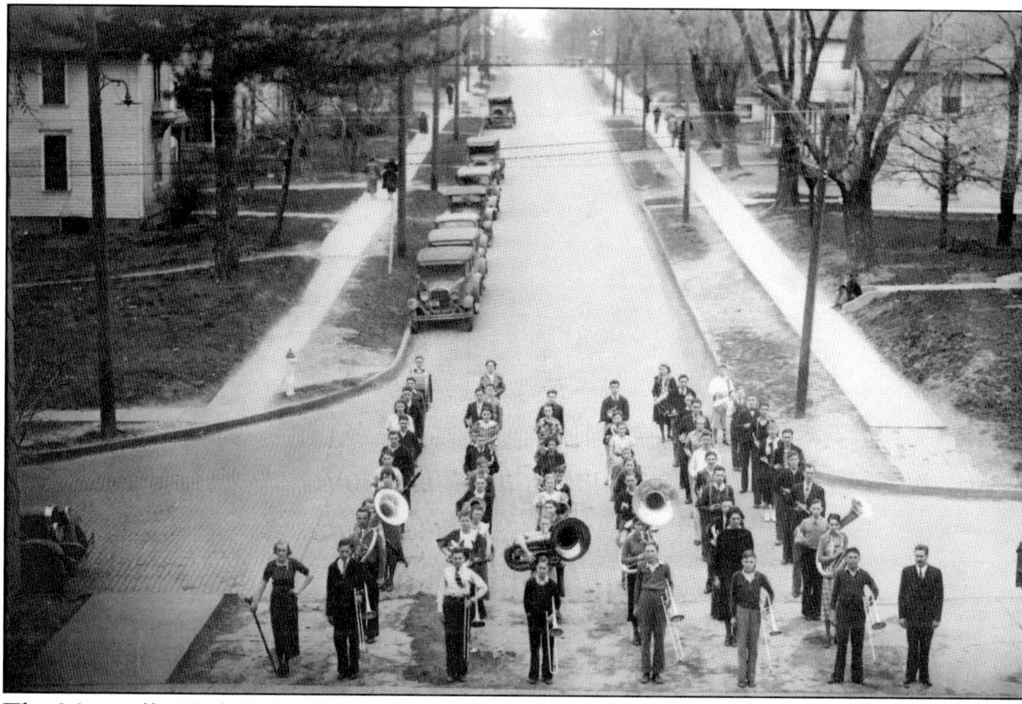

The Maryville High School marching band poses in the fall of 1934 on East First Street, photographed from an upper floor of the school building. In addition to the familiar marching instrumentation, this band marched with a bassoon and, among the bass horns, two helicons, a sousaphone, and an impressive young woman hefting a concert tuba.

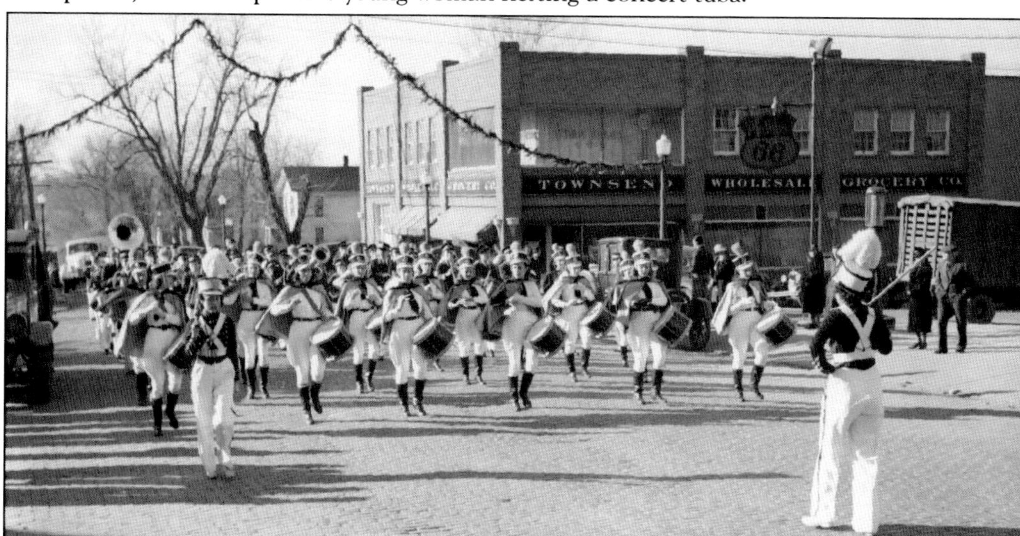

The Maryville Girls Drum and Bugle Corps passes by Townsend grocery at the corner of Fourth and Buchanan Streets in a 1939 parade, leading the regular high school marching band behind them. The girls' corps was inspired by the popular municipal corps of the 1930s, including Maryville's own adult men's corps.

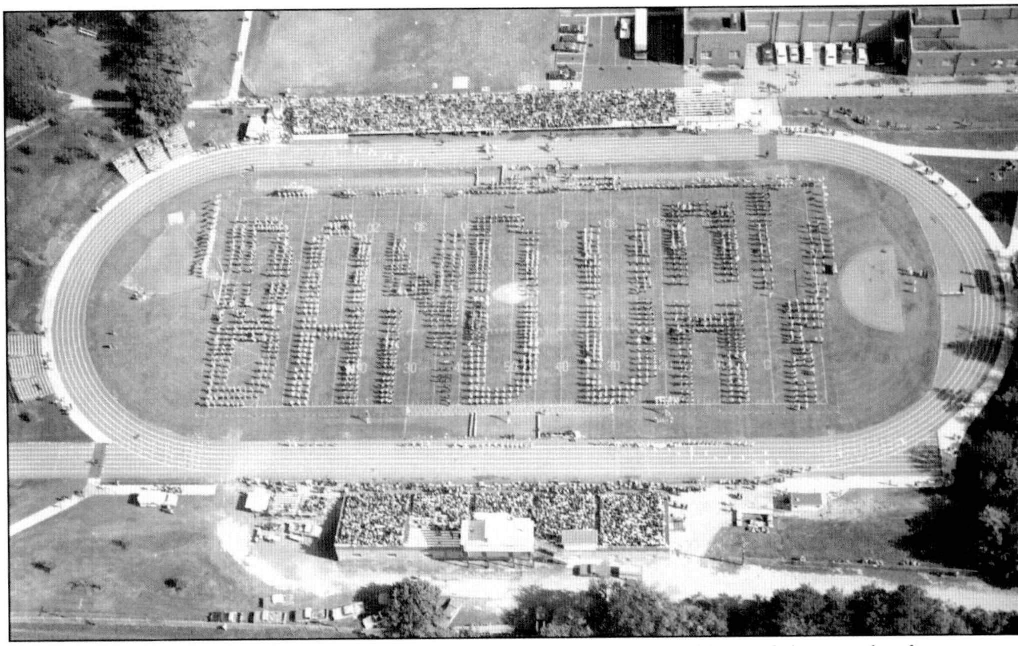

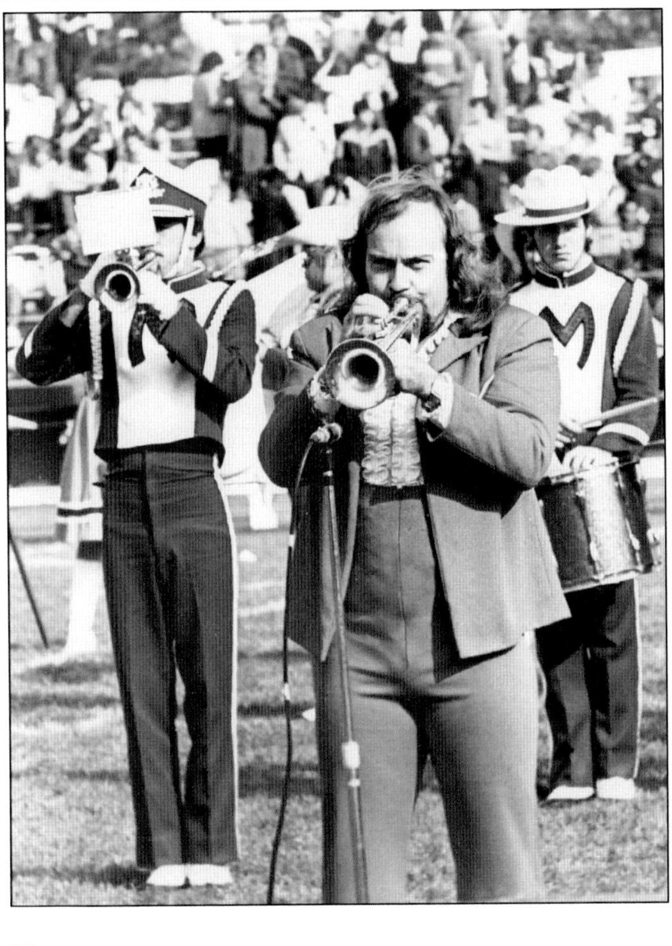

One of the regular features of the fall sports and marching band season through the 1960s and 1970s were the "mass bands" that accompanied a Fall Band Day competition. Bands from all of the participating schools joined together in a half-time performance that brought together the university, community, and surrounding schools.

Music has served for over a century as a community experience in Maryville, strengthened by local performers, public school programs, and the state university. Often, they come together in parades, contests, and performances at athletic events. In this example, Don Struve, member of the area show band Festival, joins college students and new friends at a half-time performance at a 1983 Northwest Missouri State University football game.

Five

Folks, Ordinary and Unusual

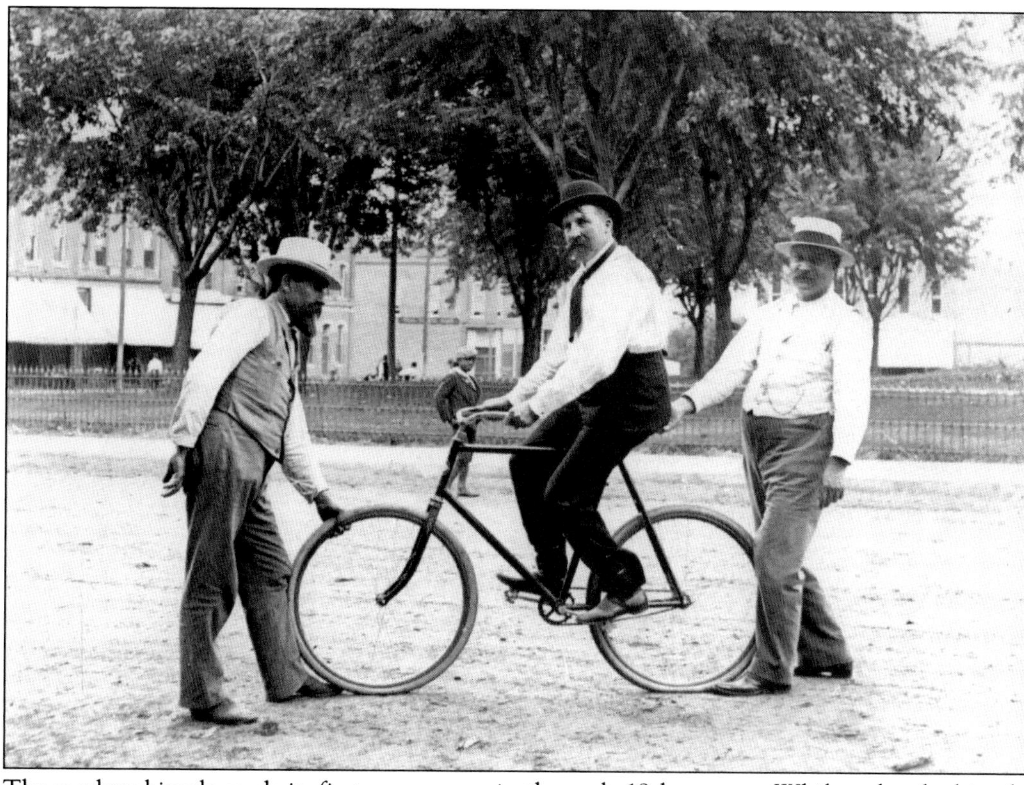

The modern bicycle made its first appearance in the early 19th century. While today the bicycle is preferred by children and exercise enthusiasts, prominent citizens Captain E. Townsend, Dr. George A. Nash, and M.D. Young test the validity of this device while an on-looking young man exhibits terrific curiosity.

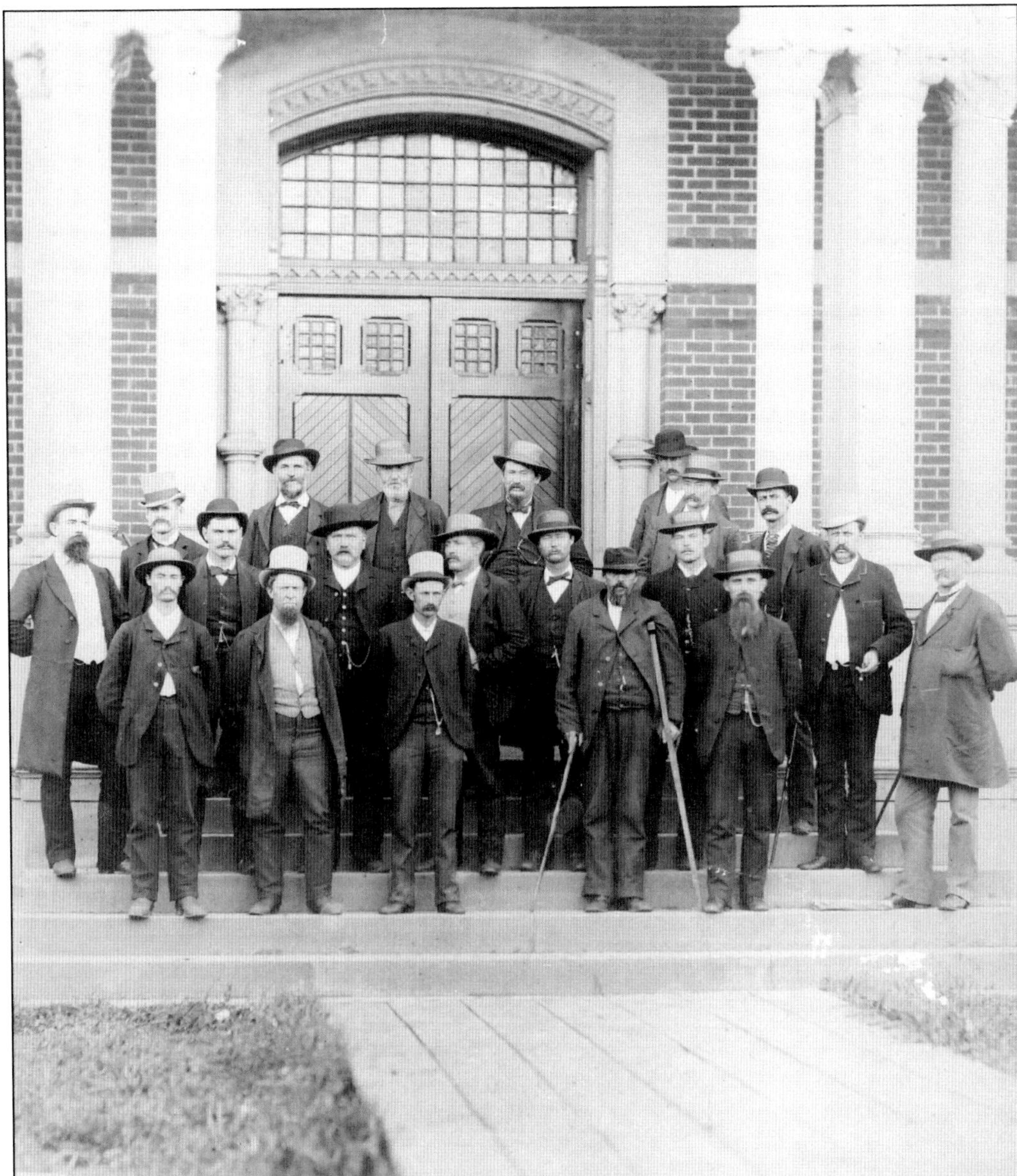

The judges and attorneys working in the Nodaway County Courthouse emerge for a group portrait in the early 1890s. The distinguished gathering, many of whom were likely veterans of the Civil War, carry on the legacy of the pioneer jurists who first held court in 1845 in the home of Isaac N. Prather. For these heirs to frontier bench and bar, vested suits and pocket watches were the order of the day, as they were among the few in town, aside from the railroaders, who needed to keep hourly time.

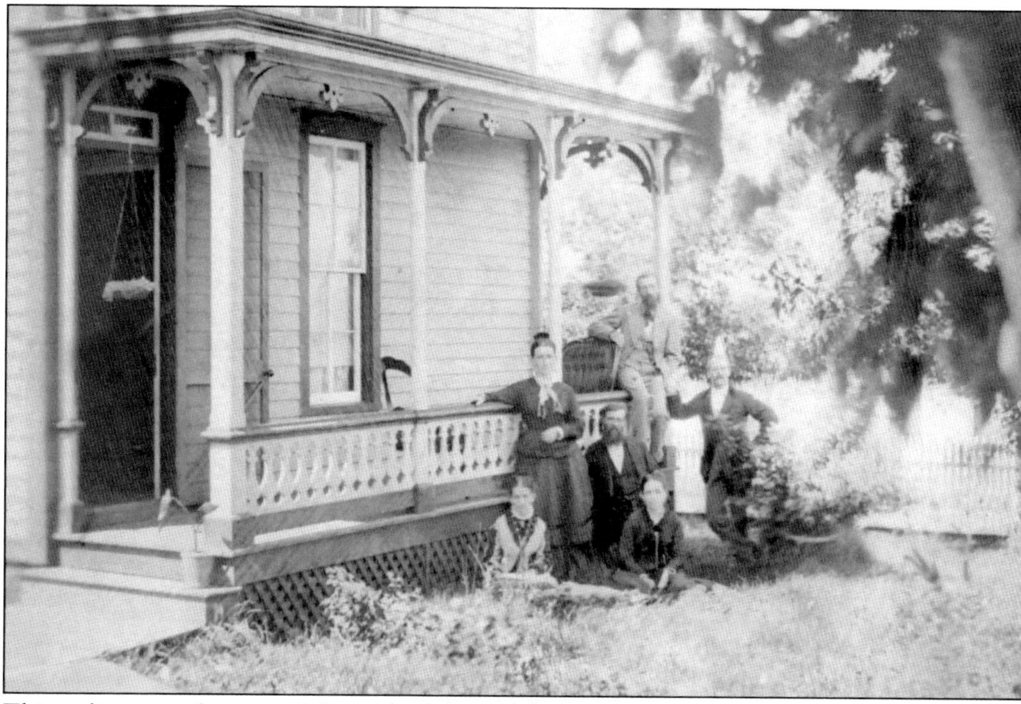

This ordinary working man's home built by Caleb Burns in 1846 still stands today and is listed in the National Register of Historic Places as the oldest home in Maryville. Caleb and his wife, Jerusah, built a home that was quite comfortable and, for its time, used sophisticated techniques. The home sat on the Burns Addition farm, near the west side of the town of Maryville that today is the site of the residential neighborhood that surrounds the property at the corner of Second and Walnut Streets.

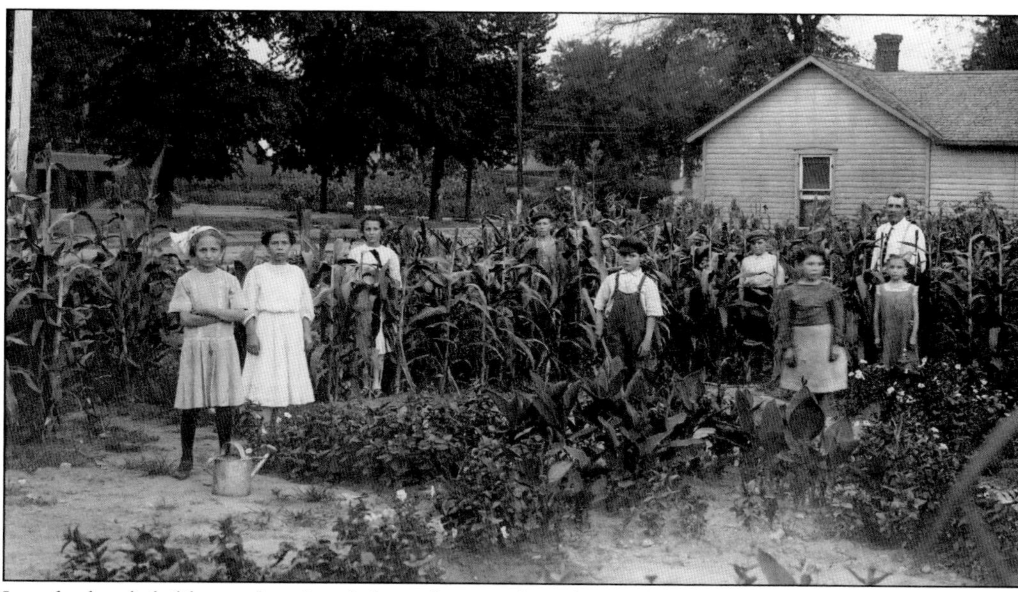

Local school children take a break from their work in the garden. While the details of this tableau are lost to history, the case seems clear that "experiential learning" has long coexisted with desks and books as a teacher looks on to supervise the efforts.

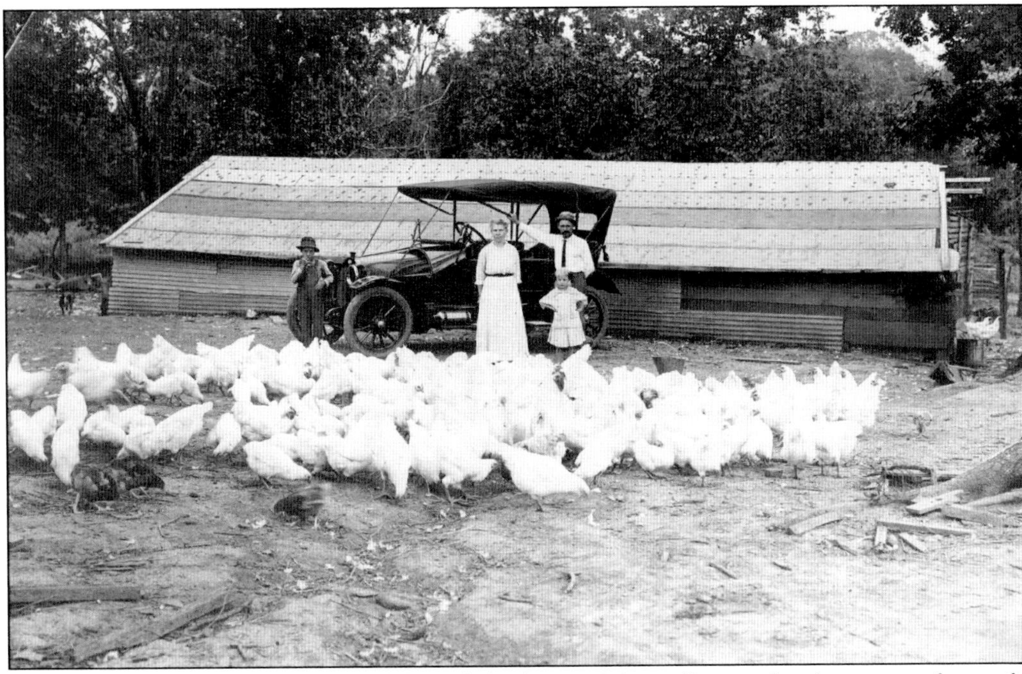

Equally proud of both their automobile and chickens, a Maryville-area family poses in front of a St. Louis-made Meteor 36, which retailed for $950. The family's White Plymouth Rock chickens, selected for both the ability to produce quality eggs and exceptional meat, not only provided breakfast and dinner, but also supplemented the household income.

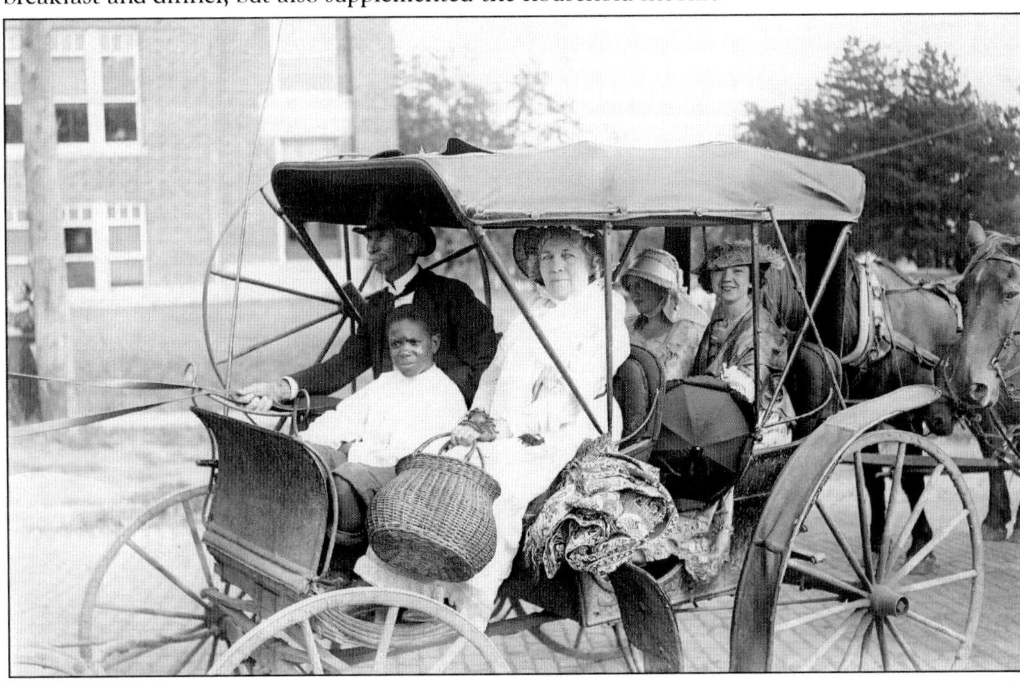

This photograph finds a contented group on a Sunday afternoon spent cruising around Maryville for entertainment in a fine but well-used buggy. Amelia Palmer Gillow, second from right, enjoys the company of a friend's family and young man who appears to have charmed his way into a ride.

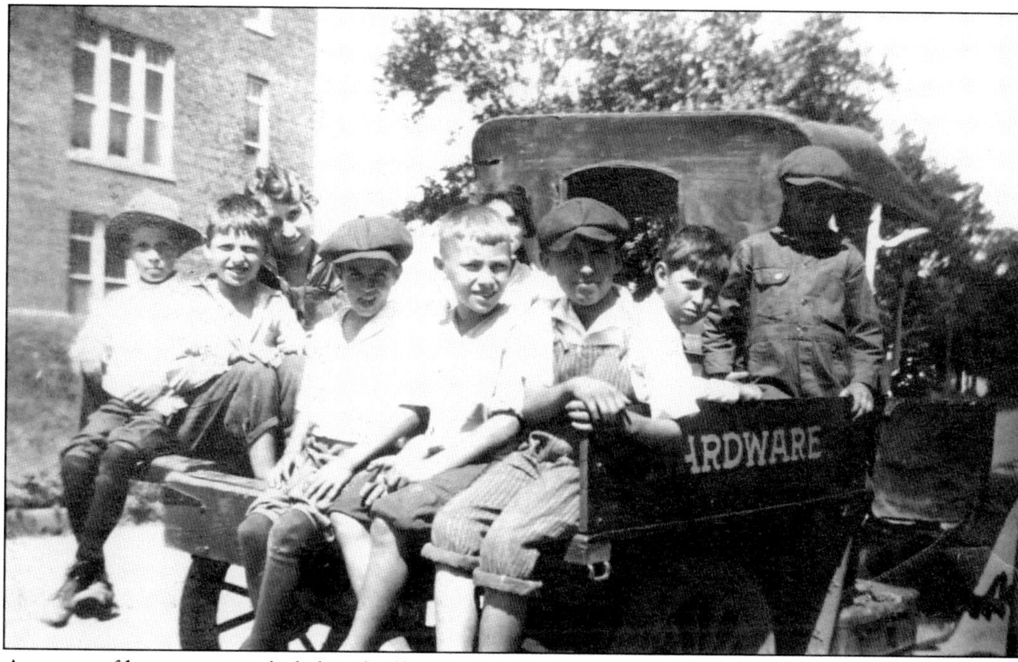

A group of happy young lads head off in 1919 for a picnic in the back of a local hardware truck. Knee pants and knickers were the order of the day as a loving mother leans in to remind the youngsters of her presence. Pants that felt too long were rolled above the knee to leave clearance for romps through mud and water without the fear of a scolding for a tough round of laundry.

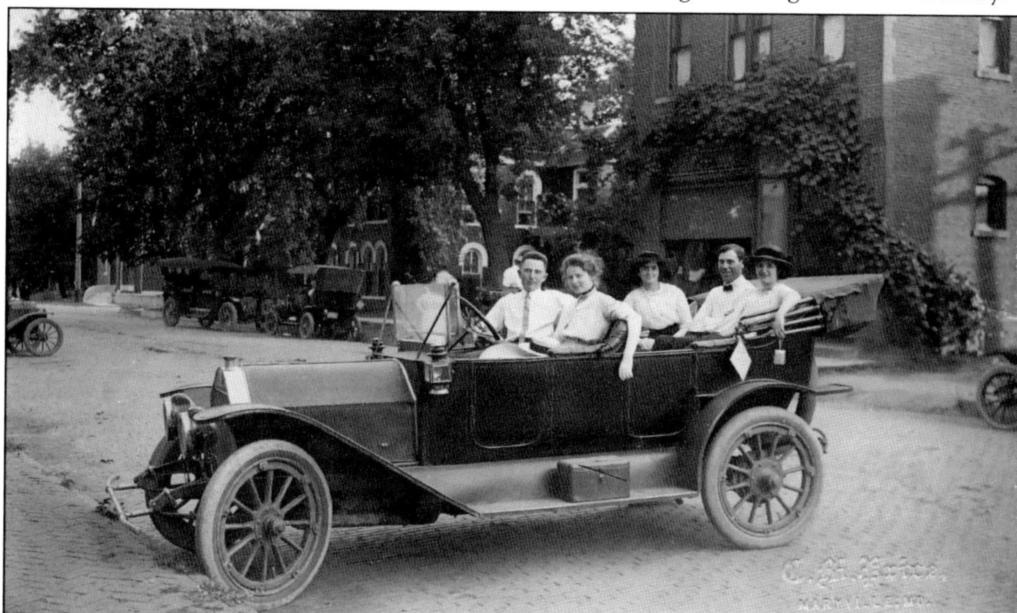

Young adults wheel their fine touring car to the curb for a photograph along Buchanan Street near St. Patrick's Church. With newly added space, it was possible to take more friends and family on pleasure drives. The toolbox on the side is indicative of the lack of both trunk space and automotive reliability. The introduction of electric starters enabled drivers to start the car without having to strenuously turn the crank.

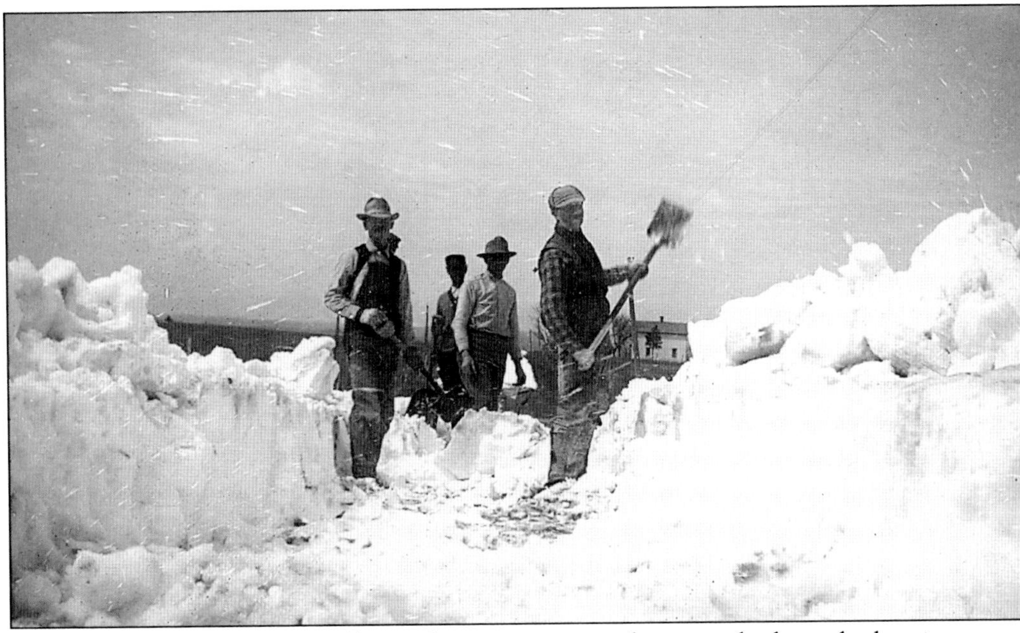

Ed Dawson and other Maryville residents attempt to clear a path through the giant snow accumulation following the March 30 snowstorm of 1912. From February to March in 1912, Missouri experienced some of the most extreme winter conditions of the century. This particular storm piled over 15.5 inches at some spots throughout Maryville and the state. This total remained unchallenged until the winter of 1982.

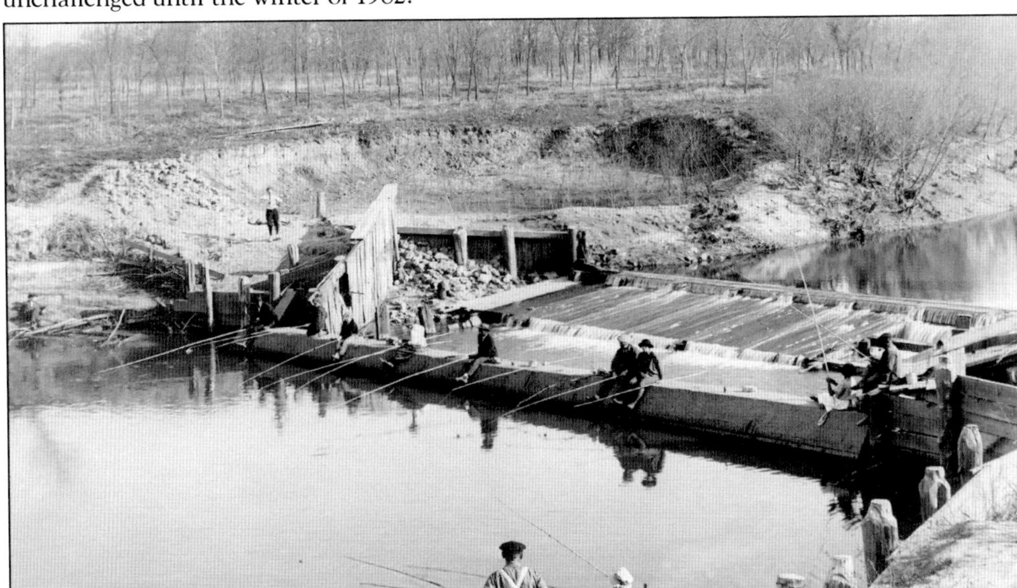

For nearly a century, the dam on the One Hundred and Two River that served the water plant has also provided a gathering spot for fishing and socializing. In this photograph from the 1920s, citizens white and black share space together in their quest for catfish to fill local frying pans.

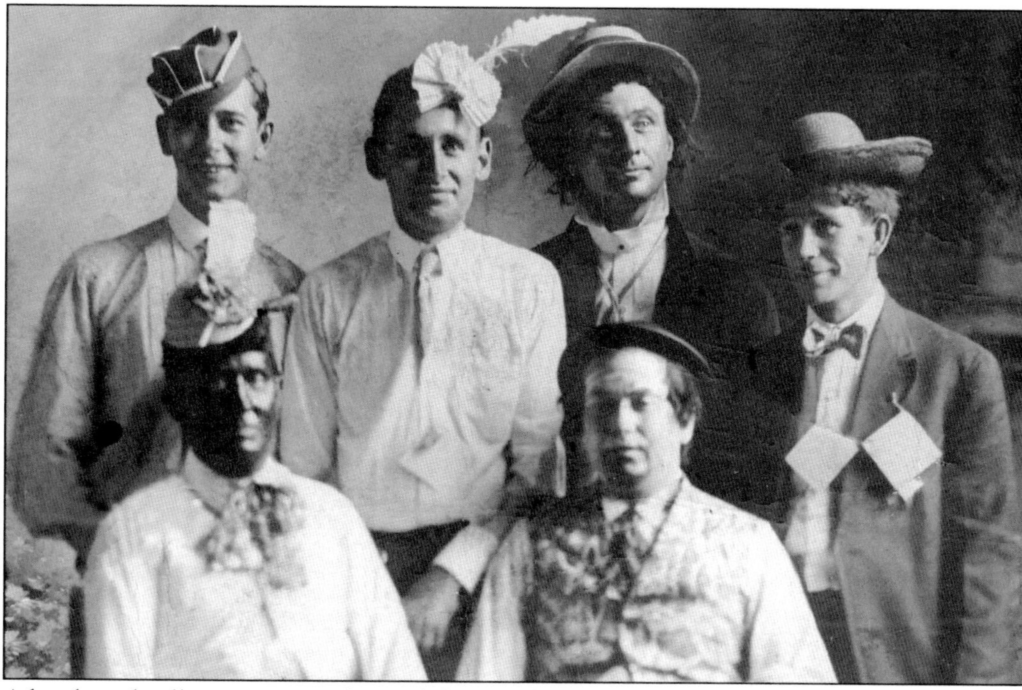

A local vaudeville troupe, one of several that overlapped in town in the 1910s and 1920s, poses in costume. Cross-dressing and blackface were common features of amateur clowns and musicians who performed in local parades and sometimes on stage in the Empire Theater.

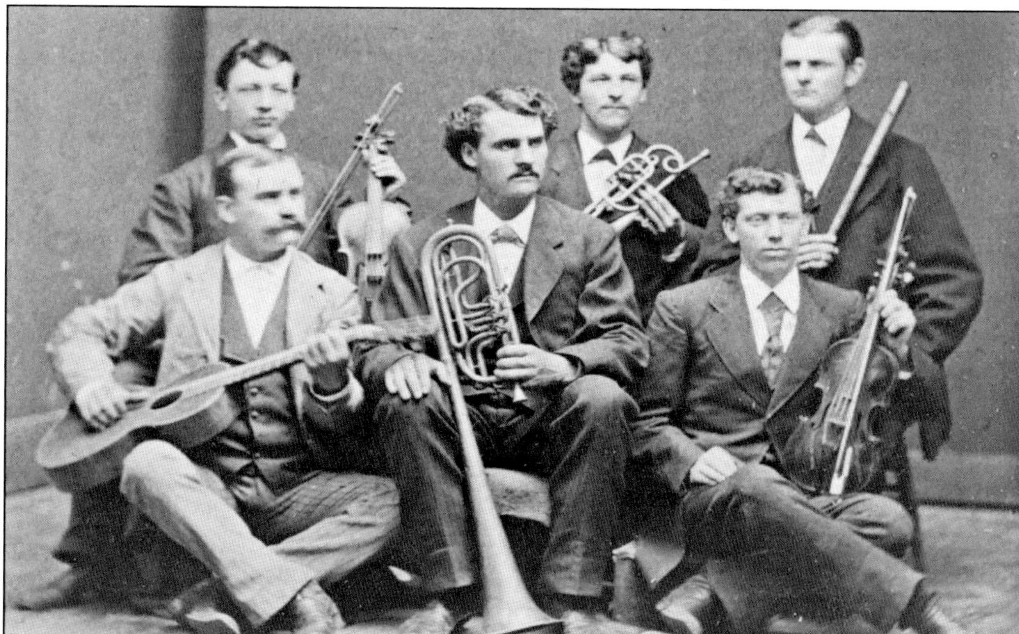

The Maryville German Boys String Band was a far more sedate, and presumably talented, ensemble than the vaudeville acts. Maryville, and the surrounding county, nurtured dozens of marching bands, brass bands, church ensembles, and the occasional stringed group. Why the name "String Band" was used for this particular group eludes us.

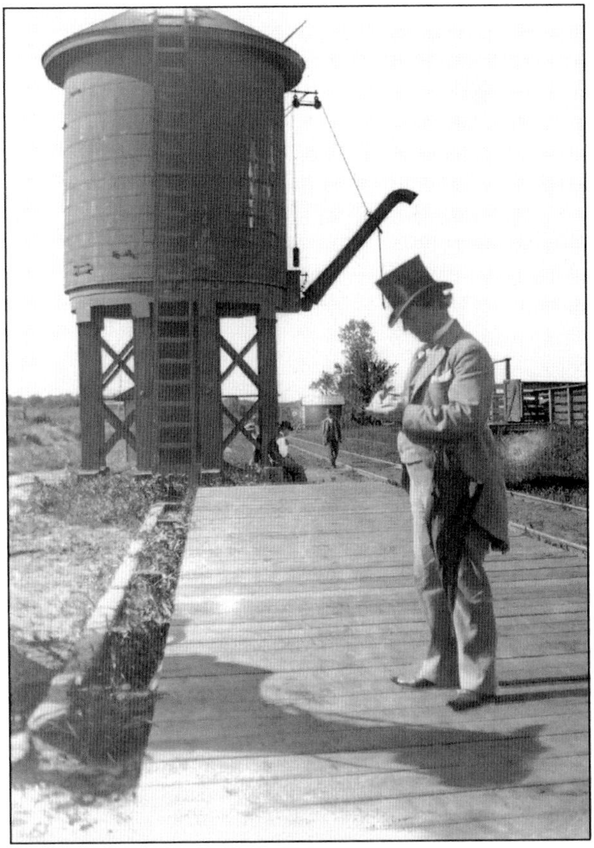

Infamous editor Frank Griffin from the *Maryville Daily Review* stops to take notes at the Burlington Station. In 1889, following some libelous attacks and improper conduct by Griffin, former Maryville druggist C.G. Jesse shot and killed Griffin. Many Maryville residents supported Jesse and his actions enough to gather funds for a defense attorney.

Iron men with wooden sticks show off the police paddy wagon, decked out for a parade in the 1910s. Jess Fisher sits at the wheel, while standing from left to right are John Wallace, Felix Grundy, Martin Borrish, Frank Bolin, and John Borrish. Newspapers suggest that the force stayed mildly busy with petty crimes, though the town history is marred by several heinous murders.

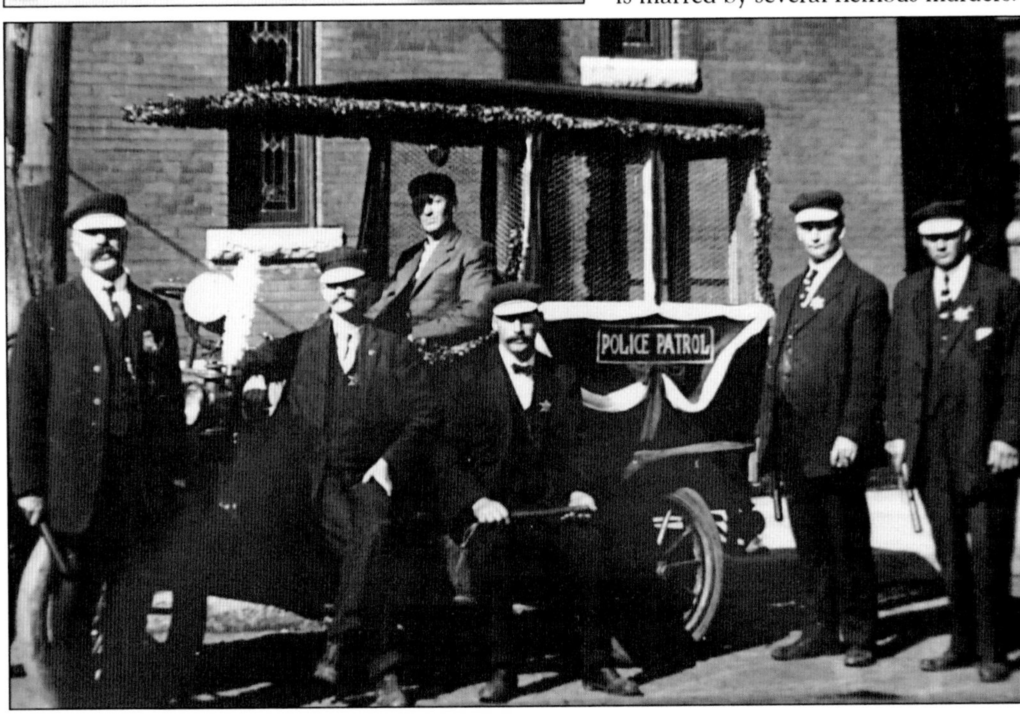

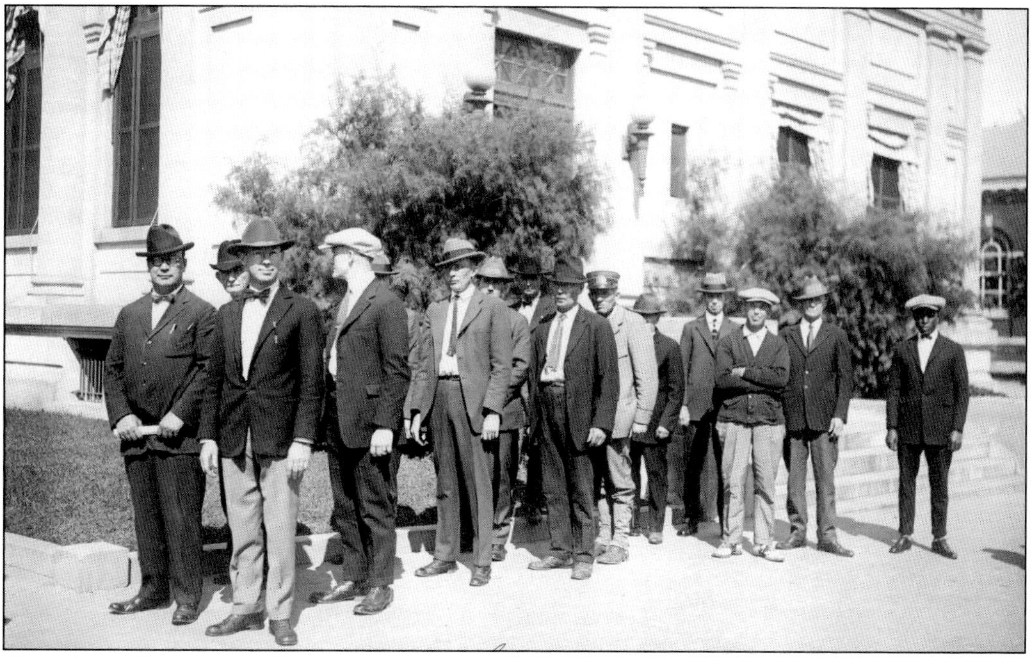

The Maryville Postal staff, seen here in the 1920s, continued a legacy started by Caleb Burns and Amos Graham, who delivered the first mail in town out of the log cabin courthouse in 1846. With the growth of the town, the post office was established in the brick block on the north side of the square and then moved in 1912 to the impressive structure seen here.

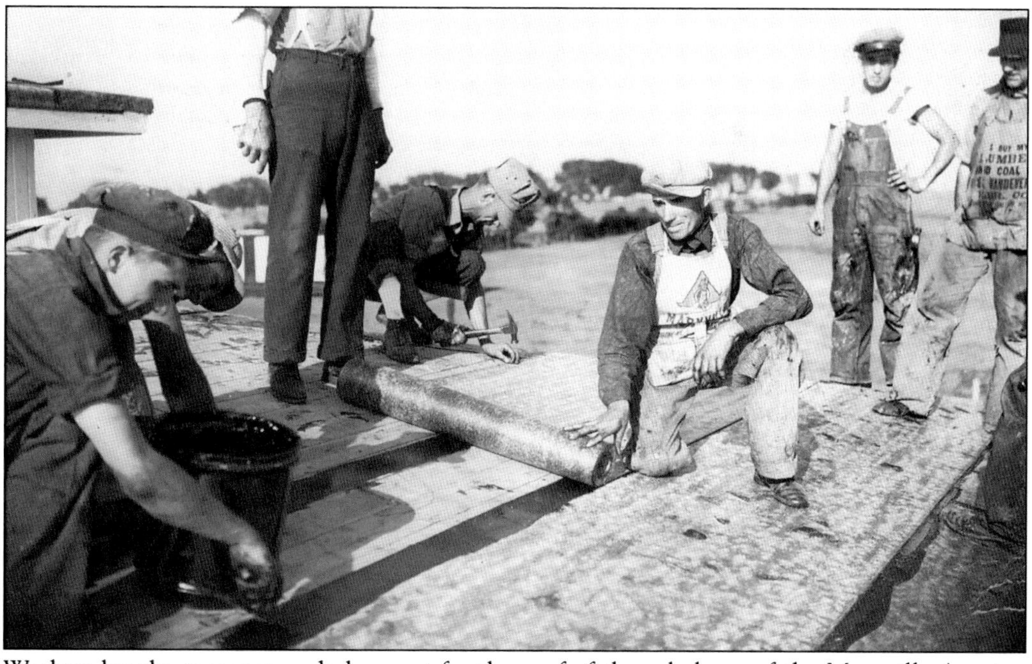

Workers lay the tarpaper underlayment for the roof of the sale barn of the Maryville Auction Company, located near the intersection of Main Street and South Avenue. Images like these comfort laborers today, who know the feeling of a job in which the messiest of tasks seem to require an equal number of men to supervise. (Courtesy of Mary Graham.)

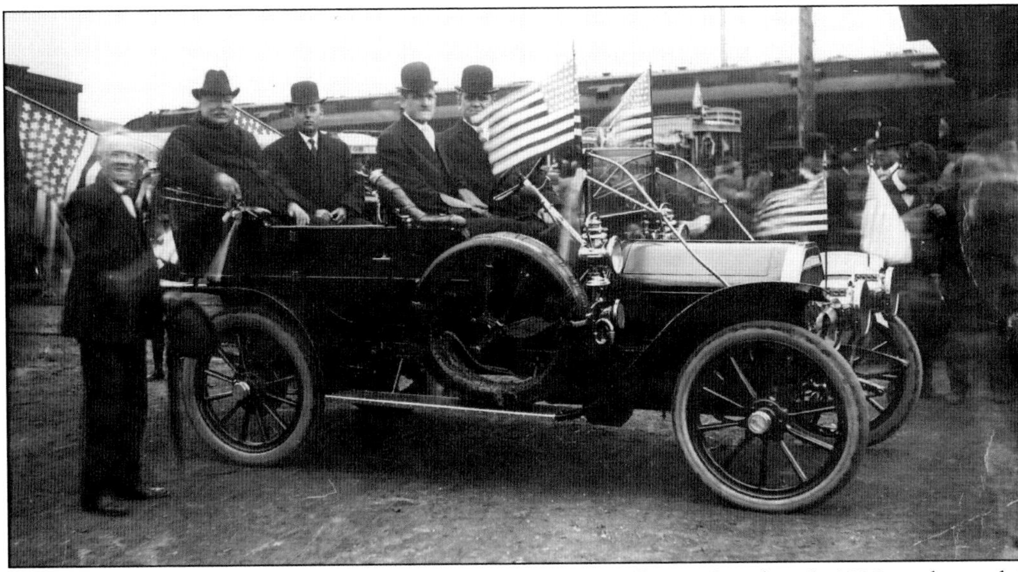

Future president William Howard Taft arrived in Maryville on October 5, 1908, to begin his campaign after receiving the Republican nomination. Taft was escorted into town by prominent Maryville citizens Ferdinand Townsend and James Shinabargar. Taft easily out-politicked his opponent William Jennings Bryan, carrying Missouri and easily winning the 1908 election.

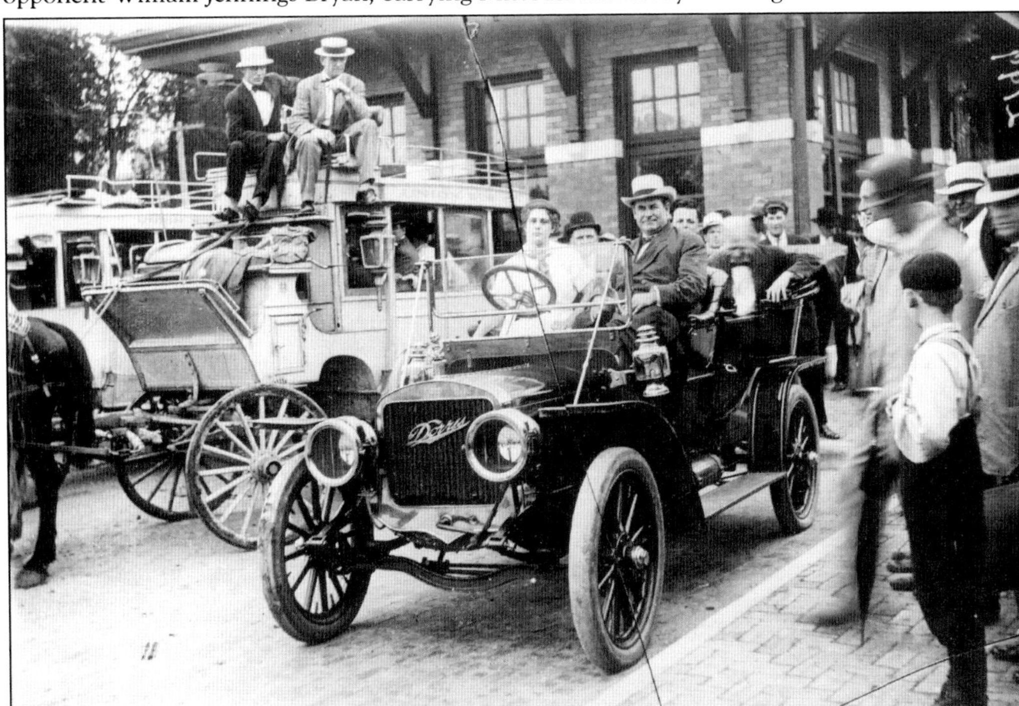

Maryville hosted three-time presidential candidate William Jenning Bryan in August 1912, seen here on his way to speak on the chautaqua grounds on the Teachers College campus. Brownie Toel Montgomery was granted the privilege of chauffeuring the former populist Democratic candidate from the Burlington Depot in a 1907 Dorris motor car. Union Bus Company coaches wait behind to carry the entourage across town.

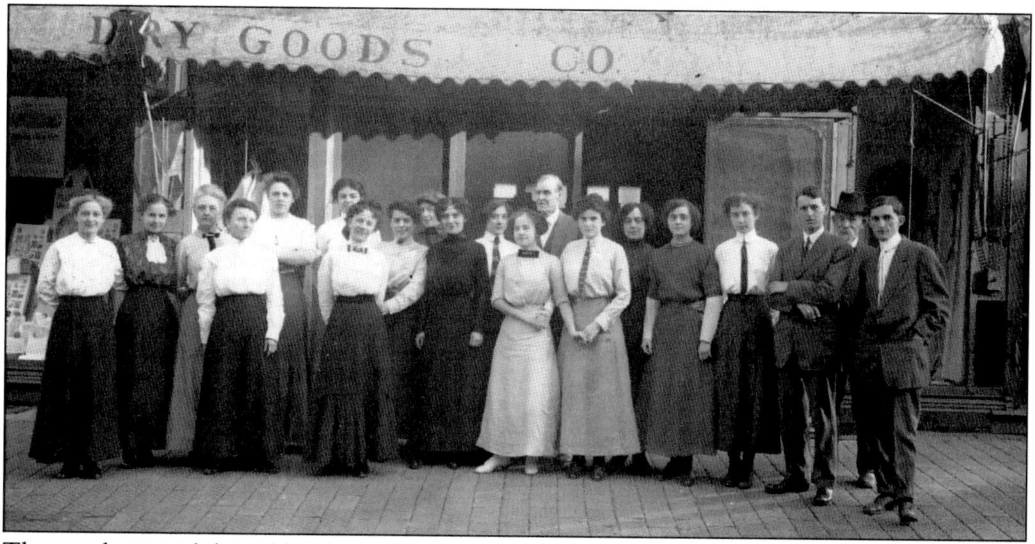

The employees of the Alderman-Yehle Dry Goods store pose in front of the establishment in the 1900s. The ladies and gentlemen of the shop themselves wear the fine garments of the era. Particularly fashionable with the younger ladies were plainer and trimmer skirts, blouses, and large collars with an assortment of neckties. Yehle, a German immigrant who came to America in 1857, moved to Maryville in 1868 and opened his own meat market.

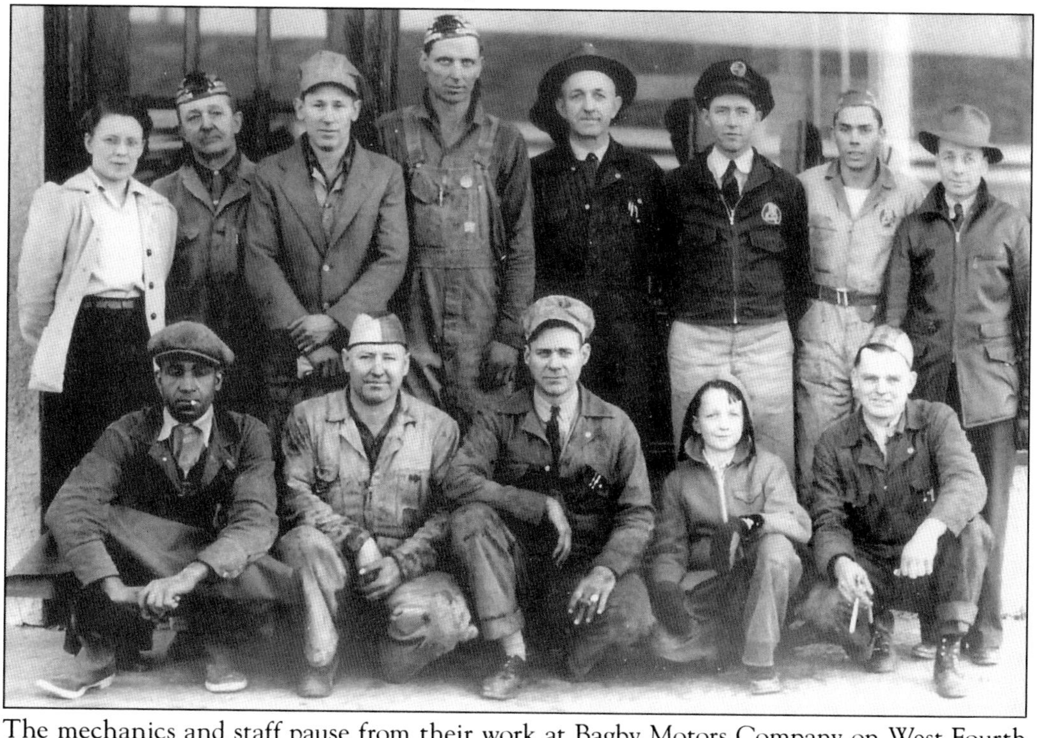

The mechanics and staff pause from their work at Bagby Motors Company on West Fourth Street at Buchanan Street. The site of the motor company was originally a livery stable called The Palace, with the structure of the livery retained in the auto garage. Pulled from their work for a snapshot, workers in varied attire and varied degrees of cleanliness suggest their roles in the shop. (Courtesy of Jim Bagby.)

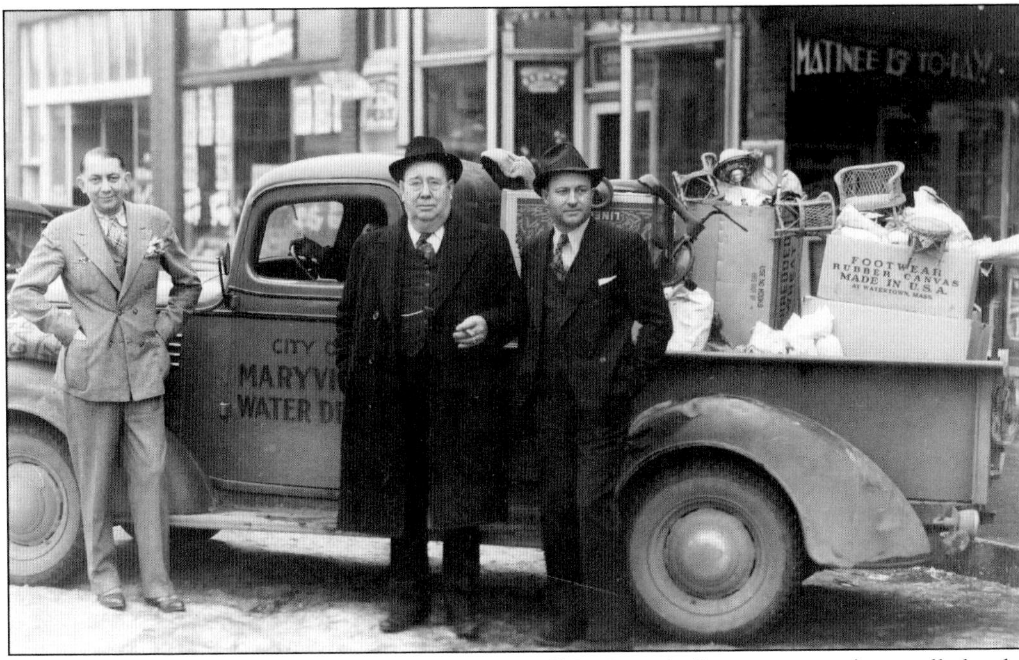

During the Christmas season of 1938, Mayor Lowell B. Campbell, center, stands proudly by the city's charity drive collection. The Missouri and Tivoli Theaters, in partnership with the city, offered free shows beginning on December 16 to patrons who brought contributions for the poor. The *Maryville Tribune* noted that the boots, toy guns, blankets, and other assorted goods seen here would make their way to homes "where Santa Claus failed to make an appearance." The pride of the Campbell administration was the new city hall, seen below, which faced repeated construction delays through 1938, postponing when Mayor Campbell and his staff could move into their offices.

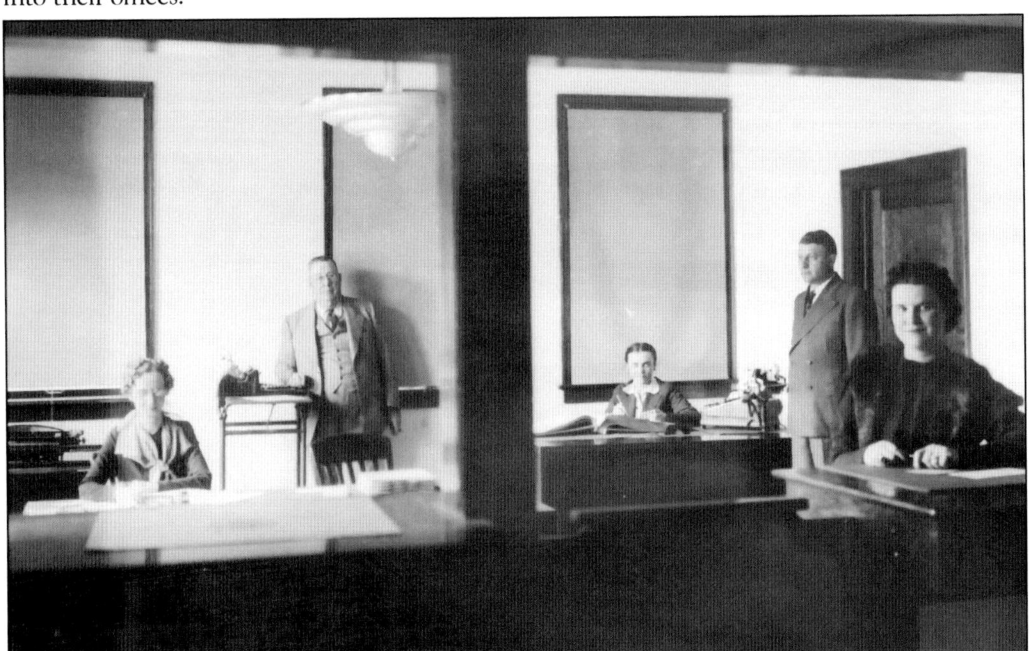

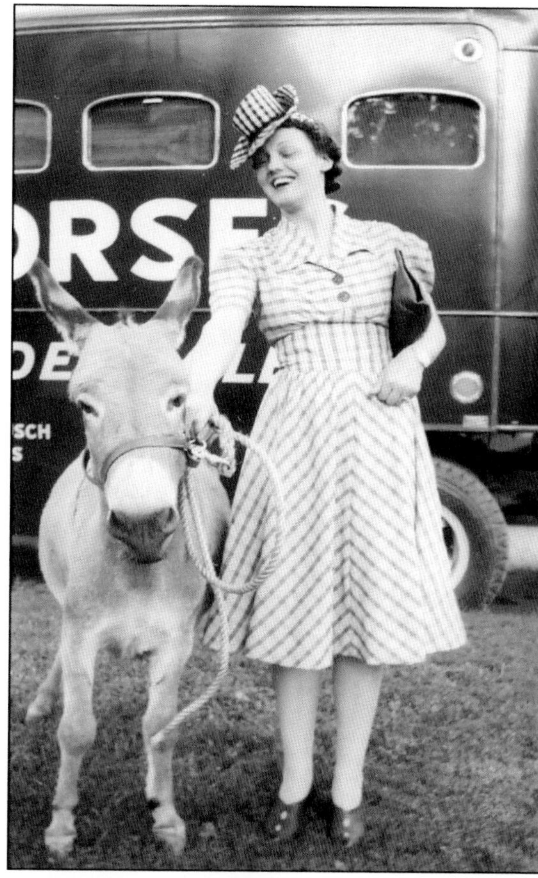

Mabel Beck holds a mascot for William "Bid" Beck's Budweiser distributorship at a Maryville fair in 1941. Though a decade of Prohibition, followed by a decade of economic depression, took its toll on Anheuser-Busch and its Budweiser label, the introduction of the metal can in 1936 added to a renewal of business. Within a year of this photograph, the company abandoned its operations in the far west to assist in making more railcar space available to the war effort.

Joseph Jackson Sr., right, influenced a lengthy stretch of town history; he was a resident for 77 years and, after purchasing a third interest in the Fisher and French Bank in 1873, spent 48 years as a leader in the local banking community. In 1884, he took the helm of the renamed First National Bank as president and served until his passing in 1921.

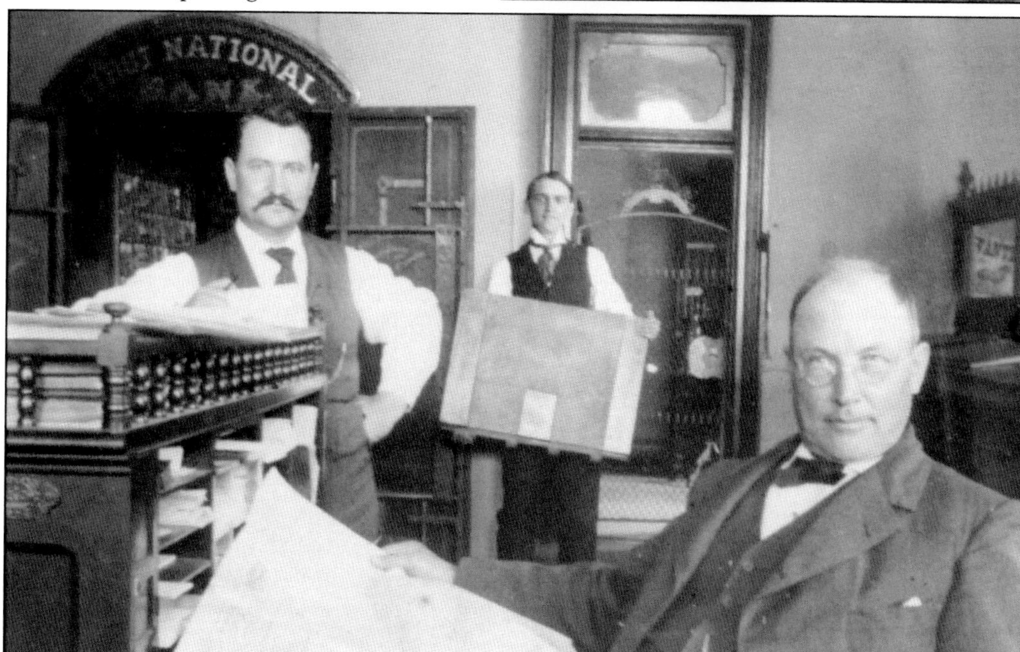

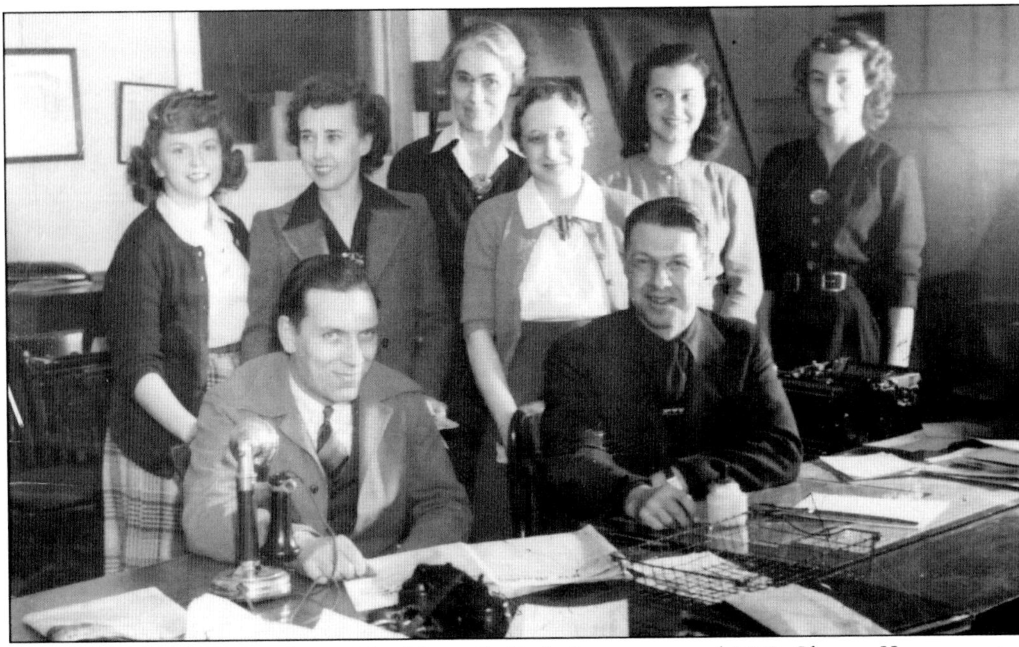

Shown here are the journalists of the *Maryville Daily Forum*, around 1942. Chester Krause, seated at right, was the editor of the paper and standing immediately behind him is Leola Swaney, who wrote for the paper from 1942 to 2002. Nellie Haller is in the back center. Originally the clerk and cashier for the *Daily Forum*, she also worked on the advertising and penned a gossip column in the late 1950s.

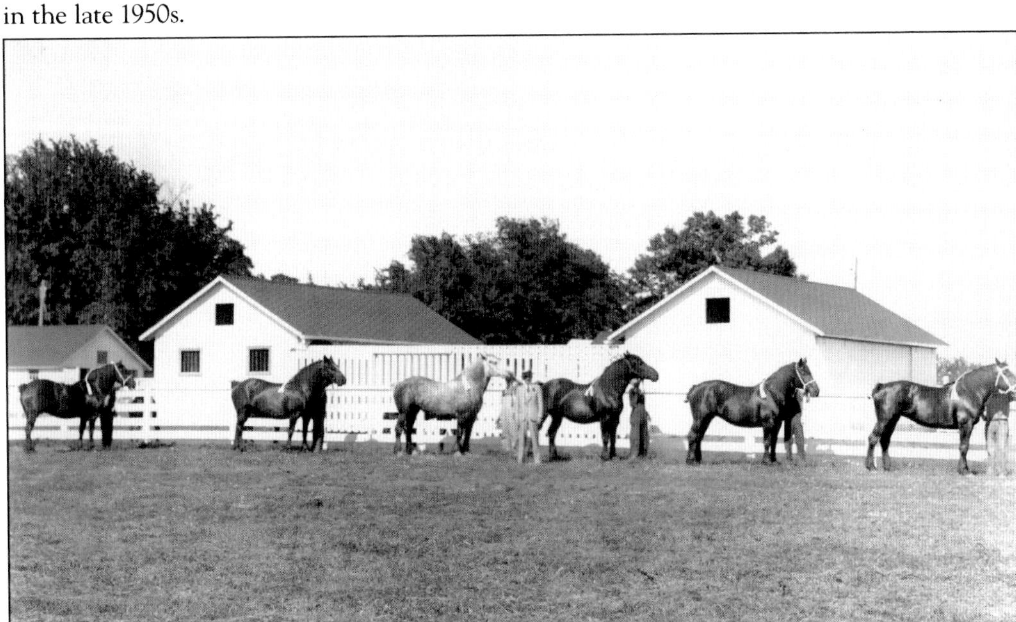

Early settlers in Nodaway County came primarily from Kentucky and Tennessee, and many, like breeder Isaac Prather, brought with them the horse culture of their home. Prather's English-bred stallion Faustus gave name to the breeding farm owned by the Townsends on the west side of Maryville from 1931 to 1964. Faustiana Farms, and stable manager Lester Swaney, cared here for famous horses like Nickel Plate, Faustiana Gardenia, Autumn Serenade, and Supreme Moment.

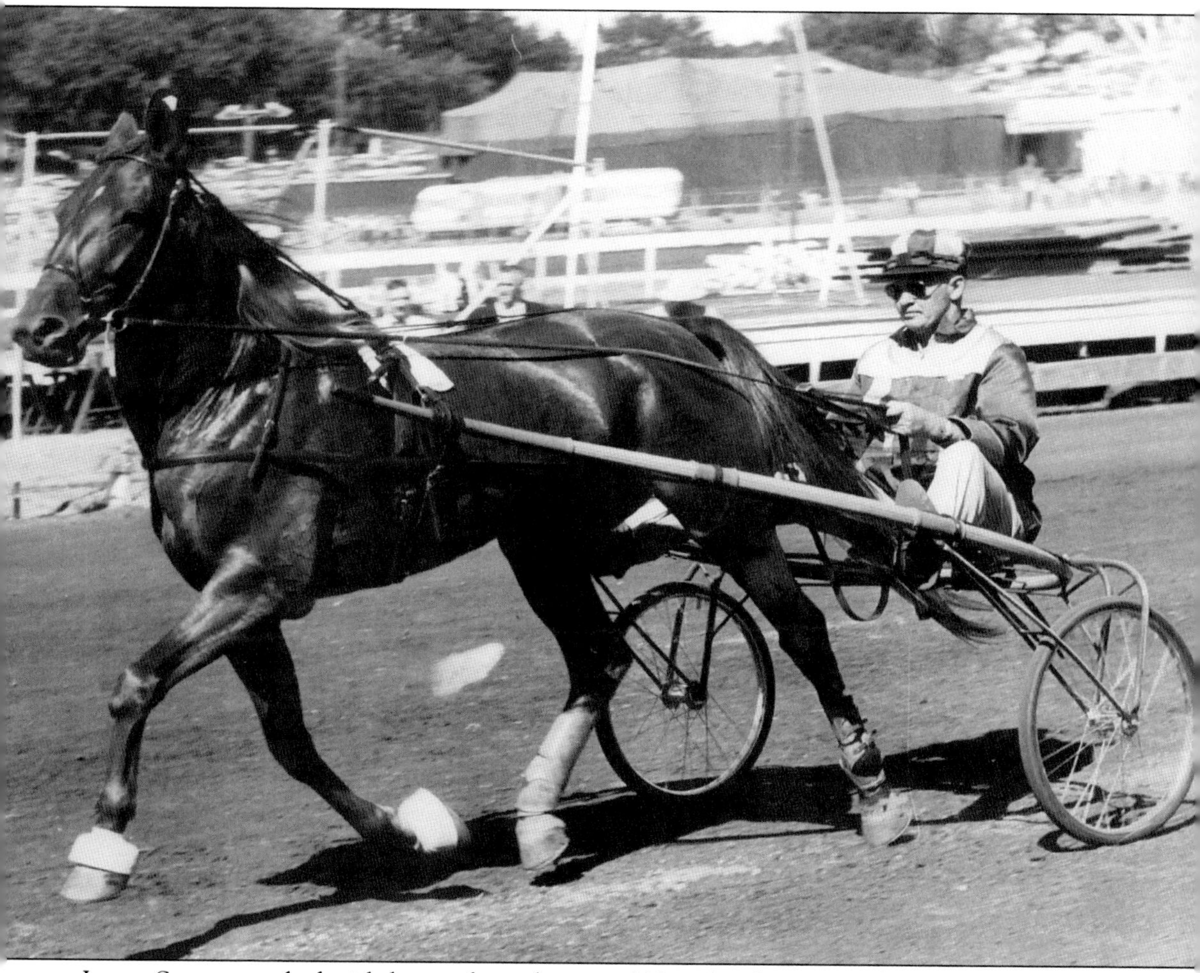

Lester Swaney worked with horses from the age of 12 under the mentorship of Jim Tapp from Nodaway County. While running his own operation in Lincoln, Nebraska, he developed a keen interest in the horses from F. M. Townsend's Faustiana Farms. Townsend convinced Swaney to come back to Maryville, where he eventually managed Faustiana Farms on the west edge of Maryville for 30 years while also establishing a national reputation as a trainer, showman, and racer.

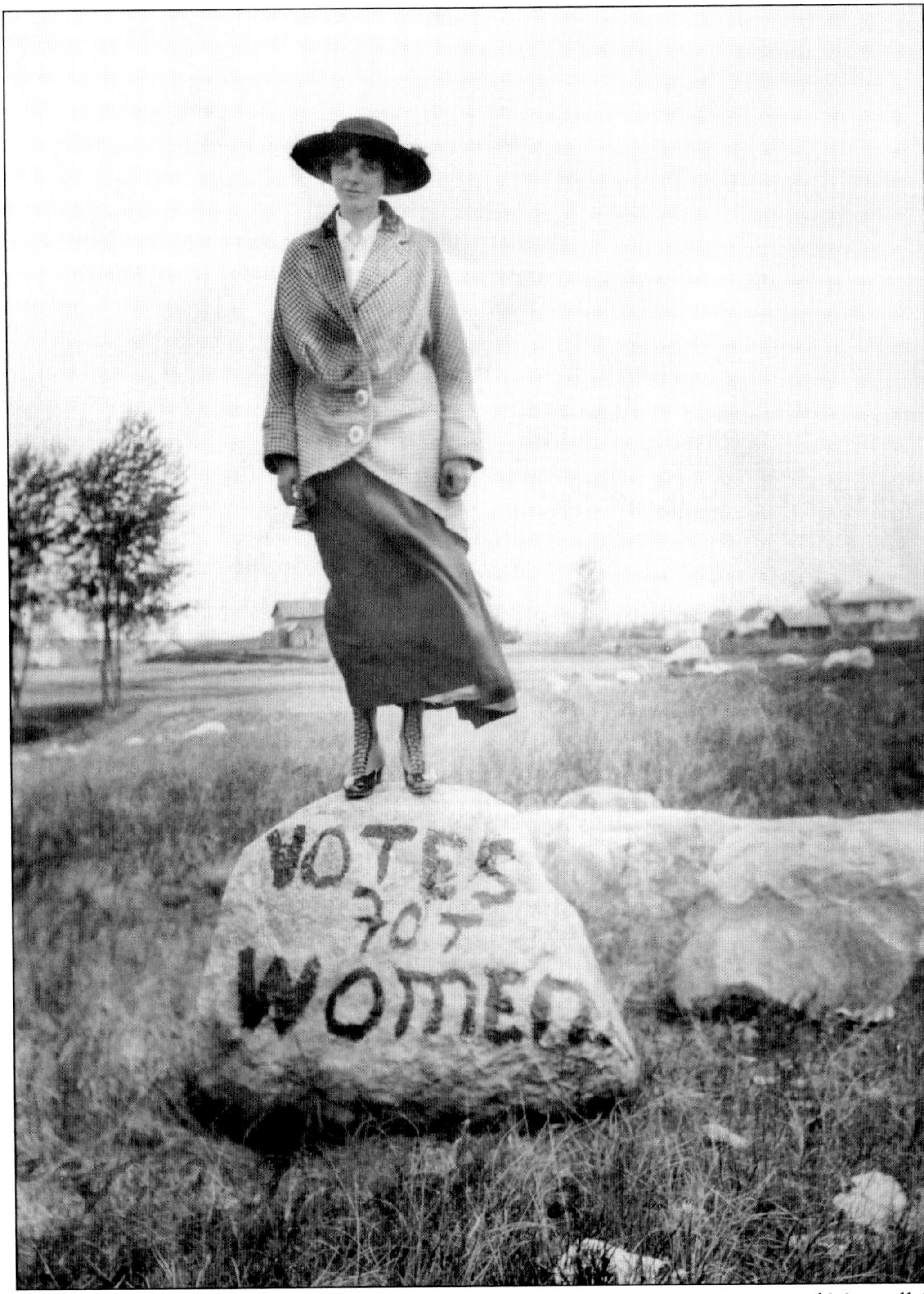

Edith Davenport Miller stands up for women's rights in 1910. Miss Davenport joined Maryville's Ladies Military Band under the leadership of Alma Nash with plans to join the group on its trip to Washington, DC, to march for women's rights. Though she did not make that trip, Miller continued for many years to be an activist for women. (Courtesy of Joyce Miller Holt.)

Six

Life Around the Square

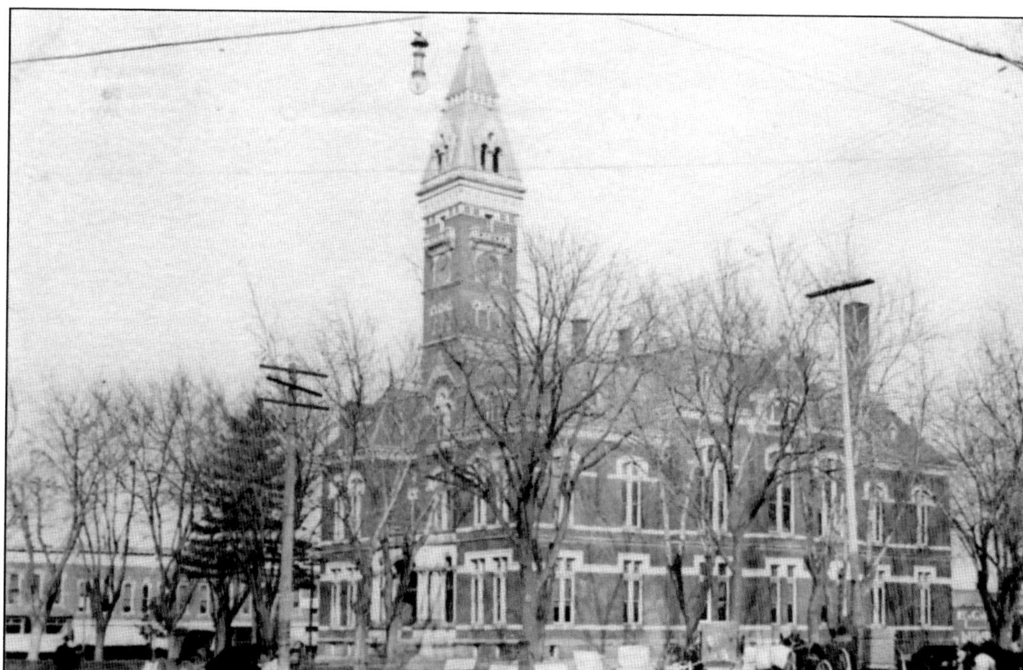

Maryville began as the county seat of Nodaway County in a 32-by-20-foot log cabin courthouse. A modest brick structure built in 1853 was replaced in 1881 with the present structure. The Italianate tower, at 111 feet, has stood for over a century as the center of the physical space and cultural life of the town. Around it, a commercial square emerged, thrived for decades, and then declined physically. Town life however, broadly around the square, continues to thrive as the people of Maryville adapt and embrace change.

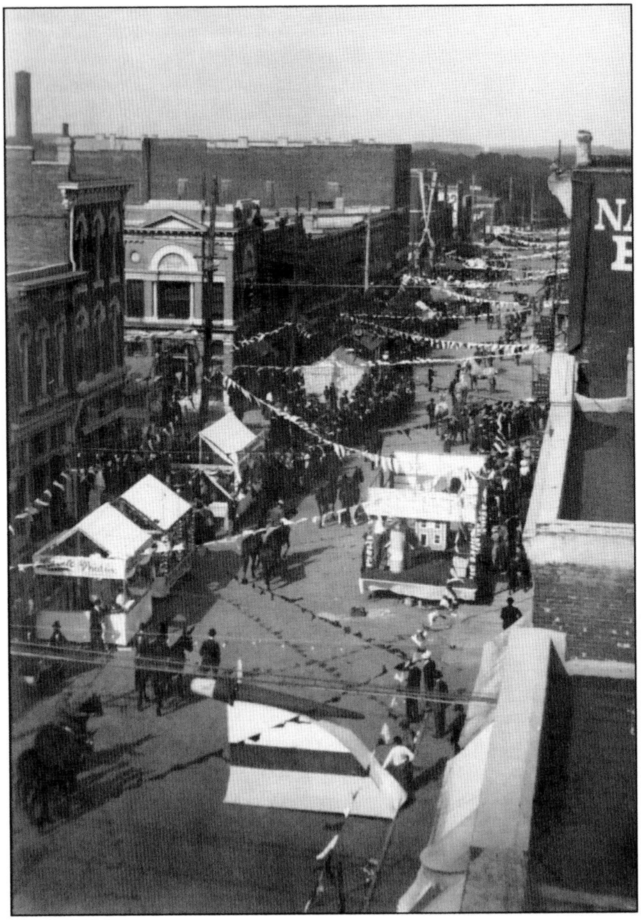

The annual street fairs in downtown were a place for people to let loose before the upcoming cold winter months. Vendors and stores throughout the town held special sales to entice new business. Photographer Ralph Marcell, responsible for many of the best images of the town during the first half of the century, likely captured the image to the left that shows his own booth, seen in the lower left portion of the image, on Main Street. In the photograph below, activities on the west side of the town square, seen in the 1900s with the block in perhaps its grandest configuration, draw large crowds, with spectators perched on ledges, rooftops, and even telephone poles. (Courtesy of Coby Lamb.)

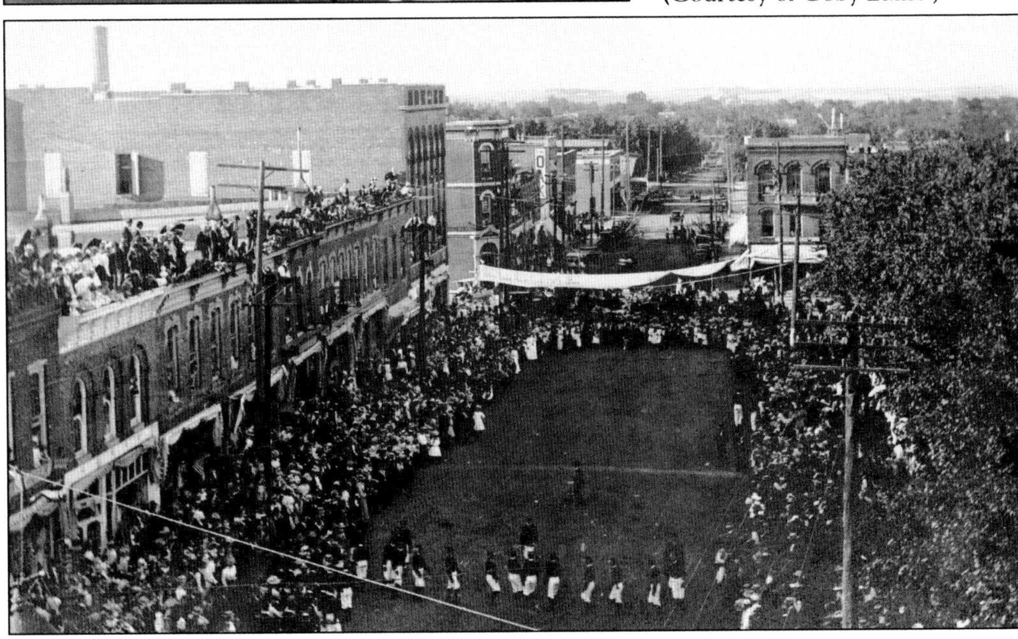

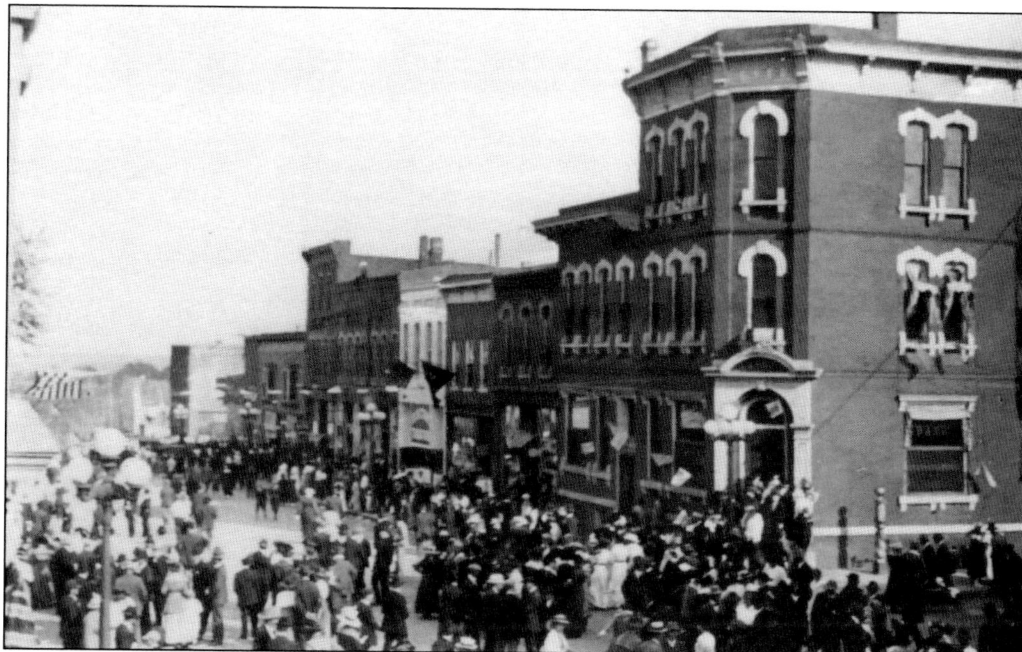

The south side of the square, as show in the image above, bustles with activity during the street fair that brought thousands of visitors to Maryville from the surrounding county and beyond. Postcards from the era testify to the invitations that went out to extended family and friends to hop a Burlington or Wabash train to come for a visit. Acrobatic teams were among the favorite headliners at local fairs, though the speed of the action challenged the best of photographers, as proven in the photograph below. Having missed or blurred the acrobats, a deft camera artist could simply ink them back in to the image to recapture the scene. The signs behind also advertise the "Old Plantation Minstrel Shows" that consisted of musical performances and skits that hearkened back to a mythical life on the old plantation.

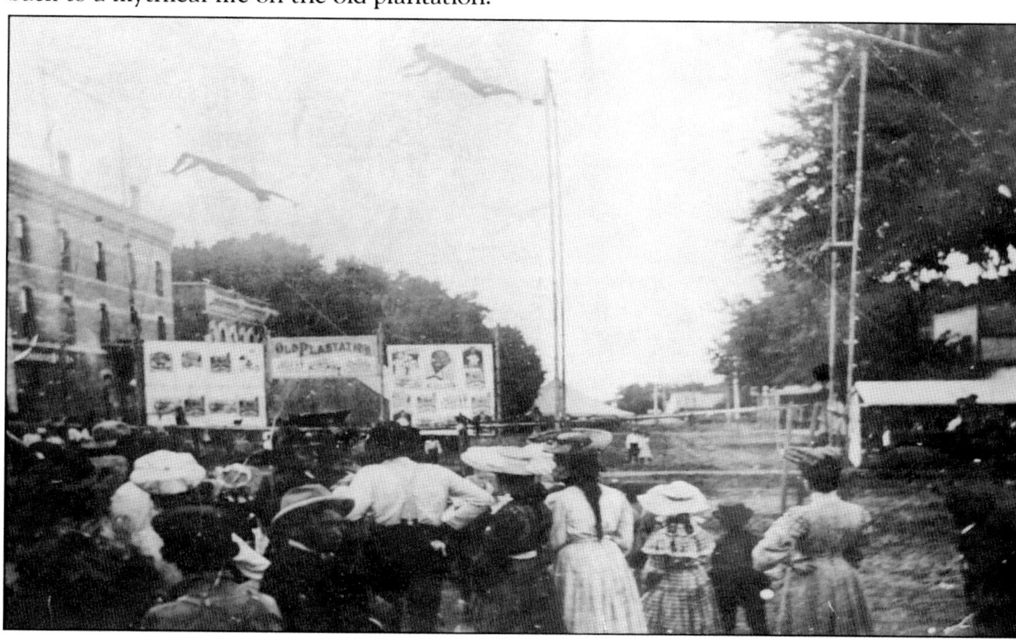

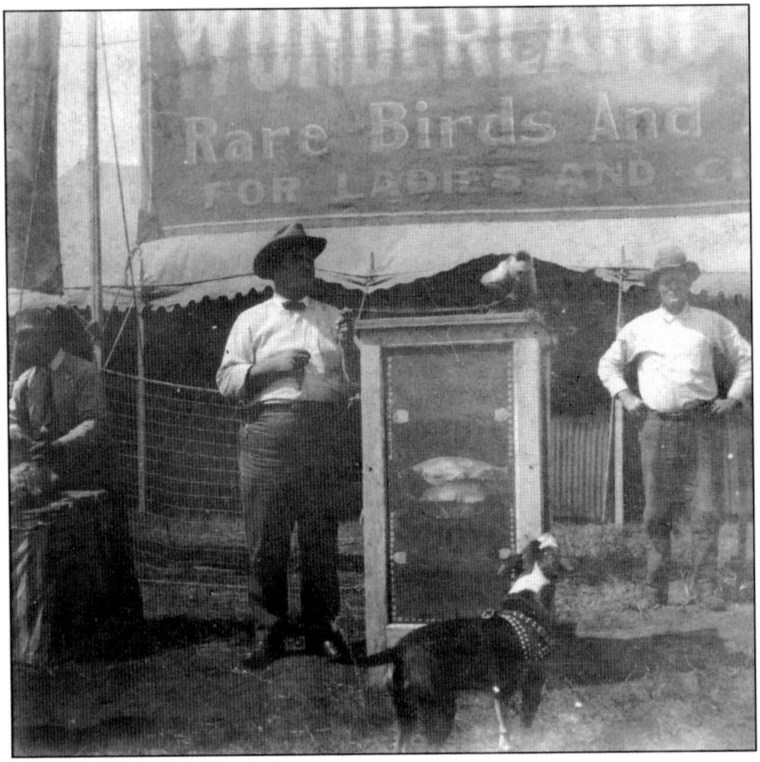

The annual street fair brought excitement in many varieties and merchants lined Main Street with elaborate front displays added to their businesses. At the fairgrounds, additional itinerant vendors raised tents and offered unique and marvelous goods. Here, Mark Turner displays for sale his "Wonderland Rare Birds and Animals for Ladies and Children."

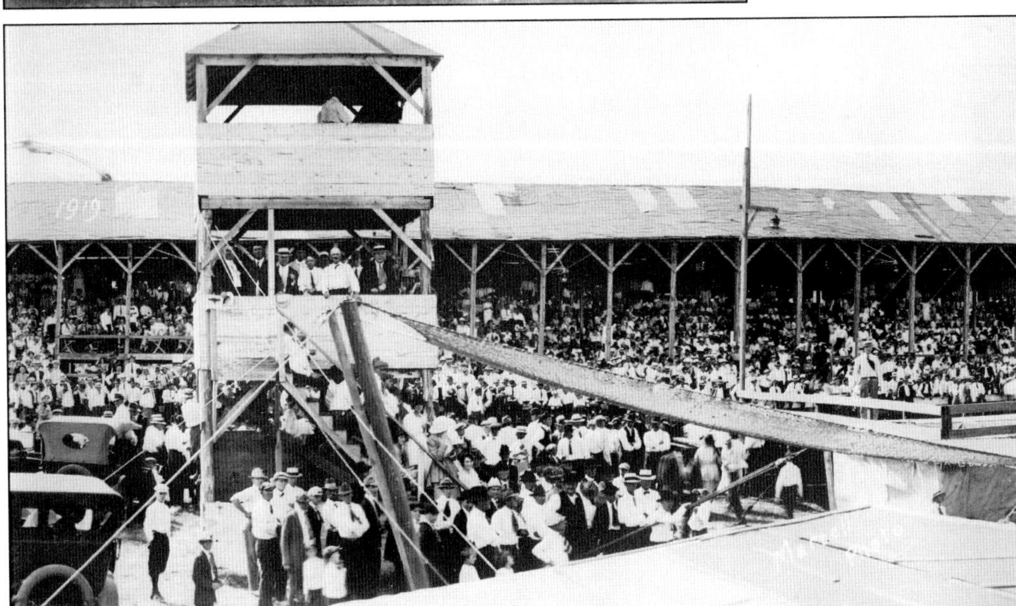

The county fair was an annual opportunity for residents from across the region to entertain themselves in myriad ways. Crowds were large for six full days of the fair in August 1919, which featured, aside from the perennial agricultural exhibits, Margaret Hill's Circus Dogs and Ponies, the "Herculanian Venus" Grom Bailey, Donald McGregor's show featuring the Great Scottish Giant, an Army aerobatics show, and trapeze artists The Original Flying Wards. Dignitaries, announcers, and the press watch from the center stand at the fairgrounds on the far eastern end of town.

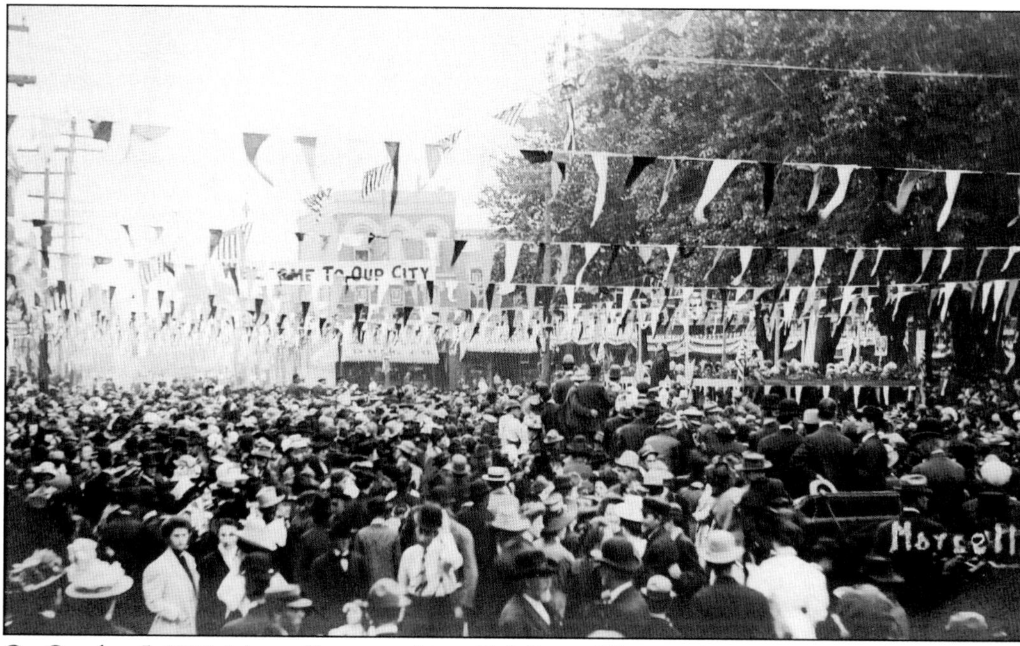

On October 5, 1908, Maryville erupted into Taft Fever. Thousands came to see William Howard Taft give his speech on this rainy day, with some considering it the greatest day in Maryville history. Despite the controversy of the time over the questionable practice, Taft planted a kiss on the cheek of Beal Roseberry's baby, which local papers proclaimed the first baby kissed on the campaign.

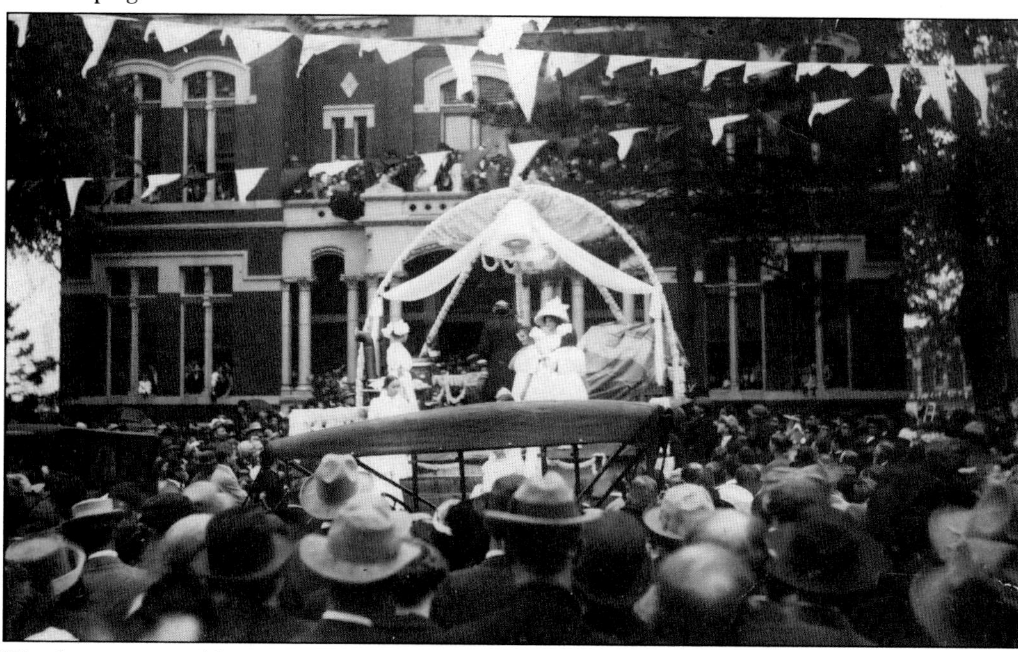

The first street wedding in town was likely that of Grace Hall and Anderson Nelson on October 8, 1903. Many others followed, well into the late 1930s, including this ceremony around 1910. Local businesses often provided gifts to the couple as a bonus for bringing additional patrons to the street fair to see the spectacle. (Courtesy of Ron and Janet Moss.)

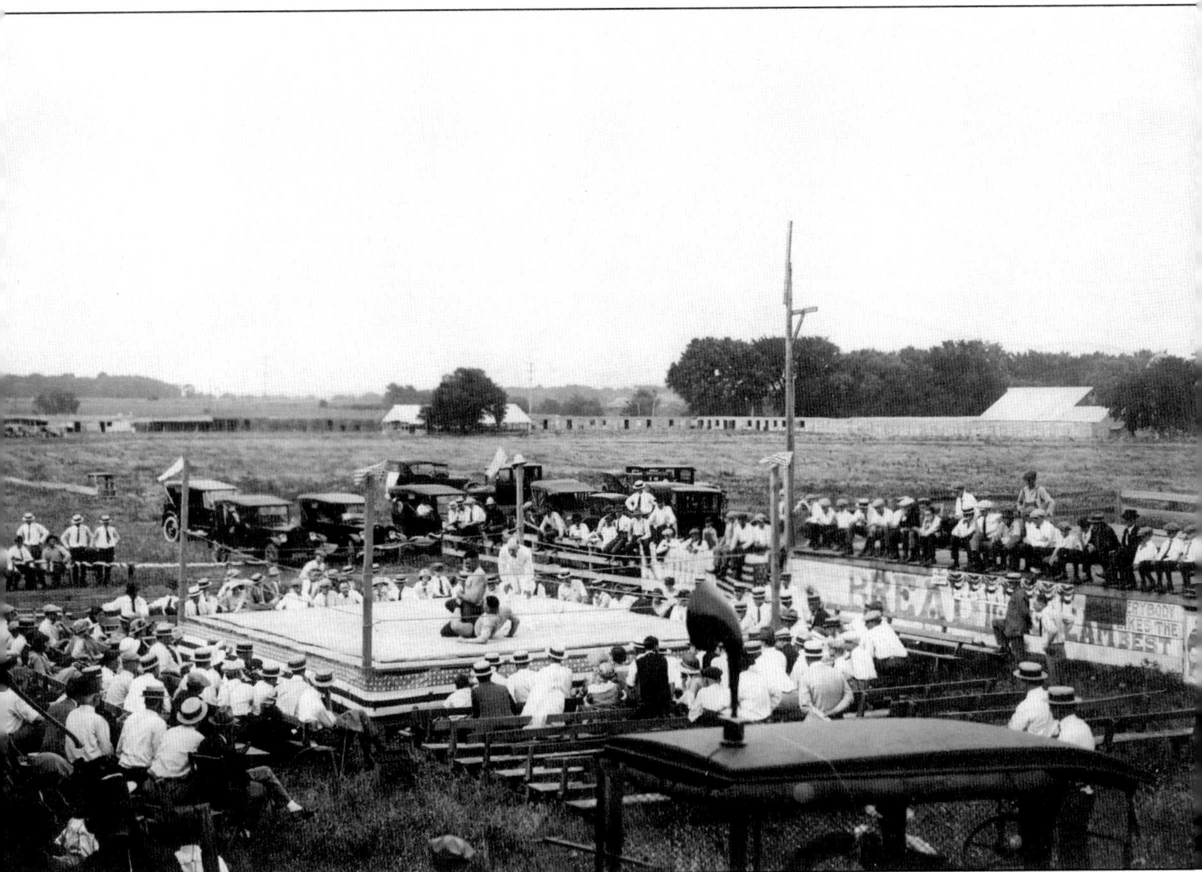

Despite the spotty popularity of staged wrestling in the 1920s due to concerns of authenticity, it remained popular in the Midwest through the middle of the century. Amusement companies toured with professional wrestlers throughout Missouri, Kansas, and Iowa. Here at a Maryville Fair, a smaller-than-expected crowd of men and a few women enjoy an open-air match.

As part of his extensive philanthropic ventures, steel magnate Andrew Carnegie seeded the cultural landscape of the Midwest with public libraries. Built in 1904 with $15,000 from Carnegie, citizens provided books and ongoing maintenance through a local tax. By 1910, the library shelved over 4,400 volumes, with an average of 63 visitors per day.

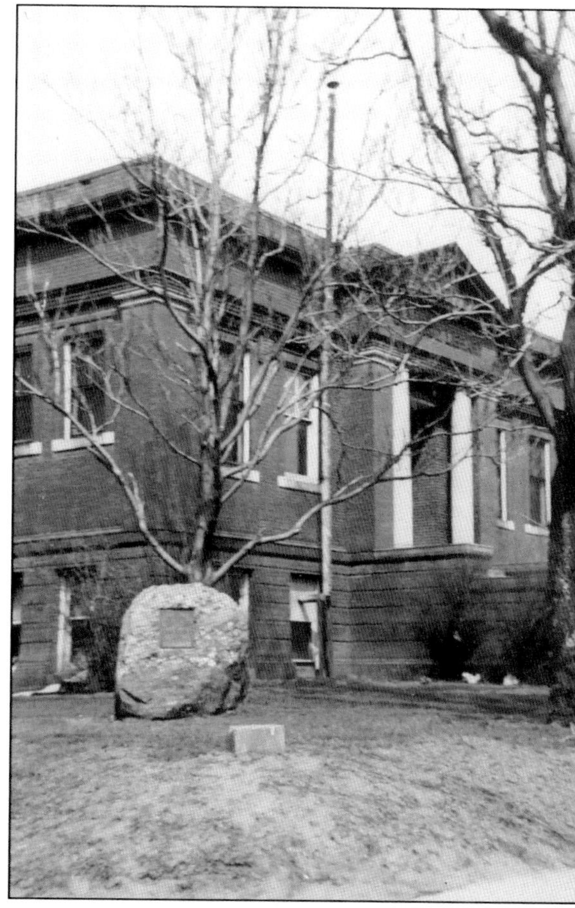

Built at the corner of Fourth and Vine Streets in 1882, the county jail utilized a novel system for allowing entrance and exit from cells by rotating the entire jail room to align the doors. When the device crushed a prisoner in 1904, it was made stationary and modified into a common cell. The facility was demolished in 1983 following the murder of a prisoner by his cell-mates.

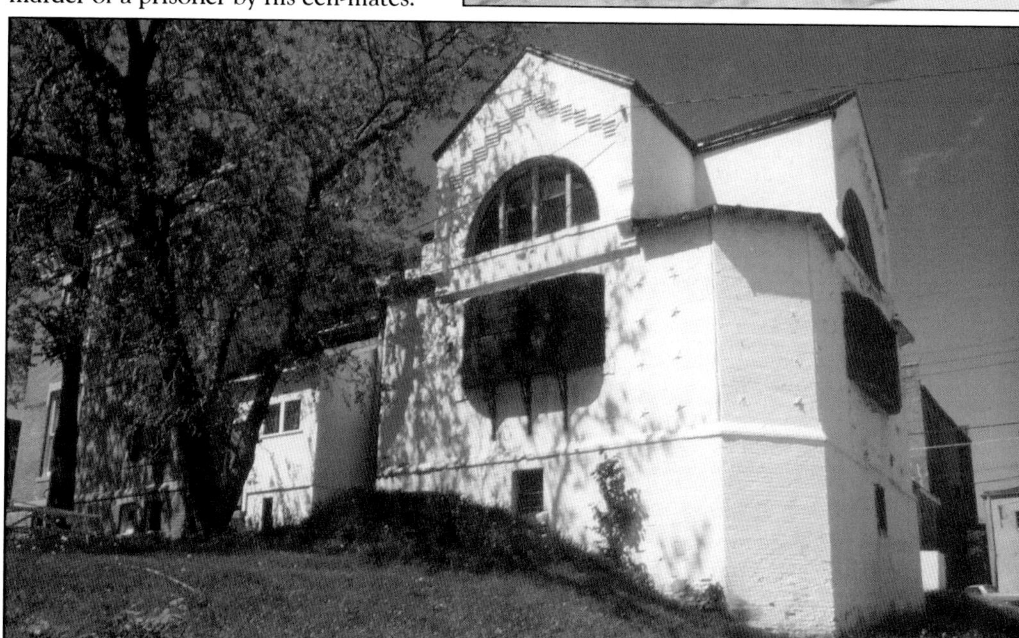

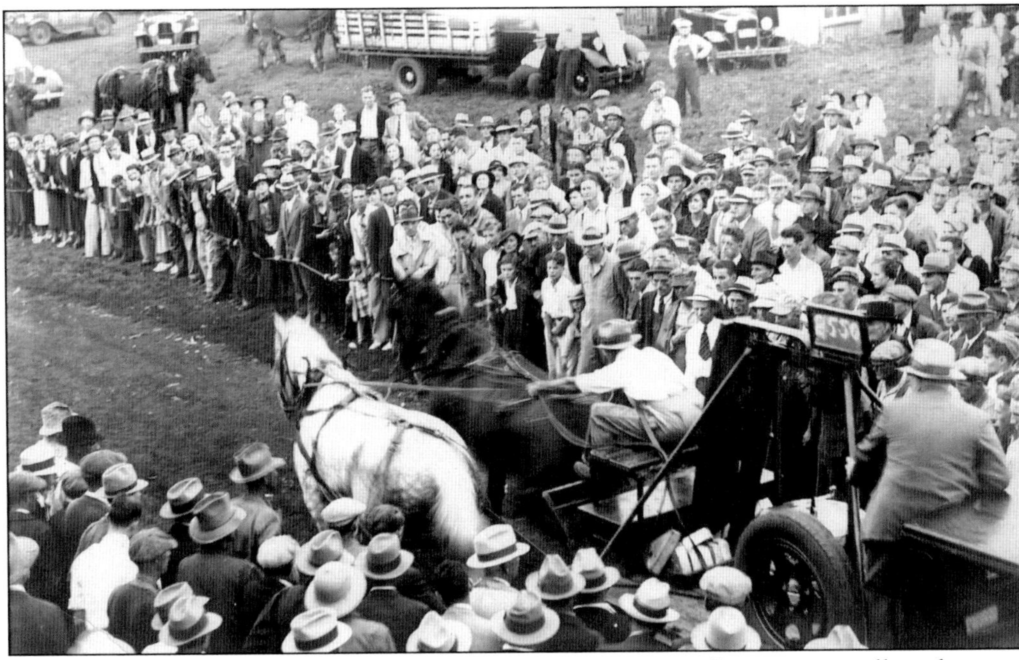

Popular in farming communities through the 1930s, amateur pulling contests allowed men to put their bragging to the test by pitting the strength of their horses against their neighbors'. A dynamometer, invented at Iowa State College in 1926 to test the strength of draft horses, was brought in for the contest and shows these animals to be pulling 2,550 pounds.

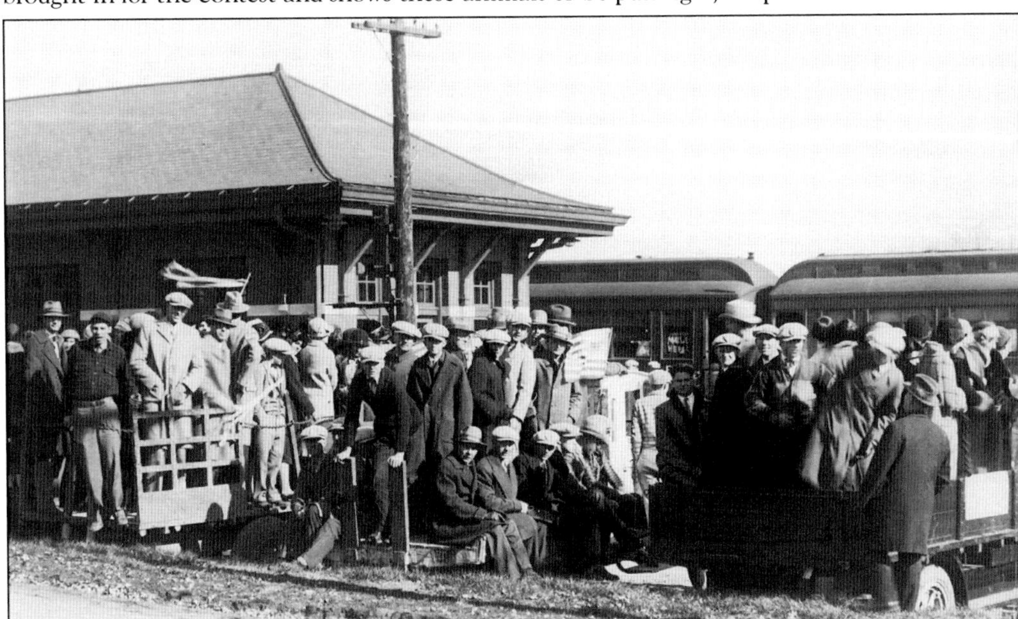

The occasion for this gathering of men at the Burlington Depot is lost to history, but well through the first quarter of the 20th century Maryville's two railroad depots were the likely ports of entry for any important visitors arriving in town. The welcoming crowd awaits on trucks, likely preparing a triumphant motorcade up the long rise from the station on the low east end to the town square a mile up the hill.

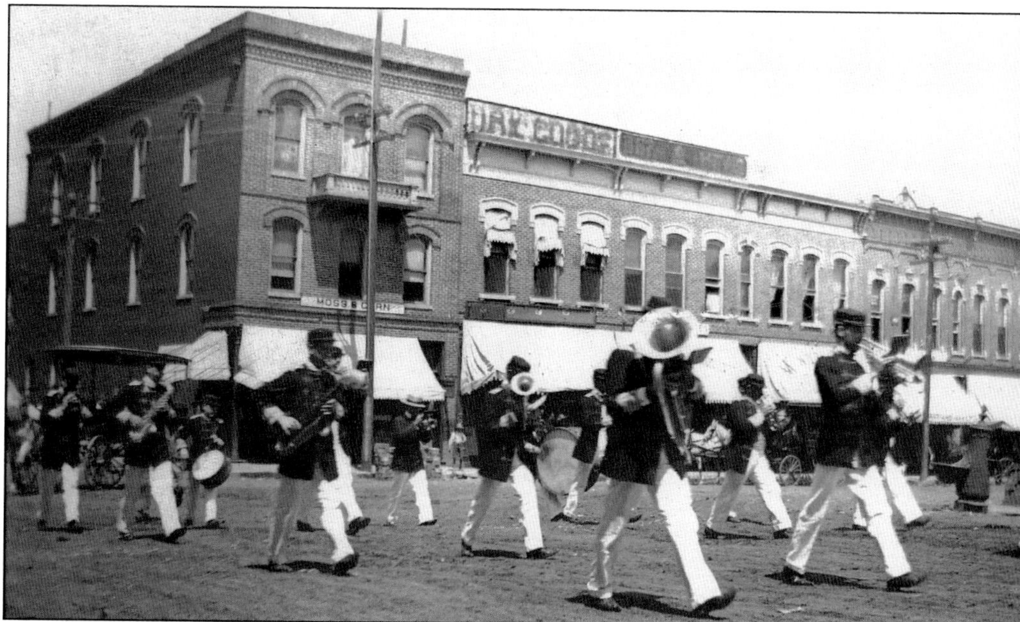

Sam Pryor's Band of St. Joseph marches in the Independent Order of Odd Fellows and Rebekah Lodge Memorial Parade in Maryville in the early 1890s. Like hundreds of similar communities, fraternal organizations and public parades stimulated civic pride and optimism. Brass bands were an essential ingredient, and while imported bands were a fine thing, respectable towns also called up at least one or two of their own.

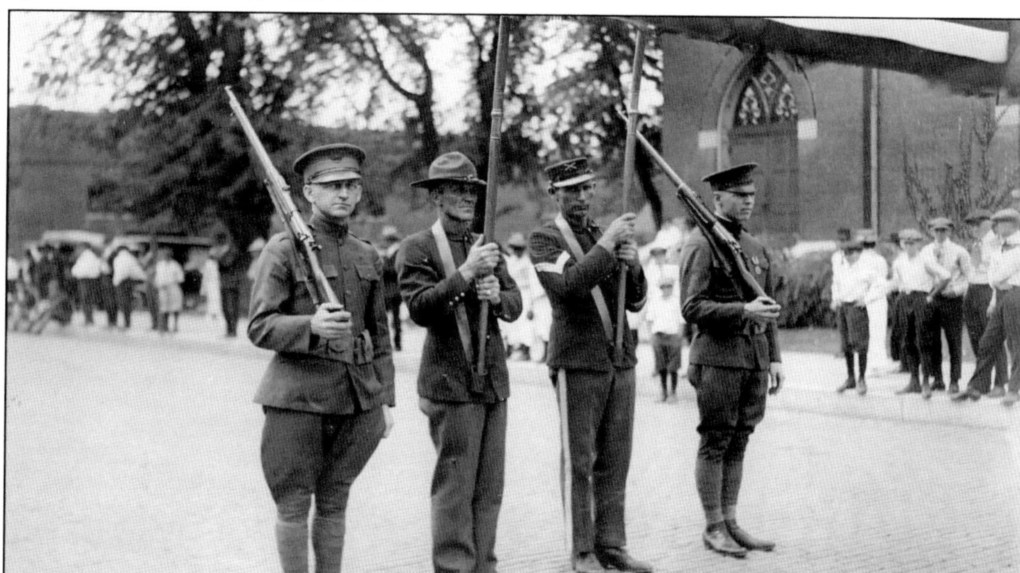

An Armistice Day parade proceeds with veterans bearing the colors on Main Street in front of the Methodist Church. Armistice Day changed to Veterans Day after Raymond Weeks led a campaign in 1947 to honor all soldiers, not just those of World War I. Congress officially approved the renaming in 1954.

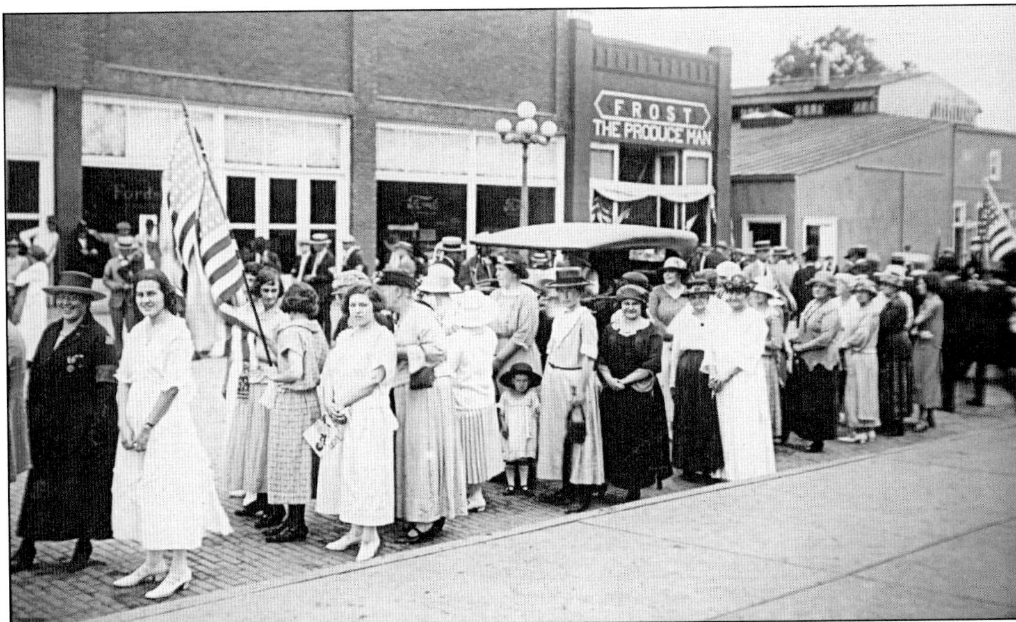

Businesses closed and 3,000 people attended the memorial march upon the sudden passing of Pres. Warren G. Harding. The strain of confronting numerous scandals as president and the rigors of an extended trip west seem to have taken a great toll on a president already in questionable health, and he died of congestive heart failure on August 2, 1923. Henry J. Allen, the former governor of Kansas, gave a speech on the Chautauqua grounds on the college campus following the march.

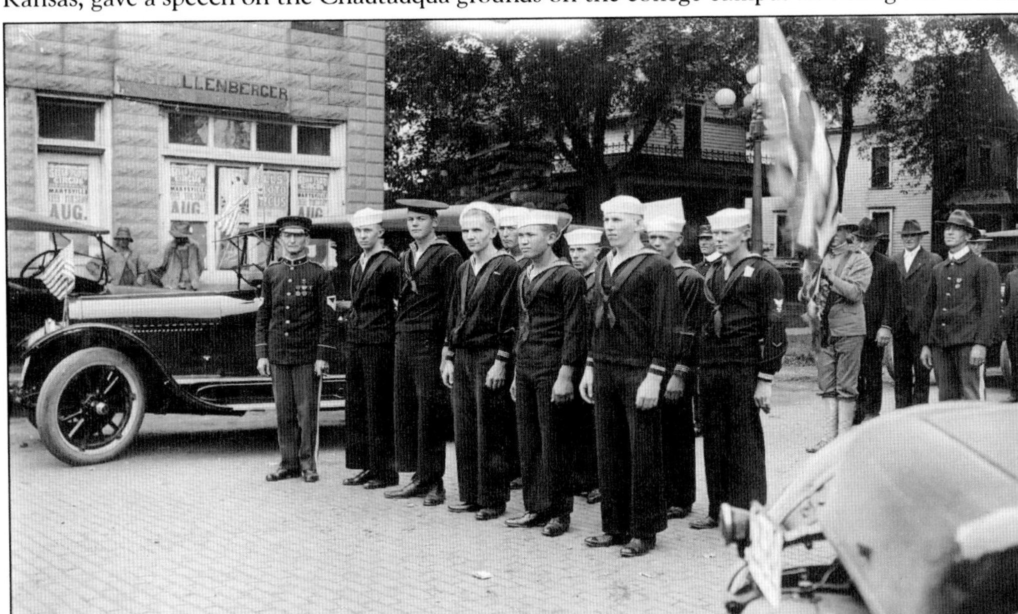

Sailors recently returned from service in World War I take the honored spot at the head of the color guard in an Armistice Day observance. The October parade brought to a close a long season of activity on the streets of Maryville. Shullenberger's old harness repair still displays posters advertising the coming of Sells-Floto Circus the previous August. Proprietors likely hung the posters despite being rankled by the circus company's misspelling of "Marysville."

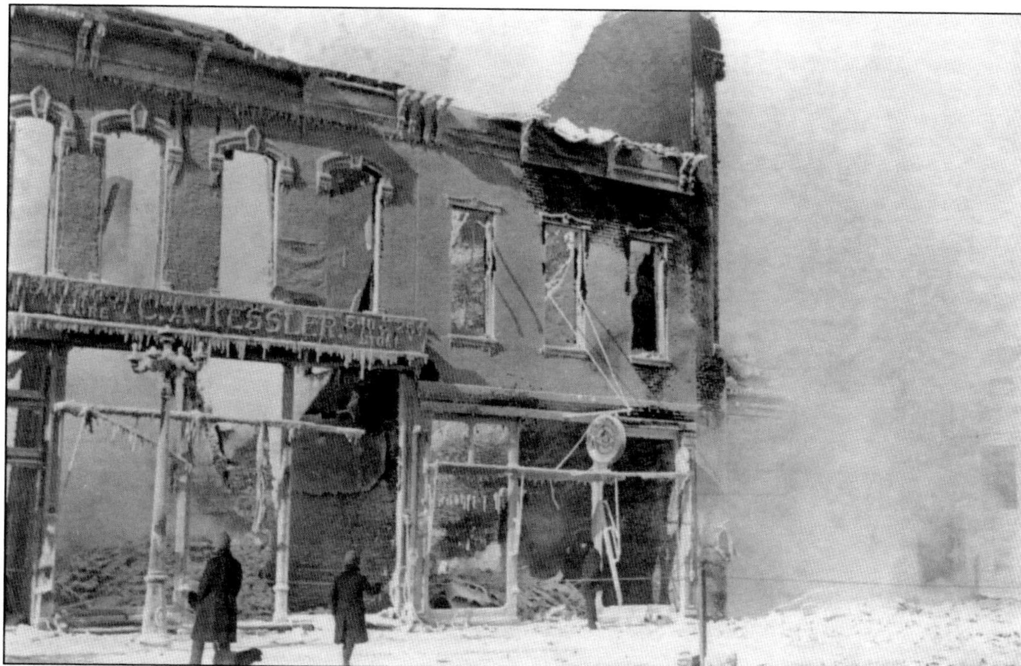

The destructive nature of fire often reared its head during the cold Maryville winters. On the evening of January 30, 1918, 25 businesses on the west side of the town square suffered damages from an uncontrollable fire. Temperatures that night plummeted to minus-20, which made quelling the fire even harder. The fire burned for over 48 hours and caused over $150,000 in damages. Residents saw the imposing three-story Michau building on the corner collapse, destroying Townsend Wholesale Grocers in the second of three disastrous fires to strike the firm in its seven decades of business. Three adjoining buildings were also destroyed, taking down half the block. The fire was first discovered in the third story occupied by the Masonic Lodge. Of the 20 people in the building, only two were injured, and no lives were lost. (Courtesy of Ron and Janet Moss.)

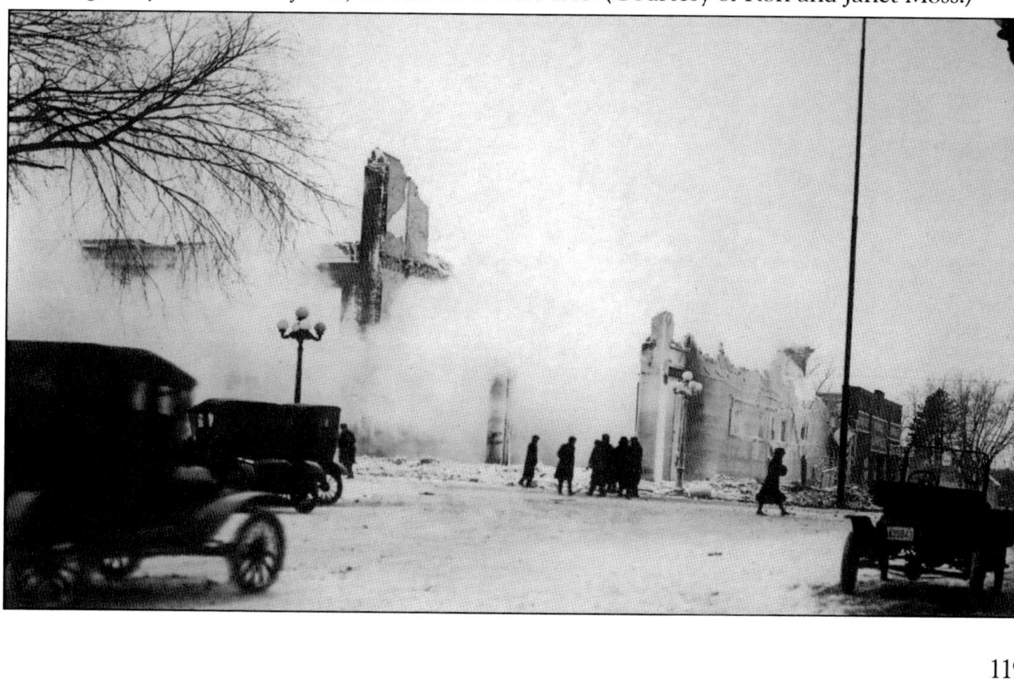

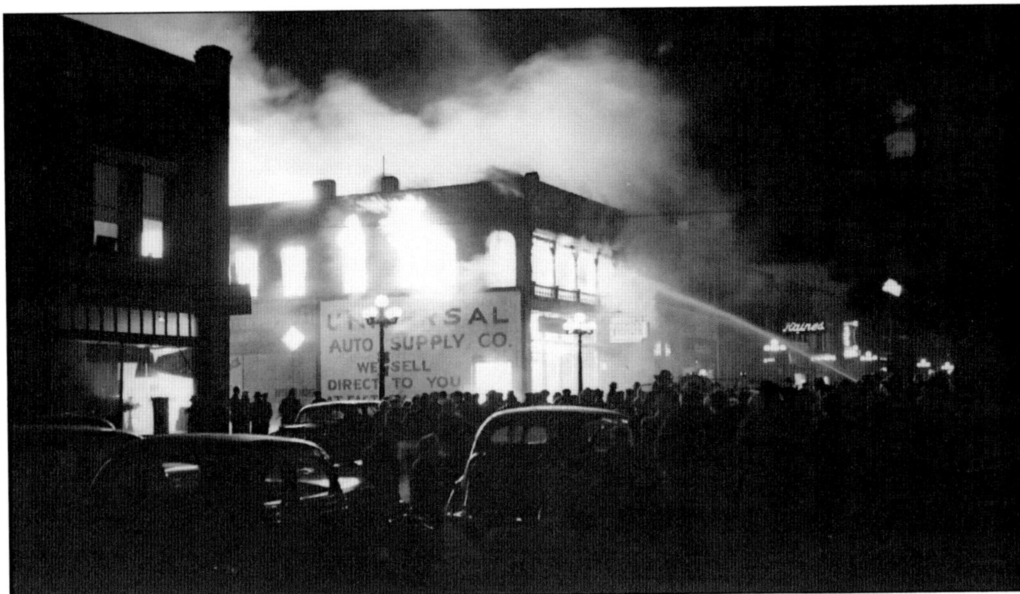

On February 16, 1939, the Sturm Building erupted into flames following an electrical malfunction in a stairway in another destructive winter fire. Onlookers reported violent explosions from oilcans in the Universal Auto Supply Company store. With the combined force of the Maryville Fire Department and the St. Joseph Fire Department, the fire was extinguished before other buildings in the square suffered damage. Spectators squeezed dangerously close to the night fire while three families initially trapped on the second floor were safely evacuated with minor injuries. Extreme weather caused local hoses to freeze and firemen from St. Joseph were called in with more flexible hose to battle a fire kept alive by brisk easterly winds. The Maryville fire department had recently purchased a new pumper, which proved effective in keeping the fire from spreading through the rest of the block.

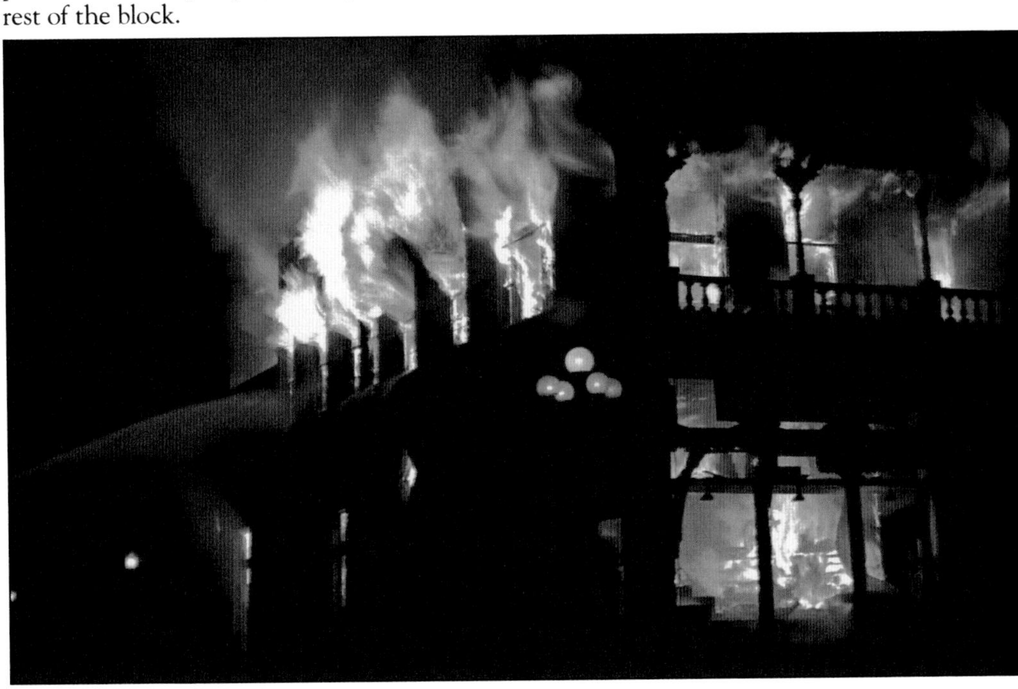

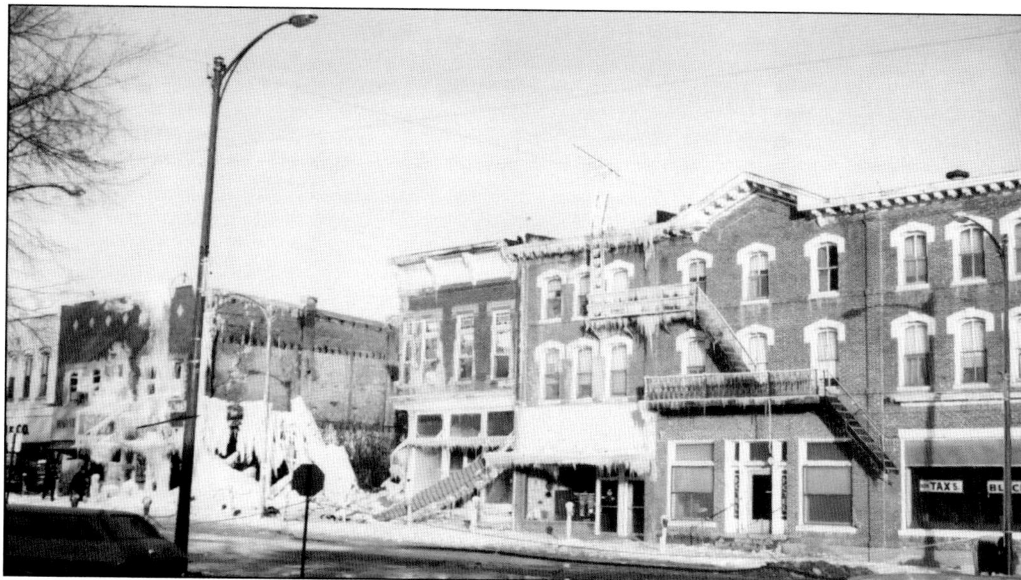

A January 4, 1972, fire destroyed a large portion of the north side of the square. Firemen in at least 12 communities responded to a blaze that started overnight in the Holt Supply Company. Numerous businesses, including the Western Auto Store, Warren Jones Drugs, and the Bainum Hotel, were damaged or destroyed.

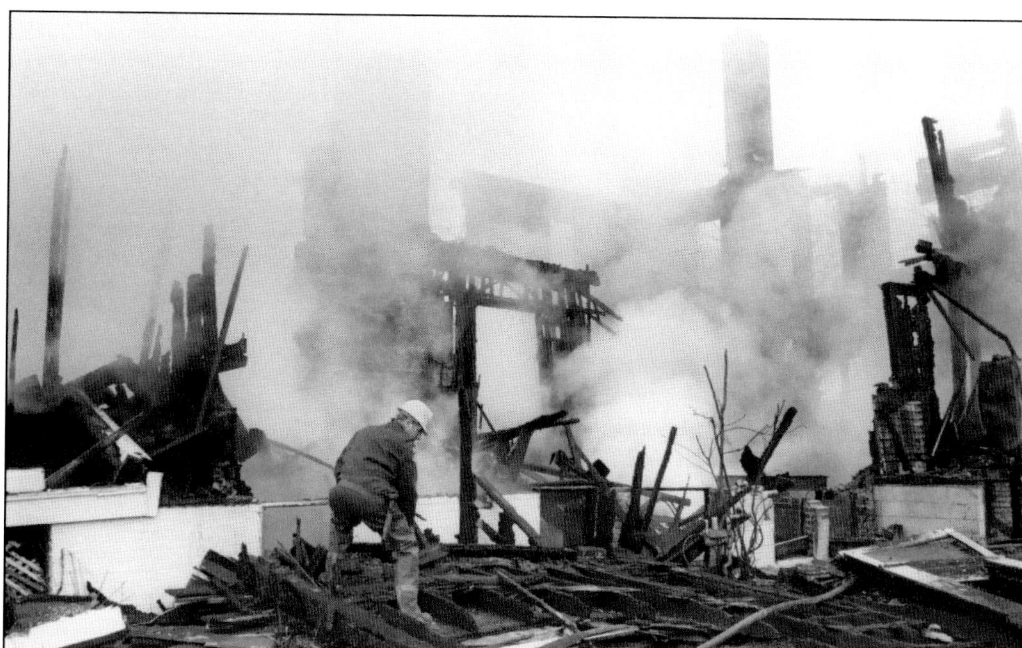

One of the misfortunes of time that plagues many communities is the loss of their fine homes, not only to neglect and decay, but also to fire. Like many of the grand homes of Maryville, the Beale home succumbed to fire in 1983. The widow Beale built the three-story home in 1893 on land purchased by her husband in 1860, with 21 rooms, 8 fireplaces, and impressive wood finishes throughout.

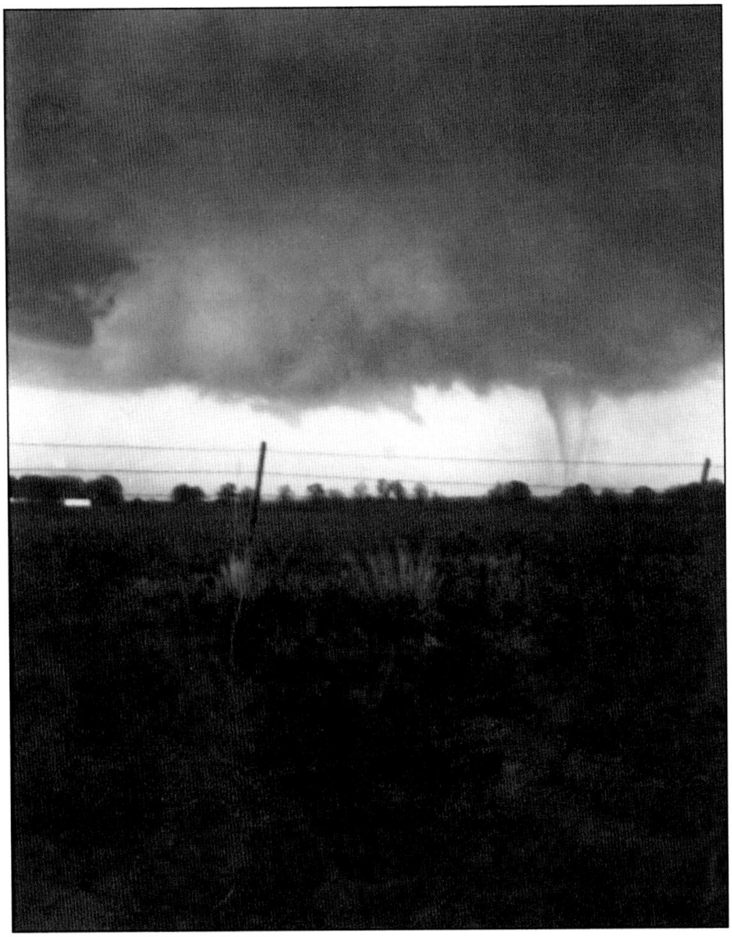

Despite suffering a record drought in 1934, Maryville was struck on October 23, 1934, by one of the most destructive storms in town history. A tornado collided with the Civilian Conservation Corps encampment on the northeast side of town, killing four young men. After tearing through town, the destructive storm left over 50 people injured and damages of over $100,000. Students of Washington High School, determined not to fall behind, attended classes in the town's churches. An amateur with a portable Kodak Brownie camera managed to capture the full view of the twister seen at left.

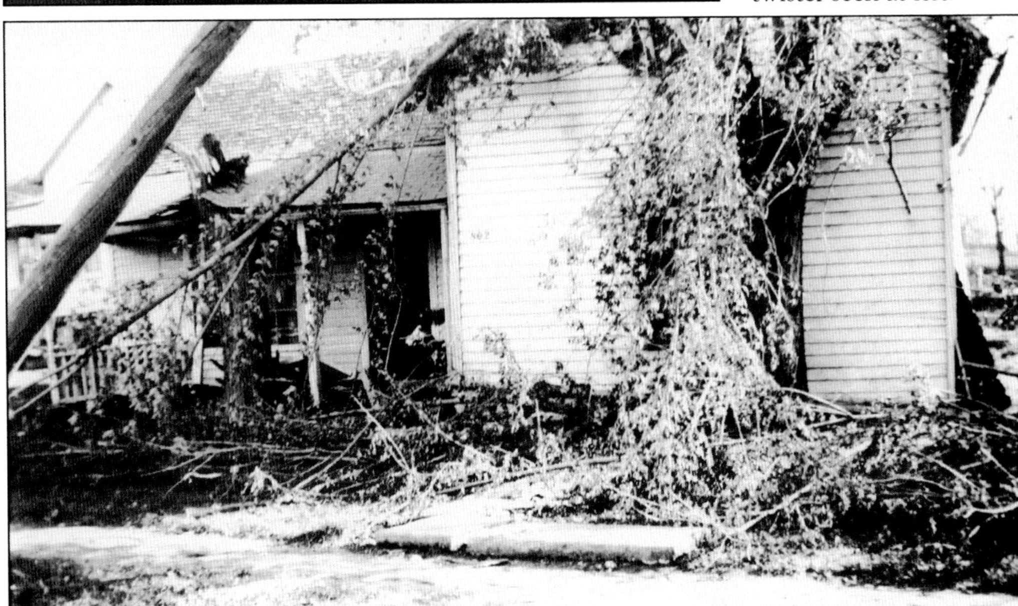

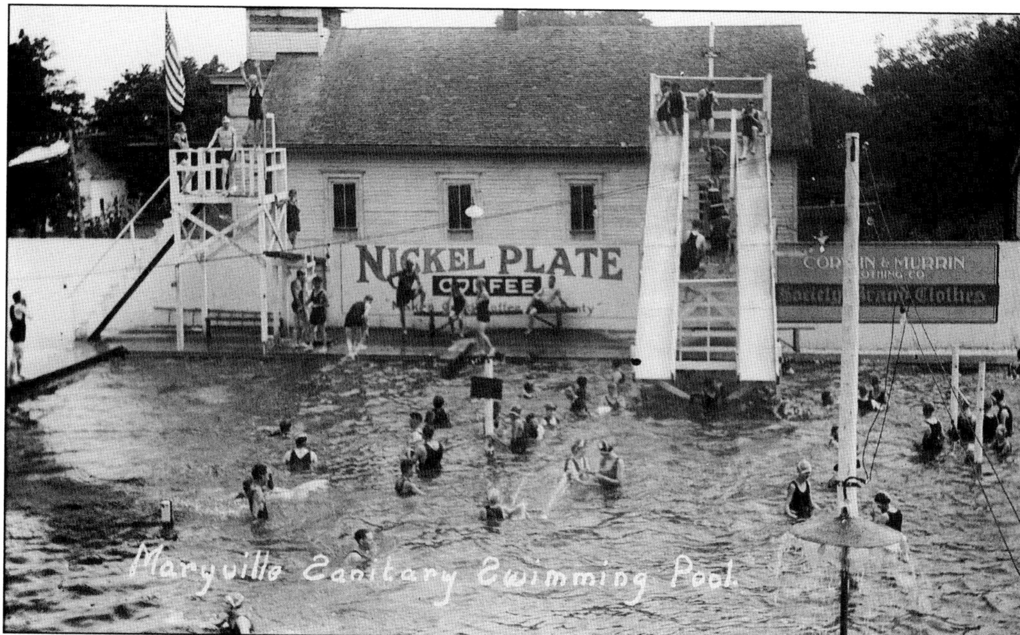

The Maryville Sanitary Swimming Pool opened on June 1, 1934, to residents' delight amid an extreme heat wave. To commemorate the opening, the town arranged for Cealo Mohawk, the "Human Seal" who delighted crowds with his swimming prowess, and trick diver Buster Strong. (Courtesy of Coby Lamb.)

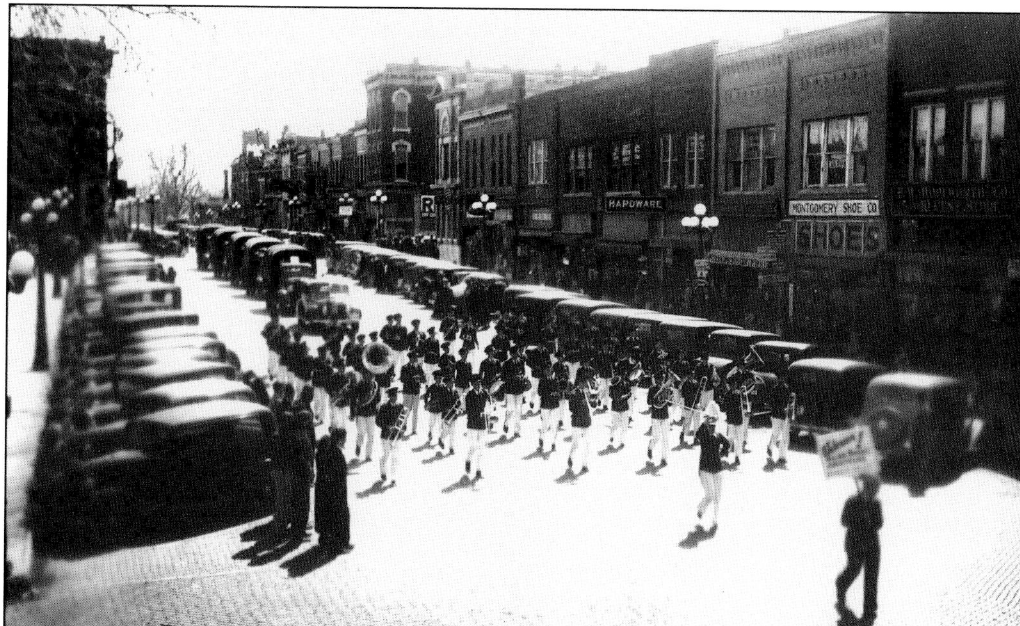

The band leads the way for the arrival of the Major Bowes 1938 Jamboree road show. The popular radio show took its amateur hour on a cross-country tour and mixed local entertainment with their own Singing Cheese Salesman, The Connecticut Four, and others. More than 3,000 spectators reportedly listened to the master of ceremonies repeat the show's catchphrase, "all right, all right!"

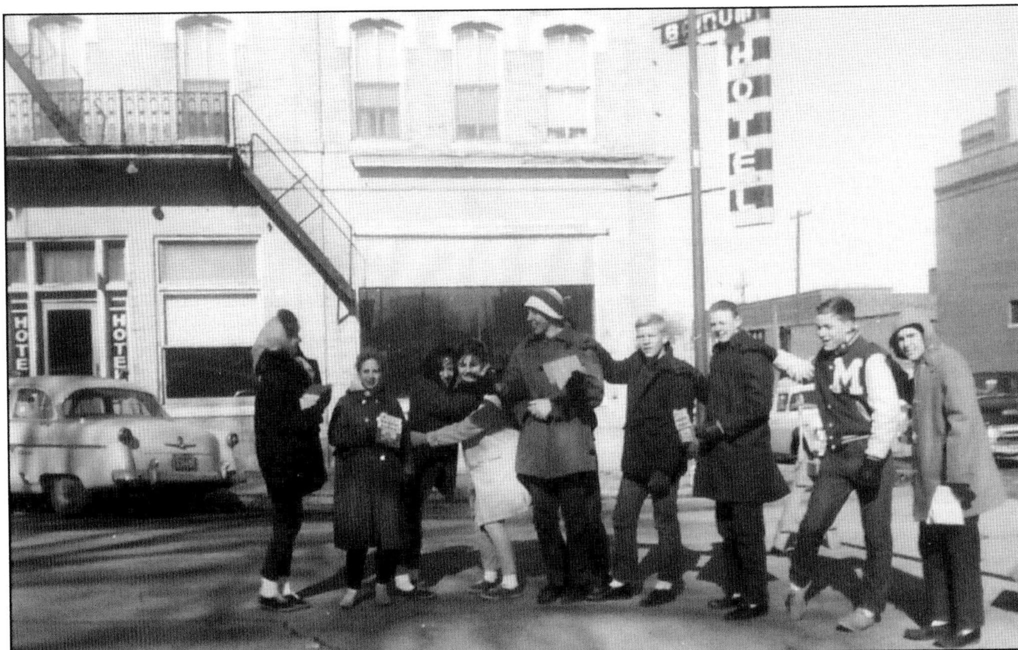

Though the early 1950s were often an age of anxiety amid the Cold War, it was nonetheless "happy days" as well for teens who found many ways to amuse themselves around the square in Maryville. Teens make fun for themselves on Fourth Street in front of the Bainum Hotel, shown above. The Dude Ranch, shown below, was Maryville's western-themed drive-in theater located on South Main. A popular spot in the late 1950s and 1960s, residents could enjoy a double feature Thursday and Friday, or enjoy the triple feature Saturday night with a hot fudge sundae. Tornado damage in the early 1960s and changing preferences put the Dude Ranch into decline.

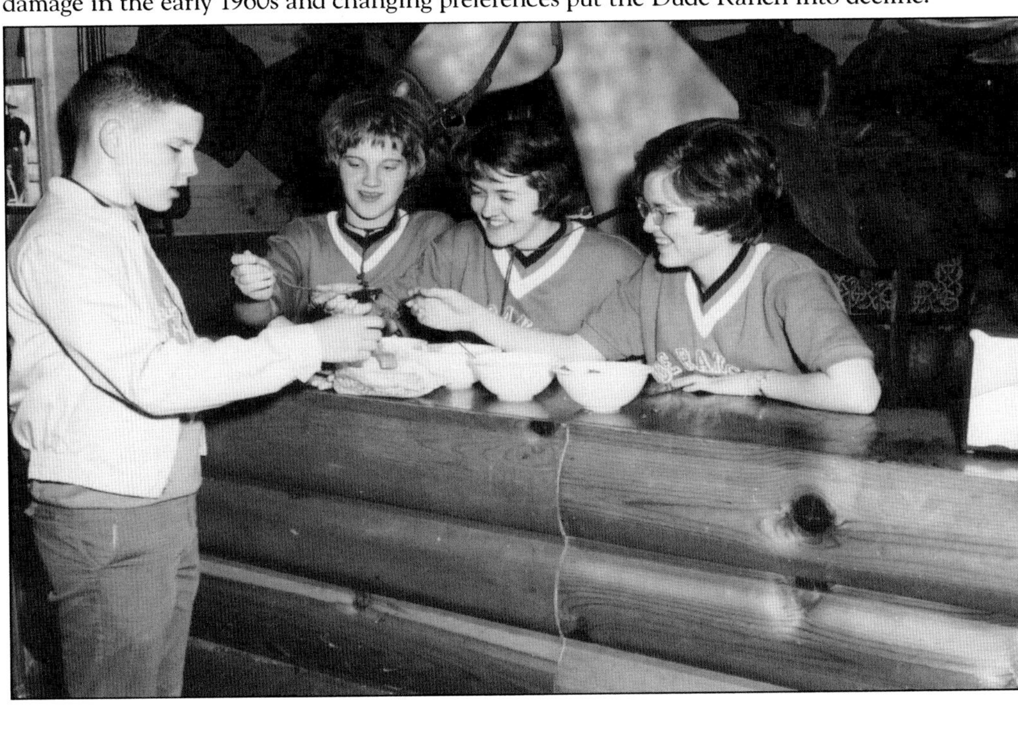

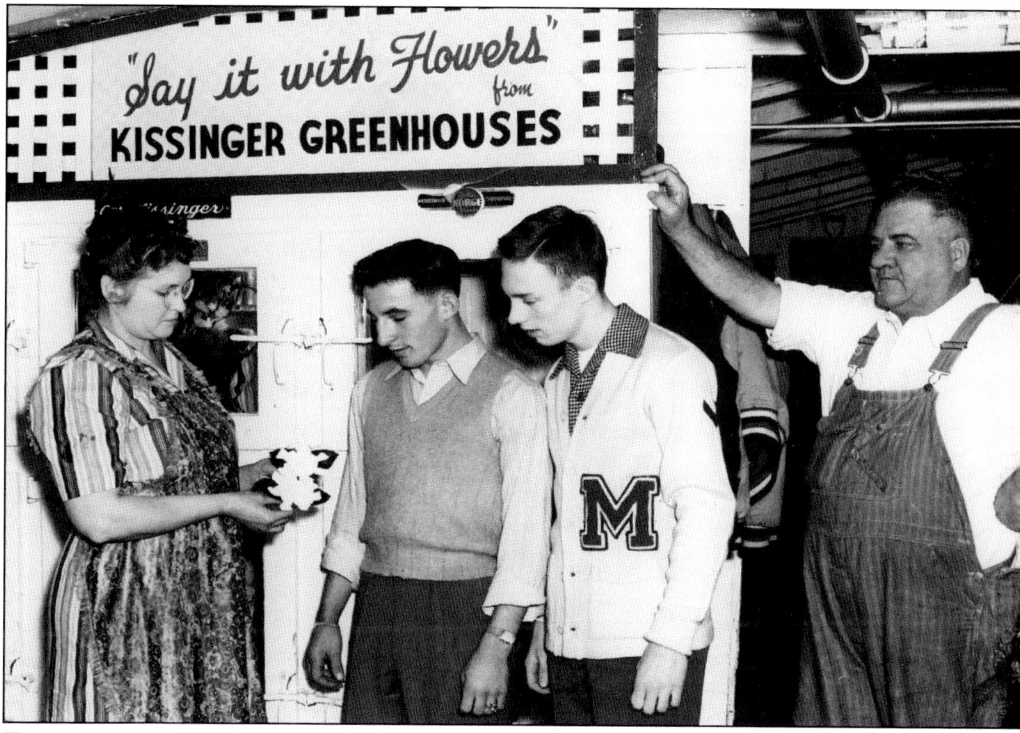

Two eager young gentlemen study the options for corsages at Kissinger's Flowers, taking part in a school dance ritual familiar to many young men and women. The Kissingers started the business with a greenhouse in 1933, and the family continued to provide Maryville with flowers and gifts for many occasions until 2003.

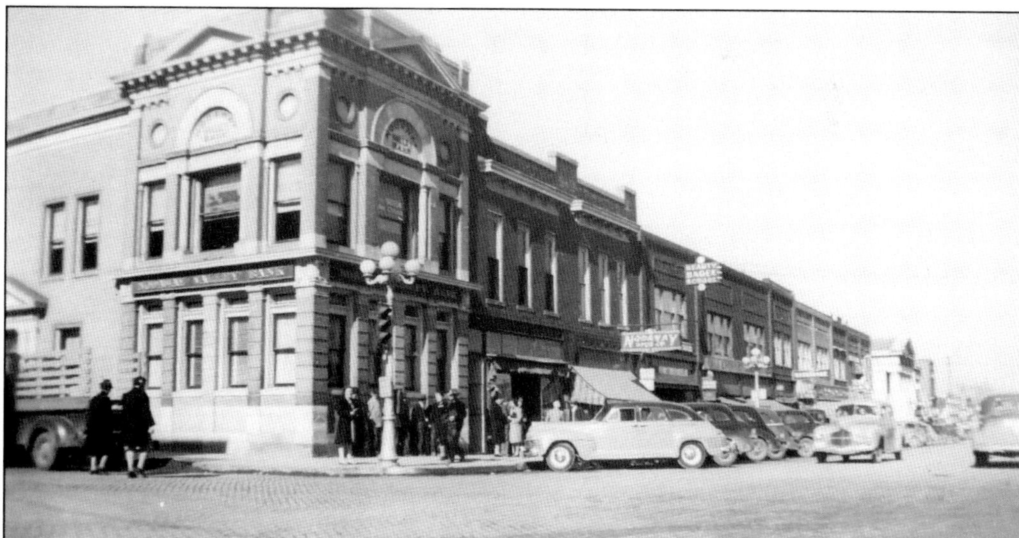

Residents in the late 1930s flock to the busy street during the day. Some head to beauty school, others handle bank duties and shopping. Already, however, the automobile and good roads tempt shoppers to travel to St. Joseph and beyond. Local businesses fought back with a newspaper campaign featuring the shop-at-home owl, who proclaimed, "Be Wise, Economize! Get your share of bargains to be found every day in Maryville."

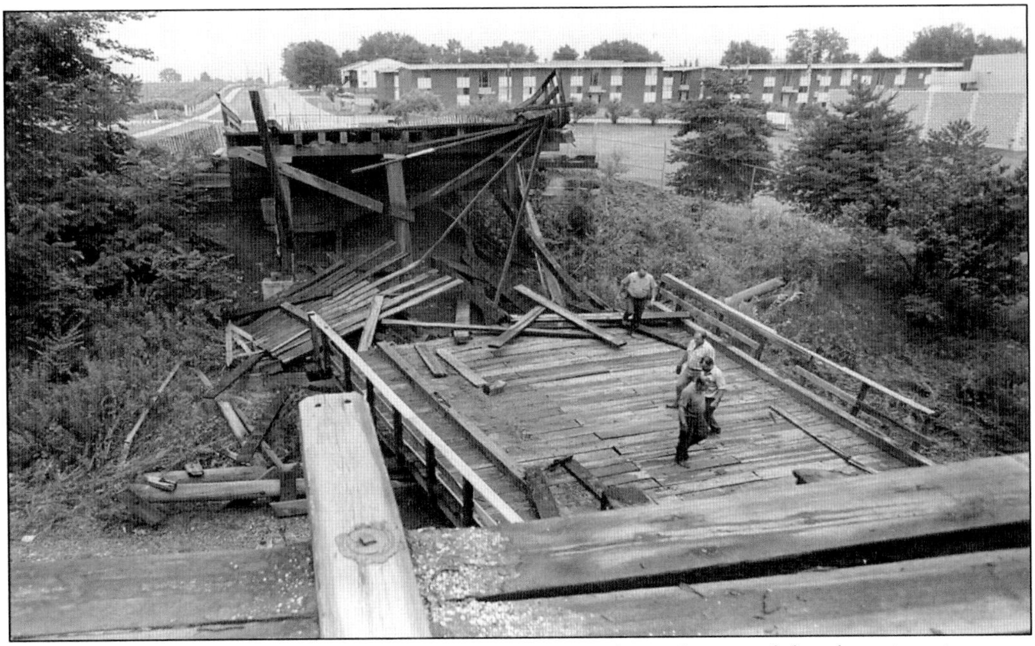

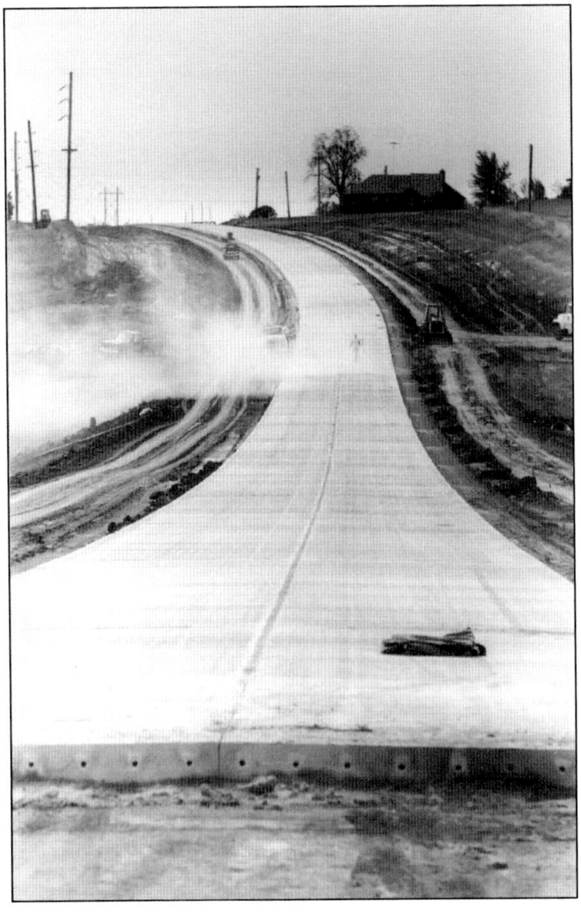

An indicator of the changing times, the bridge over the Wabash line on University Drive, just north of the campus, meets its demise. Wabash constructed the arched wooden span in 1898. With the railroad long out of service, the bridge failed to make its 100th birthday, and the gap was filled with dirt. The earthen barricade that holds the new road stands among many features of life a half-century ago that are unlikely to return.

The century-and-a-half of transformation of Maryville and its central business district saw one of its most significant changes with the simple laying of a road. Begun in 1993, the Highway 71 bypass allowed motorists to cruise past the town without the benefit of enjoying its businesses and accommodations. By no means a devastating blow, residents and businesses watched anxiously nonetheless as the route circumvented their town.

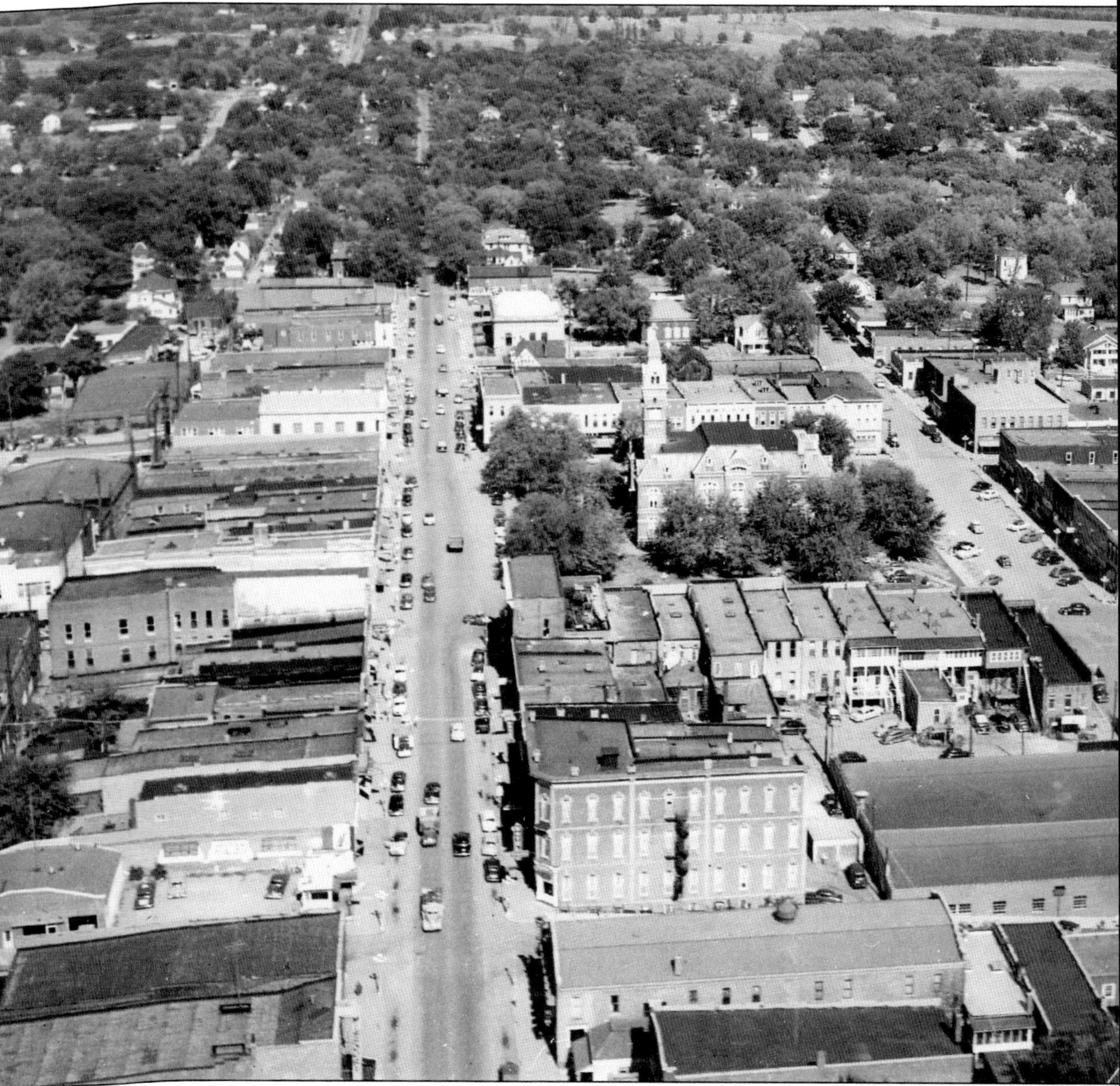

Residents of Maryville and those raised there who can remember the town as it is seen here from above in the 1940s, likely smile with the memories of all the good things, while forgetting the troubles and challenges of life before the conveniences of the 21st century. Those too young to remember will hopefully have found in these pages something not experienced first-hand, but cherished nonetheless. (Courtesy of Coby Lamb.)